THE
STORY
OF
CANADA

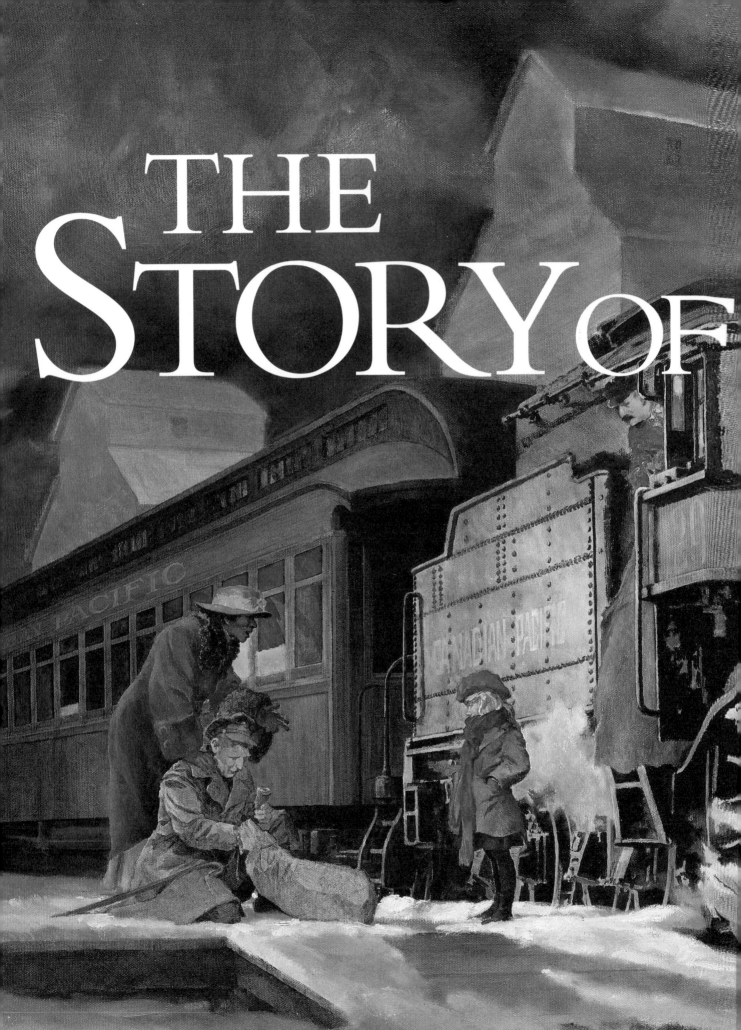

THE STORY OF

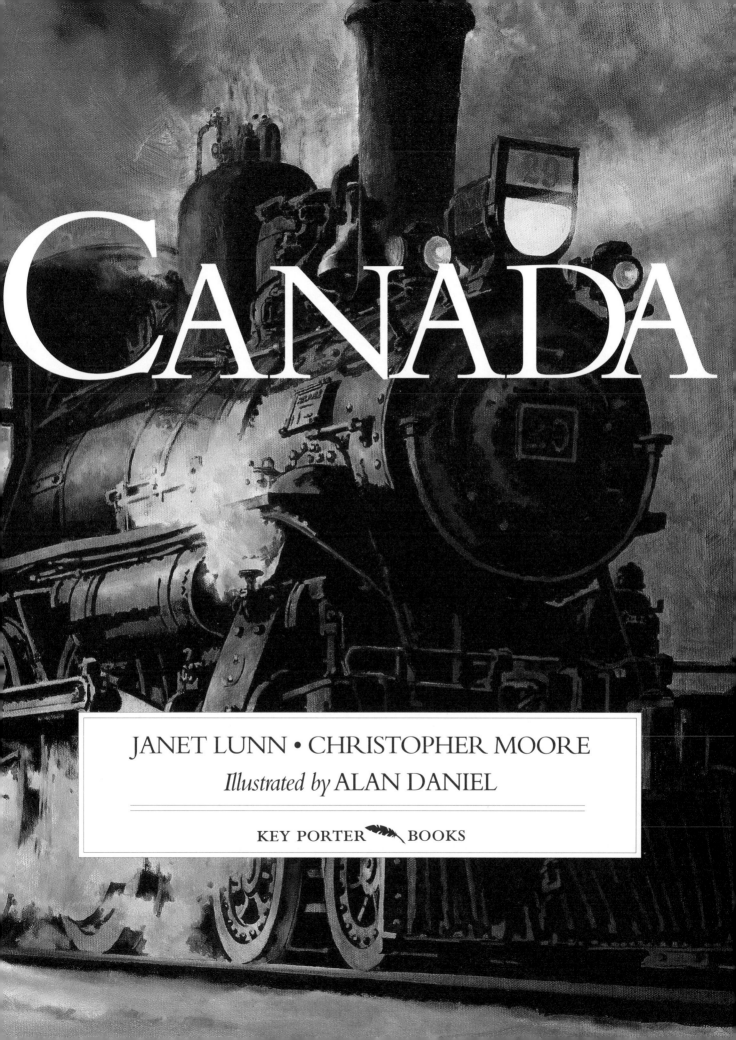

CANADA

JANET LUNN • CHRISTOPHER MOORE

Illustrated by ALAN DANIEL

KEY PORTER BOOKS

For Elizabeth, Liam, Kieran, and Joe
– born during the writing of *The Story of Canada*

Canadian Cataloguing in Publication Data

Lunn, Janet, 1928–
The story of Canada

Rev. ed.
Includes index.
ISBN 1-55263-145-1 (bound)   ISBN 1-55263-150-8 (pbk.)

1. Canada – History – Juvenile literature.
I. Moore, Christopher. II. Daniel, Alan, 1939–   .
III. Title.

FC172.L85   2000   j971   C99-933072-1
F1008.2.L85   2000

Key Porter Books Limited
70 The Esplanade
Toronto, Ontario
Canada M5E 1R2
Printed and bound in Canada

04 05 06 07 08 - 8 7 6 5 4

Page 1: A newsboy, about 1900. *Opposite:* The Young Reader. *Ozias Leduc.*

To the Reader

We have called this book
The Story of Canada,
but we know no book has
room for all the stories of
Canada. We hope you find
something of yourself in the
tales we have told – and go
on to discover more stories
of Canada for yourself.

The Authors

Contents

Chapter 1

A Hundred Centuries

Previous pages:
*As the glaciers melted more
than a hundred centuries ago,
wandering tribes discovered the
land that would one day be
Canada. The hunters in this
picture have used fire to trap a
woolly mammoth in a swamp
at the glacier's edge. The smoke
has attracted the attention of
another family, who race to
join in the kill.*

I
T HAD BEEN COLD FOR THOUSANDS OF YEARS, SO COLD THAT SNOW
barely melted in the brief summers. During the Ice Ages,
blue-white rivers of ice flowed over the northern parts of
the world. They buried almost every part of the land. Here
and there a mountain peak or high plateau rose above the
ice, but only the very highest, for the glaciers were
thousands of metres thick. As they moved, they ploughed
the ground like mighty bulldozers, scraping the rock bare.
They pushed gravel and stone ahead of them, flattening
hills, filling valleys, and carving the bedrock itself.

The glaciers must have been beautiful, but only a
cruising hawk could have seen their jagged crevasses or the
chill fogs around their grinding, roaring edges. In all those
centuries when ice covered the land, no forests, no plants,
no animals, and no people could live in the country that is
now Canada.

About twenty thousand years ago, the climate grew
warmer. Slowly the glaciers began to shrink in the sunshine. Where their farthest edges had reached, they left
heaped-up mounds of gravel. Their melting ice poured into
cold lakes, and rivers were born to carry the water away.
Seeds blew over the muddy, ploughed-out earth and took
root where they fell. Plants, shrubs, and forests began to
grow again. Animals came into the new country to graze
and hunt. Fish swam into the rivers.

*The shoreline of Grise Fiord,
the location of Canada's most
northerly Inuit community,
conjures up visions of the Ice
Age, thousands of years ago.*

Hunting Dinosaurs in Alberta

Seventy-five million years ago, steamy forests and warm seas covered many parts of Canada, and dinosaurs roamed the land. They were mostly big animals – few were smaller than humans, and a few giants weighed as much as fifty tonnes. Many were peaceable herbivores, or plant-eaters, who grazed in herds. However, it was the fierce carnivores, or meat-eaters, with their long talons and sharp teeth, who gave the group its name of dinosaur, which means terrible lizard.

After dominating the world for millions of years, the dinosaurs suddenly died out about 65 million years ago. It was only 150 years ago that scientists first began to suspect they had ever existed.

In 1884, scientist and explorer Joseph Tyrrell was studying the geology of Alberta's badlands, a strange landscape where the Red Deer River has eroded the ground into cliffs, gullies, and towers called hoodoos. "I was climbing up a steep rock face about 400 feet high," he said years later. (That's about 120 metres.) "I stuck my head around a point and there was this skull leering at me. It gave me a fright."

The skull was the first of many dinosaur fossils that Tyrrell found in the badlands, including one now called "Albertosaurus," after the province. Since then, the badlands of Alberta have become one of the world's great dinosaur "hunting grounds." Dinosaur Provincial Park has been declared a World Heritage Site by the United Nations. Today visitors come from all over the world to the Royal Tyrrell Museum of Paleontology to gaze at the enormous bones – and the very small petrified dinosaur eggs sometimes found with them.

There came a time during the melting of the glaciers when the Great Lakes swelled into one vast inland sea. Another shallow sea covered much of the Prairies. Centuries after that, the western plains were a desert where few animals could live. In some places, rising seas flooded in over the coasts. In others, the land sprang up higher as it shook off its burden of ice. There were warmer times when forests crept north across the subarctic tundra, and cooler times when the treeless tundra pushed the forest south again.

First Peoples

The first people to arrive were as old and as new as the land itself. As the glaciers retreated and the land emerged, they came across from Asia in dug-out or skin-covered boats, or on foot over a bridge of land that joined the continents. As the ice loosened its grip, people made themselves part of the new land. They hunted woolly mammoths and long-horned buffalo in the shadow of the glaciers. They learned the best places to hunt, and found the best places to shelter. They discovered where the power of the spirits was strongest. Ten thousand years ago – a hundred centuries back in time – families, bands, and tribes of the Native people of Canada were already at home.

These first people mastered the skills they needed in every place they settled. On the ocean shores, they harvested the riches of the rivers and the sea. On the plains, they grew expert in hunting the buffalo. In the evergreen forests, they learned to track woodland animals. Wherever they lived, they sought out every tasty nut or berry or medicinal herb, every sheltered spring or creek, every outcropping of flint for arrow and spear heads.

Many hundreds of lifetimes is enough time for many changes. Thousands of years ago, there were people who travelled in skin-covered canoes south along the Atlantic coast from what we now call Labrador. Where Ontario is today, there were people who buried their dead in earth

The early Native peoples left traces of their artistry on the land itself, carving masks in living trees or painting and carving images called "petroglyphs" on stone. The petroglyphs shown here are from Sproat Lake, Vancouver Island.

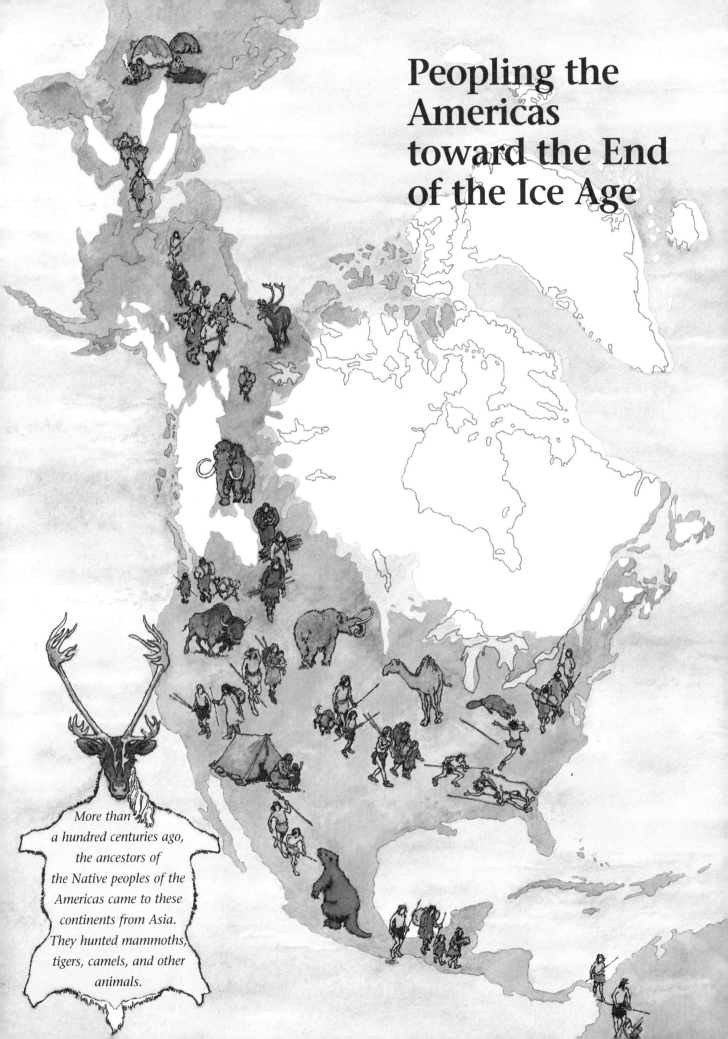

Peopling the Americas toward the End of the Ice Age

More than a hundred centuries ago, the ancestors of the Native peoples of the Americas came to these continents from Asia. They hunted mammoths, tigers, camels, and other animals.

Medicine Wheels

A brave, wise chief had died. To honour him, the people who loved him began to pile stones into a cairn on a hilltop. Around the cairn, they laid out stone lines and circles. This became a place of power. Long afterwards, newcomers to the western plains found the stone circle. Wondering what it might mean, they called it a "medicine wheel."

There are more than fifty of these mysterious landmarks in Alberta and Saskatchewan, often in high and hard-to-reach places. Some are circular, some have straight lines pointing out from the centre, and one includes an outline of a human figure. Some may point to the constellations of stars, others may honour the spirit of the buffalo. Some of the medicine wheels surely mark the death of a single leader, perhaps quite recently, but others have been visited regularly for five thousand years.

mounds that twined about the landscape like fifty-metre-long snakes. Some groups of people would leave one homeland to find another far away.

The first people became many nations, each with its own ways of doing things, its own leaders, and its own legends and heroes. Across Canada they spoke at least fifty different languages. The Dene of the Northwest could not understand the Cree of the East, and those who spoke Salish on the Pacific coast would never have heard Micmac from the Atlantic.

Centuries of Changes

Over those hundreds of lifetimes and thousands of years, the Native nations of Canada discovered and invented many things to make their lives better. People of the Pacific Northwest began to spear and net the salmon that migrated up the rivers once a year. They mastered the art of smoke-drying their catch, so that they could store up all the food they needed for the whole year. Such wealth freed them from a constant search for food. It gave them time to produce beautiful works of art, such as the totem poles that stood tall over their cedar houses.

People of the woodlands around the Great Lakes began to make clay pots and bowls to store and cook their food in. They decorated every piece with elaborate designs. The Iroquoian people of that territory became farmers, clearing and tilling the fields and planting the corn kernels that produced fat ears of sweet corn in the hot summers. Although the Iroquoians still hunted and fished, it was their fields of corn – and beans and squash, too – that kept them well fed. They lived in villages of thousands of people, close by their fields.

The people of the Pacific Northwest discovered an extinct volcano, Mount Edziza. Its lava had hardened into a glassy black rock called obsidian that was perfect for knife blades and spear points. For centuries, the people traded obsidian down the Pacific coast, east to the Prairies, and

north to the land we call Yukon. Across the continent, traders exchanged other useful goods. They traded the copper they found on Lake Superior, the shells they gathered along the Atlantic coast. Later, as people made pottery and grew vegetables and tobacco, they traded those, too. As the centuries passed, the nations came to know each other as nations do today, as allies or rivals, as trading partners, as neighbours.

Native peoples maintained a vigorous trade long before Europeans came to this continent. These Seneca traders (with the high, cropped hair) have brought corn and tobacco to exchange for the birchbark canoes crafted by Ojibwa master builders.

Chiefs and Heroes

Hundreds of years ago, before any Europeans came to Canada, a child called Dekanahwideh was born by the Bay of Quinte on the north shore of Lake Ontario. At his birth, his mother had a vision that her son would plant the Tree of Peace among the Iroquoian nations. When Dekanahwideh grew up, he set forth to fulfil his destiny.

According to the Iroquois stories, Dekanahwideh crossed Lake Ontario in a canoe of stone, and began spreading his message of peace. At Onondaga, Dekanahwideh planted his Tree of Peace, a giant white pine whose

TLINGIT

MACKENZIE DELTA INUIT

KUTCHIN

COPPER INUIT

CARIBOU INUIT

TSIMSHIAN

TAHLTAN

DENE

CHIPEWYAN

HAIDA

BELLA COOLA

CARRIER

BEAVER

KWAKIUTL

BLACKFOOT

SALISH

KUTENAI

ASSINIBOINE

SIOUX

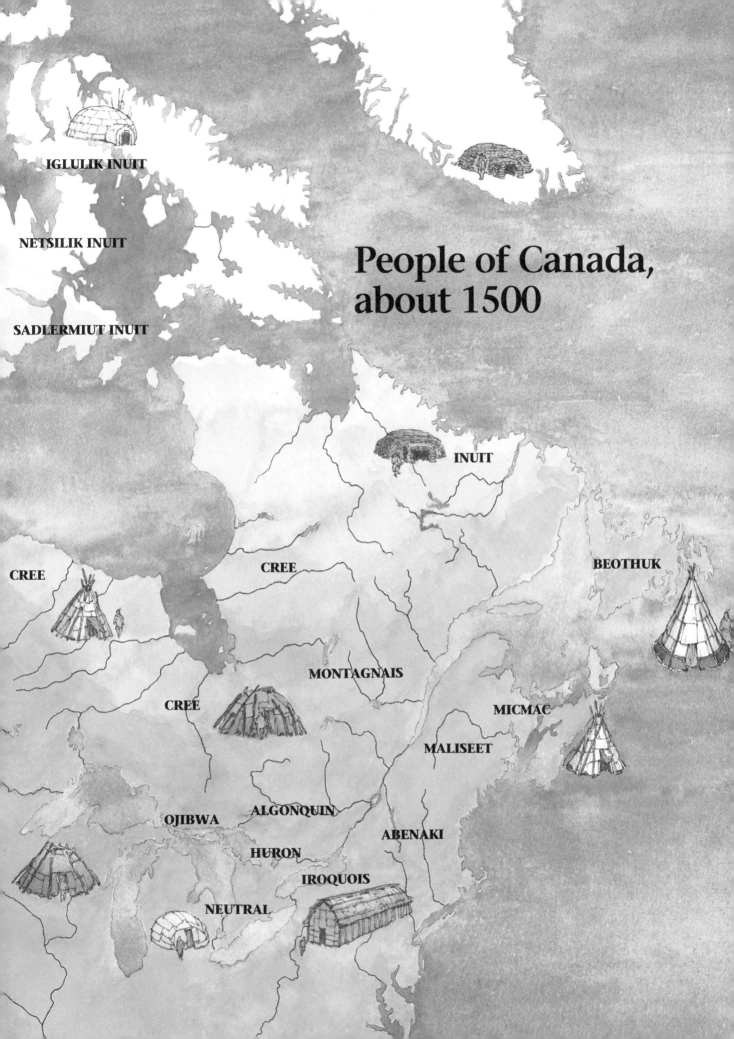

IGLULIK INUIT

NETSILIK INUIT

SADLERMIUT INUIT

People of Canada, about 1500

INUIT

CREE

CREE

BEOTHUK

MONTAGNAIS

CREE

MICMAC

MALISEET

OJIBWA

ALGONQUIN

ABENAKI

HURON

IROQUOIS

NEUTRAL

Native artists of the Woodland nations of Ontario have always been inspired by the changing, teasing, guiding spirit Nanabush.

branches touched the sky and whose roots reached out to all the world. Above the tree an eagle circled night and day, spying out any danger that might threaten the peace. Beneath the tree lay a pit where Dekanahwideh threw the weapons of war. He brought five nations together – the Mohawk, the Oneida, the Onondaga, the Cayuga, and the Seneca – to form a confederacy. "Live together," he said, "like families in a single longhouse, its rafters extending to shelter you all."

The mothers of the five nations chose fifty chiefs for a great council. Dekanahwideh gave them the law that has governed the People of the Longhouse ever since. His followers – the people we call Iroquois – called him Peacemaker. They still attempt to follow his law and his teaching.

Dekanahwideh is one of the very first heroes we can name in the story of Canada, but every Native nation revered the women and men who founded it or led it to greatness. On the Pacific coast they remember the great warrior Nekt and his fortress of Kitwanga, high above the Skeena River. Among the Hurons of southern Ontario, one leader after another took the proud name Atironta.

There were spirit heroes, too. There were tricksters – Raven on the Pacific coast, the old man Napi on the plains, and Nanabush in the spruce forests. Sometimes tricksters helped and taught the people, sometimes they teased and tested them. There were giants like Glooscap on the Atlantic shore – when he lay down to sleep, Glooscap piled up Minagoo (we call it Prince Edward Island) for a pillow. Spirits ruled the animals, too. They brought animals to the hunters, but they could take the animals away if the people offended them. Spirits also gave guidance, speaking in dreams and visions to those who sought them. Some men and women earned the power to visit and talk with the spirits and learn ways to heal the sick. Around the fire, on long winter nights, storytellers taught the young and reminded the adults of the spirits all around them. Elders passed along the history and the wisdom that guided each nation.

A Northern Passage

In several waves, over thousands of years, explorers came from Asia into the Arctic. The first Arctic pioneers followed caribou and muskox into the North about four thousand years ago. They lived hard lives. They had no dogs to hunt with them and pull their sleds. They did not even have lamps to light their skin tents. But gradually they learned how to live better in this unforgiving land. They learned that snow houses would keep them warmer in winter than skins. They braved the seas in skin-covered boats, catching fish and seals. They carved lamps from soapstone and burned seal oil in them for heat and light. They carved many other things from the soft stone, to show the magic and power that were in the land. Often they carved the powerful white bears of the North. They hunted these bears – but they knew that

On the taiga, "the land of little sticks," people and animals alike headed for shelter when winter's blast came down. Dene people moved from camp to camp, carrying their few possessions and relying on the land and on their skills to provide for them. Details: a girl's embroidered hood and a drinking tube.

The Magical Art of a Vanished People

A thousand years ago, as the Inuit came into what is now Arctic Canada, they found people they called Tunit living there. Were the Tunit conquered, killed, or driven away, or did they give up their own customs and adopt Inuit ways? No one knows.

Here and there across the Arctic, archeologists find the remains of the Tunit people's camps. Because the first camps studied were near Cape Dorset, Baffin Island, archeologists call the Tunit the Dorset people. The Tunit or Dorset people knew how to survive in the Arctic, but what impresses the archeologists most is the sculptures they left behind. The carvings are small, skilfully made – and strange. The Dorset people are gone, but the power of their art is still haunting.

polar bears also hunted them. The people hoped the magic in their carvings would keep them safe.

The people called Inuit came into the Arctic from the west long after these first arrivals, and they were better prepared than those who had come before. They had skilfully made harpoons. Out on the ice, an Inuit hunter might crouch all day at a breathing hole, harpoon in hand, waiting for a seal to pop up. When the hunter struck, the sharp point would come off the harpoon shaft easily. But the point was attached to a float by a piece of twine, so the seal's body could not sink back through the hole in the ice and be lost. With float harpoons and snow houses, Inuit families made the Arctic into a good home. They travelled over the snow and ice on dogsleds in winter, and their kayaks and umiaks carried them through open water in the brief summer.

The Inuit hunted whales in the Arctic Ocean. A thousand years ago, the climate was warmer than it is now. Whales found open water through northern channels far into the Arctic, and Inuit whalers followed them. In a few generations, Inuit explorers discovered all of the Arctic region and made it their home. Did they fight with the people who were there before them? In Inuit tales, the Tunit, as they called the earlier people, simply went away.

The Inuit made the last great Native migration across Canada. By the time they had settled the North, Canada's first nations had made their homes in every part of the land: the lush raincoast, the dry shortgrass prairie, the northern evergreen forest, the woodlands and cornfields of the Great Lakes, the bays and inlets of Atlantic Canada, and the Arctic islands.

Like the people in every other part of Canada, the Inuit of a thousand years ago were explorers and adventurers, always learning new magic, new ways to live with the land. Then, just about the time the Inuit reached the Atlantic shores, other explorers came from the east, across the Atlantic Ocean from Europe. They too had many skills, and much to learn about the continent.

A Day in the Arctic, Seven Hundred Years Ago

A skin-covered boat called an *umiak* threads its way through the narrow channels of the High Arctic islands. The women are paddling, while children and dogs sit at their feet. The men follow, riding the waves in swift kayaks. They are all wearing clothes of caribou skin, with the soft hair warm against their skin and the supple hide facing the chilly breeze that whips up the water.

Later, in their summer shelter of arched whale-bones, turf, and skins, the women work around the cooking pot. (Snow houses are only for winter.) The mother has filled and lit the *kudlik*, the soapstone lamp, which brightens the shelter with a soft glow. She and the grandmother have taken off their outdoor furs. As the room grows warm, the small children run around naked.

When the men return, they feed their dogs some of the fish they have caught. Then they come inside, taking off their furs and hugging the children. Soon everyone is dipping fingers into the fragrant pot of sealmeat and oil the women have prepared.

After the meal, the mother picks up the *qulittaq*, the outside layer of the parka she is making. She pieces together different kinds of fur in an intricate design, beautiful as well as warm. The aged grandmother is attaching good-luck charms to the parka of the youngest child, to keep her safe from evil. The grandfather picks up his bone shaper and works on his carving of a stone seal. As he works, he tells the story of Sedna, the woman who lives beneath the sea. She has power over the whales and seals, and she rewards hunters who respect the spirits of the animals they hunt.

The children try to stay awake to hear the end of the story, but they soon drift into sleep, tucked into their furs on the sleeping platform. The wind outside is icy cold, the land stark and treeless. The late summer days are already short, and soon the night will last all winter long.

Chapter 2
Strangers on the Coast

O N A DAY IN LATE SUMMER, A THOUSAND YEARS AGO, LEIF ERICSSON gripped the tiller of his wave-skimming ship. There it was, rising from the ocean like a great humpback whale: Bjarni's western land!

Leif Ericsson's people were Norsemen from Scandinavia, in the north of Europe, and everyone in Europe feared them. From Russia to the Mediterranean Sea, the fierce Norsemen went raiding in their dragon-prowed longships. Their word for raiding, *viking*, became the name by which they were known. The Norsemen were bold explorers, too. At a time when most European sailors scarcely dared go beyond their own shores, the Norsemen had settled Iceland. Leif's own father, the outlaw Eric the Red, had sailed farther west to discover Greenland.

Later that year, a merchant named Bjarni Herjolfsson, sailing to Greenland, had been caught by a howling storm. Carried far to the west, he had sighted a forested land. When he finally reached the Greenland port, the story he told fascinated Leif. Leif, whose friends called him Leif the Lucky, was a big fellow, adventurous but also shrewd and careful. He bought Bjarni's ship, put it in good repair, and went with his crew in search of the unknown land.

Leif was as lucky as his friends said, for now he had found Bjarni Herjolfsson's land. Early one morning, the weary, salt-caked adventurers waded ashore on an island off this new coast. "They touched the dew with their hands," wrote a Norse *skald*, or storyteller, in *Saga of the Greenlanders*, "and they thought they had never known anything to taste so sweet." The Norsemen had come to North America.

When they pulled their ship ashore on the mainland, Leif's men found a land that was everything they had hoped for. Salmon "bigger than any they had ever seen before" ran in the rivers. Deep forests covered the hills. Soon after they arrived, Tyrker, a German who had sailed with Leif, decided to go exploring. When he returned, he was brandishing what looked like grapes and vines. What a marvellous country, far richer than cold Greenland! Leif named it Vinland the Good and decided to spend

Previous pages:

The crew of a Portuguese fishing boat, sheltering from a storm on a summer day in 1500, is startled by the arrival of Micmac traders eager to exchange their pelts for the newcomers' wares.

Where Was Vinland?

To visit the only place in Canada where we know Vikings lived, travellers follow the long road up Newfoundland's Great Northern Peninsula to L'Anse aux Meadows, at the tip of the island. In 1961,

archeologists discovered the ruins of a Norse settlement there. L'Anse aux Meadows has been named a World Heritage Site by the United Nations. It is famous as one of the first places where the people of Europe and North America bridged an ocean and met one another.

Was L'Anse aux Meadows Leif Ericsson's Vinland? Many archeologists say no.

It may have been one of the places where Thorfinn and Gudrid wintered, maybe even where Snorri was born. But grapes never grew at the northern tip of Newfoundland, and L'Anse aux Meadows rarely has a winter without frost. Leif's Vinland may still be waiting for some lucky archeologist to discover.

the winter. He set the men to building huts. The saga says there was no frost that winter, and the cattle were able to browse outdoors.

The following spring, Leif loaded his ship with timber and sailed back to Greenland. Soon there were new expeditions setting out for Vinland. Leif's brother Thorvald led one the next year. But his expedition was not as lucky as Leif's. One day Thorvald and his men found strange men sleeping under upturned kayaks. The Norsemen killed eight of the Native men, but one escaped and soon returned with many more men in kayaks. Thorvald's men fought them from their longship, sheltering behind a row of shields, but an arrow flew between the shields and struck Thorvald. He realized that he was going to die. "We have found a good country," he said, "but we will not be able to benefit from it." His men buried him on a high headland and went home.

Norse fighting men valued bravery and laughed at death, but they did not always win their battles. In North America they could not defeat the Skraelings.

Thorfinn Karlsefni led a large fleet from Greenland to the new land a year or so later, carrying 250 men and women. They spent several years there, living in houses of sod and stone to keep out the cold winds that raged across the headland. Their sheep and goats grazed on the natural meadows. They made rough clothing from the sheep's wool and drank nourishing goat's milk. The first winter, Thorfinn's wife, Gudrid, gave birth to a baby boy named Snorri – the first European child born in North America.

The winter was harsh. People grew hungry and sick, and they fought with each other. They too met the Native people of the land. They called them *Skraelings*, and fought with them. The Skraelings fought back, and soon the settlers were afraid to stay in this new land. Snorri was three years old when he returned to Greenland.

After that, Norse sailors seldom visited the land west of Greenland. The seas were rough, the climate was getting colder, and the Skraelings fought hard to defend their land. In Greenland, the cold and lonely Norse settlements slowly dwindled away, defeated by the worsening climate. The Norse people retreated to Iceland, or the countries of their ancestors: Norway, Sweden, and Denmark. So the Vikings went no more to Vinland the Good, and remembered it only in the sagas the skalds told in the great halls at night.

Not long after the Norse had abandoned Vinland the Good for ever, Inuit in their kayaks began exploring the coast of Labrador, the places where Leif and Thorvald had been. It would be hundreds of years before Europeans returned to the shores of Canada.

The Explorers

About five hundred years after Leif Ericsson's time, Native people must have stood among the trees along the coast of Newfoundland, watching in astonishment as a sailing ship came up over the horizon, its grey sails waving like the wings of a great wooden bird.

Native people had been living on the Atlantic shores

for about nine thousand years. They understood the land and the sea and how to live well from both. Micmacs, Maliseets, and Abenakis shared the mainland and the islands south of the great river that would later be called the St. Lawrence. North of the river lay the country of the Montagnais. On the island of Newfoundland lived the Beothuk. Farther to the north was the territory of the Inuit.

In winter and spring, when floating ice packs from the Arctic came drifting and grinding along the shore, people lived inland, in the forests, taking shelter in skin-covered wigwams. Dressed in bearskin cloaks and beaver furs, they hunted moose, deer, caribou, and small game. When summer came, they moved to bays along the coast. There they wore cooler deerskin clothes, or nothing at all in the hottest weather. They caught salmon and eels in the river and gathered clams and mussels by the shore. Although the different tribes spoke different languages, they shared quite a few words and they understood each other's ways.

Then, on a spring day in 1497, a ship called *Mathew*, commanded by a man named John Cabot, reached their shores from Europe.

What made European sailors set out across the oceans of the world? Europe had changed since Leif Ericsson's day. Learning had spread. Ships now plied the coasts of Europe, and adventurers gazed at maps and wondered what lay beyond. Some five hundred years after the Norsemen had

These Beothuk men are heading for Funk Island, Newfoundland, to gather birds' eggs. Their bodies smeared with red ochre, they brave the rough Atlantic in their distinctive high-sided canoe. Detail: *bone ornaments found in Beothuk sites; their purpose is unknown.*

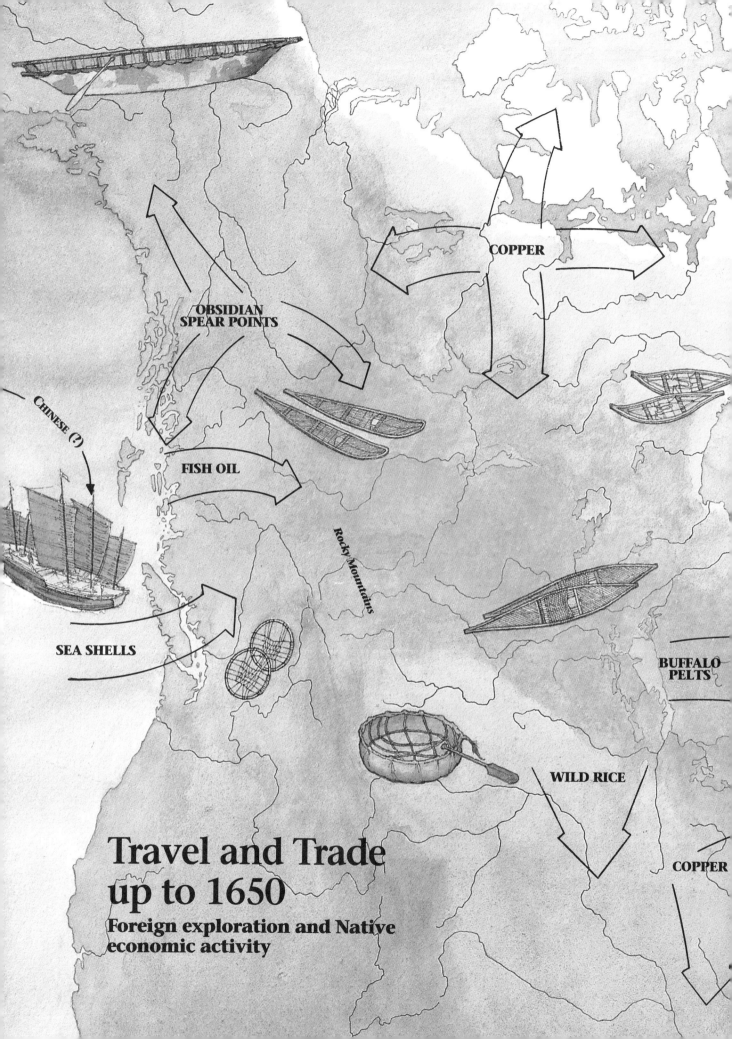

CHINESE (?)

COPPER

OBSIDIAN
SPEAR POINTS

FISH OIL

Rocky Mountains

SEA SHELLS

WILD RICE

BUFFALO
PELTS

COPPER

Travel and Trade
up to 1650
**Foreign exploration and Native
economic activity**

Greenland

Baffin Island

Davis Strait

NORSE

DAVIS, 1585

FROBISHER, 1576

HUDSON, 1610

Hudson Strait

ARROWHEAD FLINTS

CABOT, 1497

Hudson Bay

Labrador

L'Anse aux Meadows

Red Bay

Strait of
Belle Isle

St. John's

Newfoundland

CARTIER, 1535

Gulf of
St. Lawrence

Cape Breton Island

Gaspe Peninsula

TOBACCO

Acadia

Stadacona

Ste. Croix

Port-Royal

SILVER

St. Lawrence River

Hochelaga

CORN

BIRCHBARK
CANOES

SEA
SHELLS

How Sailors Found Their Way

Until recent times, sailors had only the wind in their sails to drive them. Any navigator worth his pay could find the North Star and judge from it just how far north his ship had reached. In daytime, he could measure by the sun with instruments called astrolabes, backstaffs, and quadrants. After the compass (shown above) was invented in the 1100s, a navigator could steer a straight course in any direction.

Judging how far east or west a ship had travelled was almost impossible. To cross from Europe to Canada, sailors headed west until they saw land. The best signs that land was near were the flights of birds, the smell of forests, and the mariner's sixth sense.

ventured to Vinland, Christopher Columbus sailed from Spain, out into the Atlantic. Sailors and navigators knew the world was round, and Columbus thought that if he sailed west, he should reach the Far East – the home of rare and precious spices treasured by Europe. Instead of China and the Spice Islands of the East, he found another land blocking the way – the Americas. It was a new world to Europeans, though millions of Native North and South Americans had called it home for a hundred centuries.

Five years after Columbus, John Cabot set out from Bristol, England, in the *Mathew*. Taking a more northerly route that he hoped would bring him to the Far East, he found instead the island we call Newfoundland. Cabot sailed along its coast. Along the rugged, forested shore, his men discovered that they could catch codfish just by trailing baskets over the side of the ship.

When they returned to England, King Henry VII rewarded Cabot with money and ships, and he set out once more for another look at his New Found Land. In England they awaited his return, but Cabot and his ships never came back, and no one ever found out what happened to them.

Still, the merchants of Europe remembered those baskets crammed with codfish, and Cabot's fate did not stop fleets of fishing boats from setting out for his new land. They found what they were looking for – and more. Big black whales and white belugas spouted and dived in the coastal waters. Walruses, seals, and sea lions bellowed from the rocks. White clouds of seabirds wheeled and shrieked over the cliffs, and fat, flightless auks waddled over the islands. The rivers were rich with salmon. Off the east coast stretched a vast, submerged continent the sailors called the Grand Banks. More cod than they had ever imagined swam there. Within a few years, hundreds of ships were heading for the new land every spring.

The sailors called it many names – Newfoundland, Terre-Neuve, Tierra Nueva – because they spoke English,

Gaelic, French, Basque, Spanish, or Portuguese. They fished at Labrador (named for a Portuguese explorer) and the Strait of Belle Isle. They fished from Cape Breton Island. But thousands chose the bays and harbours of Newfoundland. When Sir Humphrey Gilbert came to Newfoundland in 1583, he said he found "men of all nations" gathered in the harbour at St. John's. He could buy all the food and supplies he needed "as if we had been in a city." But St. John's and all the other harbours were only summer colonies, abandoned every fall when the sailors went home with their catch.

In 1534, François I, the King of France, sent Jacques Cartier to explore this Terre-Neuve where the fishermen were going. In France, they had heard tales of the Spanish warriors called *conquistadores*, or conquerors, who had followed Columbus. In Mexico the Spanish had seized the golden empire of the Aztecs, and in Peru they had overthrown the Incas and plundered their treasures. Were there golden empires for the French to find and conquer in the lands beyond Terre-Neuve?

Cartier explored and mapped and named, everywhere he went. When he explored the St. Lawrence River, he asked the people he met what they called their land. They answered, "Canada." The word meant "the village" in their language, but Cartier thought it was the name of the whole country, and he put "Canada" on the map.

The Micmacs of Atlantic Canada were among the first Native people to encounter the newcomers from Europe. They traded furs for such items as these firearms, which became part of their culture, just as the European settlers adopted canoes and snowshoes.

Days of the Whalers

Any summer day in the 1500s, the Labrador harbour of Red Bay was one of the busiest places on the coast. Ships swung at anchor on the choppy waters of the bay. Wharfs, huts, and houses crowded the shore. Hot ovens belched black smoke, and the sea breeze whipped it away. Hundreds of sweating, shouting men were hard at work.

Red Bay was a whaling port. Out in the Strait of Belle Isle, whalers rowing fast boats called *chalupas* chased the whales that migrated through the strait all summer long. If they caught up with one, they drove their harpoons deep into it. Then, with the dead whale in tow, they struggled back to Red Bay. Fat cauldrons simmered with thick slabs of blubber, and out poured rich whale oil. When the oil cooled, the whaling men poured it

into barrels and loaded the barrels aboard waiting galleons. Back home, the oil would become lamp fuel and soap and a hundred other useful things.

These whalers were Basques, and their home was the hill country between Spain and France. They spoke a language no one else understood, and they lived by the bounty of the sea. Once their ancestors had hunted whales on their own coasts. Now those whales were gone, and the whalers came instead to this new land, which they called Terranova.

For almost a hundred years, whales remained plentiful in Terranova, and the Basques came every spring. But about the time Samuel de Champlain came to Canada to found New France, the overhunted whales were becoming rare in the Strait of Belle Isle. The day of the Basque whalers was ending.

At Stadacona

When Jacques Cartier sailed into the Gulf of St. Lawrence in 1534, word of his arrival spread to the nearby village of Stadacona, which stood high on a cape above the great river (where Quebec City is now). Donnacona's people had always lived there, planting fields of corn, beans, and squash beyond their longhouses. Now, in his old age, Donnacona had a problem no other chief had faced. There were strangers on the coast, travelling in great wooden houses that moved over the water. They came from the sea. Did they come from the underwater world, where the spirits of the dead dwelt?

Although the strangers had not yet come to Stadacona, they had been seen downriver, where the water turned salt. Some years they stayed all summer, fishing and hunting whales. If they were angered, they pointed magic sticks that roared and flamed, and death flew where they pointed. If they were friendly, they offered beautiful beads, and blades stronger than stone. Traders from neighbouring tribes who had met the strangers had shown Donnacona the wonderful gifts they had received.

Summer came. Donnacona and his people took their canoes downriver to Gaspé to fish, and there they finally met the strangers. The young men paddled canoes out to the floating vessels, and the strangers gave them mirrors and sharp knives. Then the sailors came ashore and gave every woman a little bell. Donnacona's people danced and sang a welcome, but the strangers met this hospitality with rudeness. They put up a tall cross on the shore. Although Donnacona did not know exactly what that meant, he understood that these men were claiming his people's land as their own. From his canoe, he made an angry speech telling them that this land had been his people's forever. But the strangers did not seem to understand.

The strangers were Jacques Cartier and his men, and they wanted something from Donnacona: his sons, Domagaya and Taignoagny. By signs and gestures, Cartier asked whether the two would go with him to France, and promised they would come back the next spring. Donnacona did not know where they were going, but he could not stop Cartier from taking them. So Domagaya and Taignoagny sailed away. The tribe went back to Stadacona fearing they would never again see the chief's sons.

A year passed. At last news came to Stadacona that Cartier's ships had been seen coming up the river. Domagaya and Taignoagny were aboard! Donnacona greeted his sons joyfully and welcomed Jacques Cartier back. Perhaps they would become friends after all. Cartier's men would bring their gifts, and Donnacona's people would feed them and give them furs. Other tribes would come to Stadacona from all over the country to trade and share the new magic of the strangers.

But Taignoagny and Domagaya soon reported that their year among the French, though exciting, had not been happy. The land across the ocean was huge and rich and the great cities were full of amazing sights, but the people there were cruel. Donnacona also learned from his sons that Jacques Cartier intended to stay and to make this land his own. Meanwhile, Cartier and his men travelled farther upriver and visited a rival village called Hochelaga (where Montreal is now). Then they returned to spend the winter near Stadacona.

When autumn came, Cartier's sailors were startled and delighted to see the blazing scarlet and gold woods, but the

At Stadacona, in 1535, Chief Donnacona comes out to meet Jacques Cartier.

winter that followed terrified them. They had never known such snowfalls, never felt such cold, and the food they had brought with them did not keep them strong. One by one, they grew weak and sick with scurvy. Donnacona's people healed them with tea brewed from spruce bark. In the spring, the weakened, disappointed explorers set sail for home. They had discovered no golden empires in Canada, and no sea passage to the Far East.

Yet Stadacona's troubles were not over. European sailors continued to come from over the sea. The Native people who lived along the river fought over the valuable trade goods the strangers offered, until their way of life was destroyed. When Samuel de Champlain sailed up the St. Lawrence about fifty years later, no one lived at Stadacona. Where there had been bustling villages along the river, Champlain found only meadows.

Donnacona never knew of this disaster. At the end of his second trip to Canada, Jacques Cartier had seized the chief and carried him back to France. Donnacona had died there without ever seeing his homeland again. It was as if, by meeting the strangers, Donnacona and all his people – and Stadacona itself – had been dragged off to the underwater world of the dead.

Fur Traders

Jacques Cartier went home bitterly disappointed. He called the bleak, rocky shores visited by the fishermen "the land God gave to Cain." The land along the St. Lawrence River looked far better, and once Cartier thought he had found diamonds there, but when he took them to France, everyone laughed – his diamonds were only quartz. After that, few explorers came treasure-seeking in Canada. But the fishermen and whaling men continued to come every summer. Europe was hungry for the cod they caught, and eager for whale oil for lamps and soap.

Along the coast, the fishermen met the Beothuk, Micmac, and Montagnais bands who came down from the

forests to the shore each summer. Often the Native people and the European fishermen feared and distrusted each other. A Beothuk family in Newfoundland would be angry when intruders took over their stretch of shoreline. A crew of fishermen would be furious when gear they had left behind in the fall disappeared during the winter. Yet sometimes Natives and newcomers helped each other. The fishermen had iron knives that cut much better than stone, cooking pots made of hard, shiny copper, and warm blankets of bright woollen cloth. The Native people wanted all these things and they had something valuable to offer in return: the cloaks they wore, made from fine, glossy animal furs.

Slowly, cautiously, the Native people and the Europeans began to trade. Beaver pelts were the ones fishermen wanted most. "The beaver does everything perfectly," said one Montagnais trader, when he saw how much the fishermen would give for beaver skins. "It makes kettles, hatchets, swords, knives, and bread. It makes everything." Gradually those furs drew adventurers, traders, and explorers to Canada, leading them far inland from the New Found Land of the fishermen and the whalers.

Guided ashore by a fire, merchant fishermen show their wares to Montagnais traders. Native traders did well selling their old clothes for axes, blankets, cloth, and other manufactured goods from Europe.

Beavers, Beaver Hair, and Beaver Hats

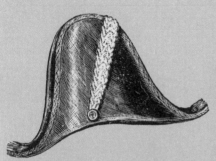

The European fur traders who came to Canada wanted beaver more than any other fur, and these pelts were made into hats. Does this mean that everyone in Europe walked around wearing furry hats? Not at all. What the hatters needed was the *hair* from the beaver skins, which they used to make felt.

To keep a beaver warm in cold northern waters, its hairs are covered with microscopic hooks or barbs that trap an insulating layer of air. Long ago, hatters learned to shave beaver hair off the pelt, chop it up finely, and crush it together into a kind of stiff felt that could be pressed into any shape. It was waterproof

and would hold its shape longer than any other material. Beaver felt made fashionable broad-brimmed tricornes, sometimes decorated with a feather.

The best hairs for felt were the short underhairs, so early fur traders paid the highest prices for old furs that had been used as cloaks until the long outer hairs had worn off. At first the Native traders laughed and said, "See what treasures they give us for our old clothes." But they soon learned to drive hard bargains.

Northern Seas

The Northwest Passage! A shortcut to the Far East, to Asia and India, to spices, silks, wealth, and glory. From the time of Cabot and Cartier, every boy in Europe dreamed of sailing west and finding it. Since Canada was in the way, sailors sought the passage farther and farther north.

Some explorers refused to believe that whole oceans could be covered with ice, and set out to sail right over the North Pole to Asia. In 1576, the English explorer Martin Frobisher thought he had found the passage, and named it Frobisher's Strait, but it turned out to be just a bay on Baffin Island. Even the "gold" he thought he had found was worthless.

A few years later, another Englishman, John Davis, led four ships with the names *Sunshine, Moonshine, Mermaid,*

Pistol and sword in hand,
fighting sailor Martin Frobisher
roamed the seas. When he
reached Frobisher Bay on
Baffin Island, the hunt for gold
distracted him from the search
for the Northwest Passage.
In the end he found neither.

Seeking a passage around North America to the Pacific Ocean and the riches of Asia, John Davis sailed north along the coast of Greenland. Here, his men have gone ashore to play football with a crowd of Inuit.

and *North Star* far into the North. During hot, sunny days at the end of June, his men went ashore and played football with the Inuit. But, winter or summer, ice floes blocked the way through Davis Strait. John Davis never found the passage, either.

In 1610, twenty-five years later, Henry Hudson explored a strait that Martin Frobisher had glimpsed. For six weeks, his ship *Discovery* fought the turbulent waters. Tides fell twelve metres in a few hours, and jagged reefs thrust their teeth out of deep water. Finally, the strait opened up and the crew of the *Discovery* found themselves sailing into a great salt sea. Hudson thought he had captained his ship through North America and into the Pacific. He set his course for the Spice Islands.

But Hudson was mistaken. By October he and the *Discovery* were still far from the riches of the East. They had sailed into Hudson Bay. There was no Northwest Passage here, and winter was coming on.

Twenty-one men spent a cold, fearful winter aboard the *Discovery*. The ship was trapped in ice and buried in snow. As the men huddled in their cabins, scurvy turned their mouths black and made their teeth fall out, and they had no fresh foods to stop it. They argued and fought all winter. When spring finally came, their food was nearly gone, and most of the men believed they would never see their homes again.

Hudson's officers hatched a desperate plot. "Get rid of Hudson and the sick men," they insisted, "or the rest of us will never get home." The men hesitated, because mutiny was a terrible crime. Then they struck. Henry Hudson, his son John, and six sailors were driven into the ship's boat. One more sailor stepped into the boat beside his captain, too loyal to save his life by mutiny. The mutineers sailed away, closing their ears to the cries of their victims, and the Hudsons and the seven others were left to drift in Hudson Bay in the open boat until they died.

A few years later, Nicholas Vignau, a French explorer who was travelling on the Ottawa River, heard tales about a white man who had died by the shores of a bay far to the north. It may have been young John Hudson.

Rats, Weeds, and Viruses

When fishermen and explorers sailed from Europe to Canada, they brought small stowaways with them. Every ship had rats, and every time a ship was anchored in some sandy cove the rats had a chance to go ashore and discover the New World for themselves. Long before anyone from Europe settled in Canada, the rodents had scattered far and wide across the continent.

Rats were not the only animals aboard the ships. Soon pigs, horses, and cattle escaped to run wild in the new land. Plants arrived, too. Before the European ships came to this continent, there was not one dandelion in North America, but seeds crossed the ocean, stuck to a sailor's baggage or the mud of his boot. Once ashore, plants migrated faster than the humans they had come with. Today, if you collect ten different wild plants in a Canadian field, chances are that five will be the descendants of immigrants.

The Last Beothuk

Shawnandithit, the last of the Beothuk people, died in St. John's, Newfoundland, on June 6, 1829. She was about twenty-eight years old.

There were never many Beothuks. Newfoundland could not support many people. It had no moose and few deer, and although the Beothuks gathered shellfish on the shores, they did not have boats from which to fish for cod. Unlike other Native people, the Beothuks did not trade furs with the fishermen who came to Newfoundland. The fishermen thought they were thieves, and the two groups became enemies. When fishermen settled along the coast, life grew hard for the Beothuks, who needed the shellfish they had always gathered there. Trapped in the interior, they became hungry and sick. When they ventured out, though, they were shot at. No more than a handful had survived by 1823, when Shawnandithit's aunt, Demasduwit, died while held captive by the English. Shawnandithit was captured, starving and ill.

Her captors named her Nancy, and she stayed with them in St. John's for six years. She lived in the home of William Cormack, an explorer eager to learn more about her people. The pictures she drew and the stories she told him are almost everything we know about the Beothuks. There is no picture of Shawnandithit. This portrait, by an unknown English painter, is of Demasduwit.

Much less welcome immigrants also found their way across the ocean. For thousands of years, Europe had shared its germs and diseases with Asia and Africa. The diseases were deadly, but over the centuries many people had built up some immunity to them. This meant that a disease might not infect everybody, or that it might weaken its victims but not kill them. In the Americas, where these diseases had never existed, no one was immune.

Like rats and dandelions, measles and fevers and tuberculosis and smallpox came on the ships. The sailors and explorers did not know about bacteria and viruses or how diseases spread, but spread they did. The microscopic newcomers passed from tribe to tribe, killing thousands.

In vain, Native healers worked their medicine. In some places, everyone in the village sickened and died, leaving too few to bury the dead. Across the Americas, as many as nine out of every ten people may have died from diseases. Nations collapsed.

In the early 1600s, Membertou, a very old headman of the Micmac at Port-Royal, in Acadia, could remember back almost to the days when the strangers first came to his land. "In my youth," Membertou said, "I have seen my people as thickly planted here as the hairs on my head. Since the French mingle with us, we are dying fast."

People in Europe knew little of the destruction they had caused. They were beginning to see North America as an exciting new land, and by the early 1600s they were building permanent settlements. English fishermen began colonies in Newfoundland. Religious pilgrims from England landed in New England. The Dutch founded New Amsterdam, which was later taken over by the English and became New York. English adventurers settled in Virginia, and Spanish in Florida. The French built a colony in Acadia, and a few years later they came again up the St. Lawrence River to found Quebec where Stadacona had once been. But when they returned, North America was a land in mourning. Many of its Native people had died of imported diseases.

Fur traders and explorers were not the only newcomers to North America. Plants and animals came early and spread rapidly.

Chapter 3
Habitants and Voyageurs

I N 1603, SAMUEL DE CHAMPLAIN SAILED UP THE ST. LAWRENCE RIVER and gazed at the meadows where Stadacona and Hochelaga had once stood. "You could hardly hope to find a more beautiful country," he exclaimed. Five years later, he came again. With twenty-eight men, he landed at Quebec, which means "the place where the river narrows" in the language of the Montagnais people who lived along the river. Champlain's men built a cluster of buildings by the river's edge, and he named it the Habitation of Quebec. Samuel de Champlain had brought French settlers to Canada to stay.

During that first winter, most of these pioneers of Quebec died of cold and scurvy and lack of food. Champlain needed help. The Montagnais brought corn and meat to the Habitation, and they showed Champlain how to boil spruce bark in water to make a cure for scurvy. They also brought furs to trade. Over the years, only the

Previous pages:
In 1670, Jeanne Mance welcomes Native traders with a feast in the grounds of her hospital in Montreal. The feast is a hearty stew: meat from beavers, bears, even cats and dogs, has gone into the big pot, with corn, grapes, and raisins.

Champlain drew this complicated plan of the Habitation he had built at Quebec in 1608. This cluster of buildings grew into the oldest permanent French community in North America.

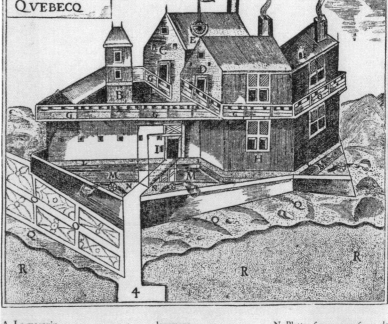

ABITATION DE QVEBECQ

A Le magazin.
B Colombier.
C Corps de logis où font nos armes, & pour loger les ouuriers.
D Autre corps de logis pour les ouuriers.
E Cadran.
F Autre corps de logis où eſt la forge, & artiſans logés.
G Galleries tout au tour des logemens.
H Logis du ſieur de Champlain.
I La porte de l'habitation, où il y a pont-leuis.
L Promenoir autour de l'habitation contenant 10. pieds de large iuſques ſur le bort du foſſé.
M Foſſés tout autour de l'habitation.
N Plattes formes, en façon de tenailles pour mettre le canon.
O Iardin du ſieur de Champlain.
P La cuiſine.
Q Place deuant l'habitation ſur le bort de la riuiere.
R La grande riuiere de ſainɛt Lorens.

p. 303.

The Pirate Admiral

In 1610, while Samuel de Champlain was building his Habitation at Quebec, Peter Easton, the Pirate Admiral, arrived at Harbour Grace, Newfoundland.

All that summer, Captain Easton was the lord of Conception Bay. He did as he pleased. He boarded fishing boats and trading ships, being cruel or generous as the mood struck him. He took food, equipment, and gunpowder. He took carpenters, whether they were willing or not, to keep his ships in fighting trim.

On the rocky headland of Harbour Grace, Easton's men built a fort to keep themselves safe from attack. When his mood was good, Easton invited fishermen and colonists to drink with him, while he boasted of his plans. Soon, he said, he would sail away in pursuit of Spanish gold. This talk of easy riches tempted many fishermen. Five hundred sailors abandoned the fishing fleet to join Easton.

In July 1612, Captain Easton was ready. With a thousand men and ten ships, he sailed away to hunt the ships that hauled gold from Spain's American empire

home to Seville. In mid-Atlantic, he found the storm-battered treasure galleons and captured three of them. His fortune was made. He sailed to France and "lived rich" for the rest of his days.

Captain Easton never returned to Harbour Grace, but some of the fishermen who had sailed with him did. Easton had been their springboard to gold and glory, and they chose to forget how he had plundered the colonists of Newfoundland. They preferred to remember the Pirate Admiral as a hero, and they kept the legend of Peter Easton alive.

When Champlain reached Huron country in 1615, he was not the first Frenchman to have arrived there. In this picture, young fur trader Etienne Brûlé is on hand to meet him. Brûlé lived among the Hurons for more than twenty years.

trade in furs would keep his little outpost going. Champlain talked with the Native people, travelled with them, and helped them in their wars. He did not know how to swim, but he rode bravely in their canoes through the wildest rapids. He wanted to endure the hardships they took for granted. Everywhere he journeyed, he recorded what he saw in his maps and diaries. He came to know Canada better than any European explorer ever had before.

In July 1615, Champlain set out on his longest voyage in this new country. He was going to the country of the Huron people, more than a thousand kilometres inland, by the shores of a freshwater sea, Lake Huron. For nearly a month, he and his Native guides and companions pushed their way up wild rivers along a route that Native traders had followed for centuries. They carried their goods and canoes over sixty portages and shot as many rapids before they reached Lake Huron. Finally they arrived in the Huron country.

Champlain was amazed by what he saw. All the Native people he knew – the Micmac, the Montagnais, the Ottawa, the Algonquin – were nomads and hunters of the wood-lands. In small bands, carrying all they owned, they roamed vast territories where they hunted, fished, and gathered plants. The Huron nation was different. In their country Champlain found tilled fields and, just beyond them, a big town surrounded by tall palisades. Crowds of men, women, and children came out to greet him. For Champlain, seeing these towns and fields and crowds of people was almost like being back in France. "The country here is all fertile and a delight to see," he wrote admiringly.

The Corngrowers

Instead of moving about in small hunting bands, the Hurons lived in one place. They grew corn, beans, squash, and tobacco in the fields that surrounded their towns. Besides being prosperous farmers, they were courageous warriors and skilful diplomats, and they had become the most powerful Native nation north of the Great Lakes. Laden with corn and tobacco, their trade canoes plied the Great Lakes and the rivers of what are now northern Ontario and Quebec. No sooner had Champlain built his Habitation at Quebec than Huron traders began bringing furs down the long river routes to trade there.

In the first town Champlain came to, he saw dozens of sturdy longhouses – each one the home of several families. In the Huron country, he soon learned, there were many towns, and some had as many as 2000 people. Their homeland was a small peninsula on Georgian Bay, in Lake Huron, and more than 20000 people lived there. The Hurons had joined several tribes and towns into a nation, the Huron Confederacy. They had dozens of chiefs, who met in great councils. The chiefs were men, but women also had power because they tended and owned the fields that produced the corn. And women chose the chiefs.

The Hurons had one great rival, a confederacy of tribes south of Lake Ontario. These tribes called themselves the People of the Longhouse, but their enemies had long ago given them the name Iroquois, which means rattlesnake. The Hurons and the Iroquois spoke similar languages and

In the Iroquoian farming nations, the fields and crops belonged to the women. Women planted them, weeded them, and harvested the corn – and kept away the birds.

lived the same way of life, but they had been enemies for hundreds of years. Their rivalry grew fiercer after the French arrived. Each feared the other could seize the routes to the coast and control the trade with the newcomers. The losers might vanish, the way Stadacona and Hochelaga had vanished. That was why there were tall palisades around the Huron towns. And that was why Champlain had come.

Atironta, a Huron war leader, had invited Champlain to the Huron country because he wanted the French to fight the Iroquois alongside the Hurons. Champlain could not refuse him. Without the Hurons there would be few furs at Quebec, and without furs there would be no colony. So Champlain's colony depended on the outcome of the Huron-Iroquois war.

That summer Atironta and Champlain travelled through the country, gathering warriors for a raid on the Iroquois. In September, 500 Hurons and a handful of Frenchmen set forth for battle. In a hundred canoes, they crossed Lake Ontario and invaded Iroquois country. Their target was a large Iroquois town crowded with longhouses, surrounded by cornfields, and, like the Huron towns, protected by rows of palisades.

Atironta and his warriors attacked, while Champlain and his French companions fired their muskets into the village. But the Iroquois defended themselves with skill and bravery, and the attack failed. Champlain was wounded in the knee by an arrow, and the defeated invaders turned homeward, carrying him on their backs. He spent the winter among the Hurons and returned to Quebec in the summer.

The French and the Hurons remained allies, for they still needed each other. Traders like Etienne Brûlé lived among the Hurons for years, and young Hurons went to live at Quebec. Missionaries went into the Huron country. The French dreamed of converting all the Native people of Canada to their own Christian faith. If the Hurons became Christians, they told themselves, other Native nations would follow. And because the Hurons wanted the friendship of the French, they agreed to be hospitable to these strange visitors. In a few years, mission houses stood among the Huron longhouses. Black-robed priests were hard at work, learning the Huron language and preaching Christianity.

Father Jean de Brébeuf arrived in the Huron country in 1626, eager to bring word of his God to the people there. At first Huron life shocked and frightened him. He hated the unfamiliar food and the dark, smoky longhouses. He knew nothing of Huron ways and customs, and even the children laughed at his ignorance. As Brébeuf and his fellow priests slowly learned the Huron language, he began to understand and admire his hosts. He still dreamed of converting them to his faith, but most Hurons preferred their own beliefs.

Jesuit missionary Jean de Brébeuf lived among the Huron people for fifteen years, fought with them against the Iroquois, and died when the Iroquois conquered the Huron nation. The Roman Catholic Church honours him as a saint and a martyr.

Champlain's Colony

While the missionaries worked among the Hurons, Samuel de Champlain had a colony to build. He wanted much more than a trading post at Quebec. He wanted many people to come from France, to raise families and to build towns and farms and businesses. He was determined to see his colony become a place worthy of the name New

France. He believed it would become large and prosperous, bringing wealth and honour to his master, the King of France.

Labourers, artisans, and farmers arrived at the Habitation. Louis and Marie Hébert and their children were the first family to settle. One of their daughters, Anne, became the first bride in New France. The Héberts began growing vegetables and herbs to support themselves and the community. So did a sailor named Abraham Martin, and the place where he started his farm became known as the Plains of Abraham. Champlain's Habitation grew into the town of Quebec, with homes, a church, warehouses, and a fort.

Some colonists were inspired by their religious faith to come. A nun named Marie de l'Incarnation had a vision that told her to do God's work in New France. Even though the son she had borne before becoming a nun beat at her convent door, crying, "Give me back my mother," Marie set sail for Quebec. She spent the rest of her life in New France, tending the sick, teaching, and praying for the settlers. A few years after Marie de l'Incarnation arrived, Paul de

Samuel de Champlain's young wife, Hélène, lived most of her life in Paris, but in 1620 she came with him to Quebec and spent four years there. The artist has imagined the welcome the handful of settlers gave her.

Maisonneuve led a group of devout colonists from France to Quebec and on up the river to where Hochelaga had stood. They founded a mission community there and named it Ville-Marie. In time it became the town of Montreal.

Samuel de Champlain nurtured his colony devotedly. Over the years, he crossed the Atlantic more than twenty times. Sometimes he would hold council with Native chiefs, then sail to France to beg support from the king, then return to encourage his pioneers at Quebec, then rush back to France to have one of his books published, all within a single year. He was much too busy to spend time with his young wife, Hélène. She had married Champlain when she was only twelve, but she continued to live in France while he was away across the ocean. Hélène visited New France only once, and after four years at Quebec, she went home to spend the rest of her life in Paris.

When Champlain died at Quebec in 1635, only a few hundred people called New France home, but he had planted the French flag in Canada and created a permanent community of European settlers here. He was the founder of New France.

The coat of arms of New France was displayed over the gates of the city of Quebec.

Louis XIV Saves New France

In the 1640s the proud Huron nation was in desperate trouble. The war with the Iroquois raged more furiously than ever. Meanwhile, smallpox and fever, unwittingly brought by the missionaries, swept the longhouses, killing half the population. The survivors were grieving and fearful. Some became Christians, hoping the new religion would comfort them. Others held to their own ways, blaming the priests for the sorrows that had come to them. Christian Hurons began to live apart from the others, and the nation became divided.

Then, in 1649, the Iroquois invaded the Huron country. They stormed the palisades, clubbed down the defenders, and burned the longhouses and cornfields. The Huron nation collapsed. Some people escaped, but

Amid the towns and cornfields of the Huron people near Georgian Bay, the French missionary priests built their own little community – Ste-Marie Among the Hurons. It was destroyed when the Iroquois attacked in 1649.

hundreds were killed and even more were taken prisoner, to be adopted into the Iroquois nation. The Christian priests burned their mission, called Ste-Marie Among the Hurons, and ran for their lives. But after more than twenty years among the Huron people, Father Brébeuf was determined to stay with them. Iroquois warriors put him to death along with Huron warriors they had captured.

Soon the Iroquois were attacking New France itself. Champlain and his soldiers had helped the enemies of the Iroquois, and the Iroquois intended to teach Champlain's colonists who the true masters of Canada were. No more furs came down to Quebec. Iroquois war parties laid siege to Montreal and raided Quebec, sending terrified farmers fleeing from their fields. Some settlers gave up in despair and went back to France. Fifty years after Champlain founded Quebec, barely 3000 colonists lived in New France, and the colony was growing weaker.

In 1663, Louis XIV was just beginning his long reign as one of France's mightiest kings. He refused to let New France collapse. Instead, he took charge of his besieged colony. He sent a powerful governor general and a regiment of soldiers to fight the Iroquois. The Iroquois were too skilled to be defeated by European soldiers who knew nothing of forest warfare, but now that the French had become stronger, the Iroquois agreed to make peace.

The French soldiers stayed on to become settlers. The king gave the army officers great tracts of land called *seigneuries*, and many of the soldiers settled down as their tenants.

The king also began sending workers to his colony. Then, since there were already six young men for every woman in New France, he set about encouraging young

Heroines of Ville-Marie

Of all the people who followed Paul de Maisonneuve to his settlement at Ville-Marie (which grew into Montreal), Jeanne Mance and Marguerite Bourgeoys are among the best remembered.

Jeanne Mance (pictured here) was among Maisonneuve's first seventy pioneers. She had one goal: to build a mission hospital. She called her hospital the Hôtel-Dieu (the hostel of God) and she worked tirelessly there for the next thirty-one years, tending the sick and injured among the Montagnais, the Hurons, and the French.

Marguerite Bourgeoys was a teacher. Like Jeanne Mance, she was already in her thirties when she came to Ville-Marie in 1653. She set up her first school in a stable. At first, there were so few girls to teach that she too looked after the sick. Then, when the first *filles du roi* arrived from France in 1665, she made a home for them. A sign on her door read "Girls to Marry," and she acted as matchmaker.

Later she recruited more teachers, and established three schools where spinning, sewing, and cooking were taught, as well as reading and writing. She was the founder of the Congregation of Notre-Dame, an order of teaching nuns.

Both Jeanne Mance and Marguerite Bourgeoys are remembered for the devotion and energy they gave their work, but even more for the love they poured into it.

women to immigrate. He offered gifts of money to help them get started, and during the 1660s nearly a thousand agreed to seek new lives across the ocean. Françoise Hobbé of Paris accepted the royal invitation to sail for Canada in 1668. Like most of the *filles du roi*, she soon found a husband. She married a young soldier named Michel Roy, and the couple settled on a farm near the town of Trois-Rivières and raised a large family.

Habitants

All the horses in New France were descendants of the twenty-one mares and two stallions (one of them pictured here) that King Louis XIV of France sent over from his stables in 1665. By the next century, most farmers owned their own horse, something only nobles could hope to do in Europe.

With peace restored and immigrants arriving every summer, New France began to recover. The Hurons no longer brought furs to Montreal, but other Native traders did. *Voyageurs* of New France went inland to meet them in the *pays d'en haut*, the upper country, which meant all the territories beyond the St. Lawrence Valley. With all the soldiers, labourers, and filles du roi sent by Louis XIV, New France had become home to more than 10000 people by the 1680s. After that, fewer immigrants crossed the ocean, so it came about that these few thousand pioneer men and women were the ancestors of millions of French Canadians.

As New France grew, most of its people did what Françoise Hobbé and Michel Roy did: they became farmers. Most farm families did nearly everything for themselves. Just to clear the trees from their land took years. They built their own homes and furniture from the wood they cut. They made their own rough homespun clothes from the wool and flax they raised, and they grew most of their food in their own fields and gardens. It was hard work, but the land was fertile and there was plenty of it. The people who lived on the farms of New France called themselves *habitants*.

Farm families were big families. Most children in New France had eight or ten sisters and brothers, crammed together in small two-room farmhouses heated only by a fireplace in the kitchen. They worked on their parents' farms until they grew up, and then cleared more land of its trees and started farms of their own.

Each year, farm families in New France had to pay part of their crop to their parish priest and another part to the *seigneur* who owned their land. Some seigneuries were owned by the king's officials, others by army officers from noble families, and others by religious orders of priests and nuns. These were powerful people, the rulers of New France. They expected the habitants who farmed the land to support them.

By the time Françoise and Michel Roy's children and grandchildren were starting their own farms, the shores of the St. Lawrence River from below Quebec to Montreal were an almost unbroken line of tidy wooden homes. In spring, the habitants and their ox teams ploughed the long, narrow fields stretching back into the hills. In summer, they tended the precious crops of wheat and let the cattle graze in the meadows. In fall, after the harvest, it was time to slaughter the fat pigs and make salt pork for the winter. Winter was the season for cutting wood and hauling grain to the seigneur's mill.

Despite the burdens, life became easier as the years passed. Often the habitants gathered at the church, with their children crowded around them, to celebrate another marriage or baptism. When they drove a wagonload of grain to the mill or spent a lively evening dancing and sharing stories, the descendants of soldiers and filles du roi could be proud of the land they had cultivated and the homes they loved.

Not everyone in New France lived on a farm. The founders of Montreal, who had come to build a mission but had found themselves in the midst of the Iroquois wars, eventually made Montreal into a busy trading town. Montreal was the centre of the fur trade, and its streets were lined with the warehouses of the merchants and the voyageurs' favourite taverns.

On the waterfront at Quebec, the site of Champlain's Habitation was now crowded with storehouses and docks. Three-masted sailing ships arrived from France with cargo, passengers, and news. Small boats sailed up and down the river, the great highway of the colony. Newly arrived

One winter, when cash ran low, the intendant of New France paid the colony's debts by writing IOUs on playing cards. After that, all paper money in New France was called "card money." This artist's impression shows what the first playing-card money might have looked like.

Quebec City

At the centre of the Place Royale, near the river's edge in Quebec City, stands the church of Notre-Dame. In 1690, when Governor Frontenac drove back English invaders, it was named "Notre-Dame-de-la-Victoire" – Our Lady of Victory. In 1711, the English once more failed in an attempt to attack the capital of New France, and the church was renamed "Notre-Dame-des-Victoires" – Our Lady of Victories.

Today, all around the church stand the homes and shops and warehouses of the people of the eighteenth-century port. The Place Royale looks much as it did in the glory days of New France. The walled city of Quebec, which rises above the Place Royale, is the heart of French culture in North America, and it has been declared a World Heritage Site by the United Nations.

sailors who had escaped storms and other dangers made pilgrimages to the shrine of Ste-Anne-de-Beaupré to give thanks to God and the saint.

Stately stone buildings lined the streets that now covered Louis Hébert's fields high above the river. In the shops, aristocratic ladies and gentlemen could visit a silversmith or have an elegant wig fitted. In the seminary, young men studied theology and Latin. In the convents, young women learned less Latin and theology, and more domestic skills. Convents and seminaries were the only schools, but because there were many convents, more women than men went to school in New France. Choirs sang in the cathedral. Companies of soldiers tramped through the street, and hard-driven slaves and servants ran about doing errands. For the aristocrats, the city of Quebec made an elegant home. When the governor general of New France entertained at the Château Saint-Louis, they arrived in silk and lace for balls almost as spectacular as those Louis XIV gave at his new palace of Versailles.

The governor general was the king's representative in New France, but Louis XIV, a shrewd man, kept a leash on his governor. He sent a man called the *intendant* to help manage the colony, and the governor could do very little without his agreement. When they worked together, the governor and intendant were powerful rulers. Their authority was as absolute in the colony as the king's was in France. They saw themselves as fathers to the people of New France, and they believed fathers should be loving but stern.

The governor general commanded the colony's troops, the Compagnies Franches de la Marine. Their officers were the young aristrocrats of New France, who made war their profession. In bright blue coats and white overcoats, the companies made a fine sight on the *place d'armes* of Montreal, Quebec, or Louisbourg – but they did more than parade. Soldiers of the Compagnies Franches had to be good with a paddle, an axe, and a pair of snowshoes. On the battlefield they carried a flintlock musket with a long

L.R. BATCHELOR.

bayonet. They became feared fighters in the wilderness warfare they learned from Native warriors, and they ranged across half of North America.

New France was often at war. The English had once captured Quebec, in Champlain's day, and they tried again in 1690. They came to Quebec in a fleet of ships and laid siege to the town. The governor general, Count Frontenac, defied them. When they demanded that he surrender, he cried, "My only reply shall come from the mouths of my cannon!" The English invaders retreated.

But New France faced another danger. The war with the Iroquois Confederacy had begun again. Frontenac's soldiers attacked the Iroquois country, and Iroquois warriors raided the settlements of New France once more. In 1692 one of their targets was the seigneurie of Verchères, downriver from Montreal.

François Jarret was seigneur of Verchères. Like many seigneurs, he had come to the colony as an army officer, and the king had rewarded him with the lands of Verchères. Jarret de Verchères granted lots to soldiers and immigrants who wanted to start farms, and he kept a share of all they grew. He built a mill to grind their grain and a fort to protect them.

Jarret de Verchères's daughter Madeleine was only fourteen in 1692, but she knew first-hand the high cost of

Soon after he arrived, Jean Talon, the first intendant of New France, took Canada's first census – to find out how many colonists there were. Talon had great plans for the colony, but he stayed only a few years.

The St-Maurice Forges, Canada's first heavy industry, were developed in the 1730s around the iron-ore deposits near Trois-Rivières, Quebec. The St-Maurice Forges are now a national historic park.

the war with the Iroquois. Her sixteen-year-old brother had been killed in the fighting. Her teenaged sister Marie-Jeanne had already been married twice, and both husbands had died in the war. Madeleine's father was often called away to fight, and her mother had taken charge of their little fort during one attack. Although most of the powerful positions were held by men, women sometimes became seigneurs, or managed businesses, or took charge of farms. The nuns who ran the hospitals, the schools, and the charities were valued leaders. Now it was Madeleine's turn to take charge.

One October morning when both Madeleine's parents were away, Iroquois raiders surprised the farmers of Verchères in the fields. Some of the farmers fell captive; the rest raced to the seigneur's fort for safety. Madeleine fired a signal gun and, with the habitants, held off the attackers until soldiers from Montreal came to their aid. Madeleine became one of the heroes of New France.

Madeleine de Verchères defends her family's fort against Iroquois raiders.

Pierre Radisson and Médard Chouart Des Groseilliers told the English merchants of a treasure trove of furs to be found around Hudson Bay. In 1668 Des Groseilliers and the Nonsuch sailed there. The rich haul they brought back persuaded London's businessmen to found the Hudson's Bay Company.

Voyageurs

While habitant families worked the long, narrow fields by the edge of the St. Lawrence, voyageurs were following the wild rivers that led far into the North and West. When Jean Nicollet went to explore the Great Lakes, he took a gorgeous Chinese cloak with him in his canoe – just in case he met the Emperor of China! René-Robert Cavelier de La Salle also dreamed of the route to China. La Salle talked of nothing else, and the Montrealers jokingly called his seigneurie just west of town "La Chine," which meant China. La Salle never reached China, but he did explore the Mississippi River all the way to the Gulf of Mexico – and the town where his seigneurie stood is still called Lachine.

Pierre-Esprit Radisson and his brother-in-law, Médard

Chouart Des Groseilliers, cared less about China than about the furs in the northern woods. Des Groseilliers had learned about fur trading while working in the Huron missions. Young Radisson's schooling had been harder – as a boy he had been captured by the Iroquois, who had taught him their language and customs. When he had tried to escape, he had been tortured, but in the end he had made his way back to New France to become a voyageur.

Once the Hurons were gone, experienced woodsmen like Radisson and Des Groseilliers went to seek furs for themselves.

Radisson and Des Groseilliers ranged the north country beyond Lake Superior until they were so far from Quebec that it seemed simpler to ship their furs to Europe by Hudson Bay. This idea infuriated Montreal's traders, who wanted the furs to come to them. To get their way, Radisson and Des Groseilliers went to London to see if the English might be interested. Indeed they were. King Charles II gave his cousin Prince Rupert and "A Company of Adventurers" a charter to trade at Hudson Bay. With Radisson's help, the Hudson's Bay Company became a permanent rival to Montreal's traders.

In those early days of the fur trade, there were furs enough for all. The voyageurs left Lachine every spring, launching canoes heavy-laden with supplies and trade goods amid wild celebrations. They followed the turbulent Ottawa and French rivers to Lake Huron. Then a month of eighteen-hour days at the paddle brought them to the trading post of Michilimackinac early in June. Some voyageurs traded for furs there, then made the fast trip downstream to Montreal in time for the harvest celebrations.

Some voyageurs scorned the men who went home to eat salt pork by the fireplace all winter. For these *hommes du nord*, or men of the north, Michilimackinac was only the start of the voyage. They would paddle on, day after day, fighting the gales of Lake Superior and the cold rivers beyond, until winter found them encamped by the shores of some distant northern lake. They would be gone from

Montreal for years, meeting distant Native nations, stealing the best furs from under the noses of those English traders on Hudson Bay, and living the wild, roving life of the pays d'en haut. Many voyageurs married Native women and joined the Native bands who trapped and traded the furs.

As the voyageurs pushed west and north, seeking new sources of beaver pelts, there was always one thought in the back of their minds. They might yet find the western ocean that Henry Hudson and Samuel de Champlain had sought.

No one took the search farther than an army officer named Pierre de La Vérendrye, who commanded a trading fort on Lake Superior. He believed that the great plains to the west stretched to the edge of the Pacific Ocean, and he set out to go there. In 1729, he asked Auchagah, a Cree trader, about the route to the plains. Auchagah drew a map for him, and La Vérendrye began his journeys.

La Vérendrye and his sons spent years exploring the rivers west of Lake Superior and out across the plains. They met people of many Native nations, they built trading forts on the plains, and they kept on exploring westward. Slowly La Vérendrye realized that the western ocean was not just ahead of him; beyond the plains rose the Rocky Mountains, and he never even quite reached the mountains. However, canoe after canoe laden with beaver pelts went back east to Montreal from the places he explored.

By the early 1700s, the territory of the fur trade stretched northwest from Montreal to the Prairies, and south to Louisiana and the mouth of the Mississippi, through the land of the Ojibwa, Assiniboine, Winnebago, and Cree. The voyageurs hauled furs that Native traders and trappers brought to the trading posts. The trading posts sheltered traders and voyageurs, but they were also forts manned by soldiers sent by the governor general – soldiers who carried gifts and offered treaties to the chiefs on whom the fur trade depended. For the Native nations were still the masters of the fur trade. Although New France's influence stretched across half a continent, Canada was still a Native land.

When Pierre de La Vérendrye went seeking the glory of discovering the "Western Sea," he had no idea that mountains – like the Coastal Range and the Rockies – would be in his way.

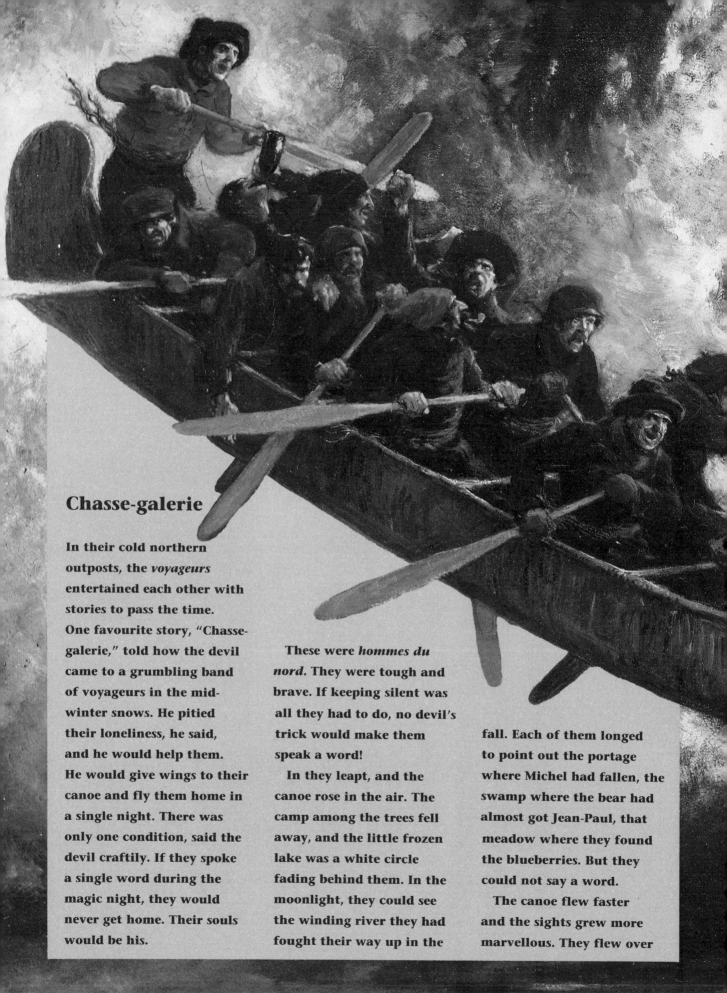

Chasse-galerie

In their cold northern
outposts, the *voyageurs*
entertained each other with
stories to pass the time.
One favourite story, "Chasse-
galerie," told how the devil
came to a grumbling band
of voyageurs in the mid-
winter snows. He pitied
their loneliness, he said,
and he would help them.
He would give wings to their
canoe and fly them home in
a single night. There was
only one condition, said the
devil craftily. If they spoke
a single word during the
magic night, they would
never get home. Their souls
would be his.

These were *hommes du
nord*. They were tough and
brave. If keeping silent was
all they had to do, no devil's
trick would make them
speak a word!

In they leapt, and the
canoe rose in the air. The
camp among the trees fell
away, and the little frozen
lake was a white circle
fading behind them. In the
moonlight, they could see
the winding river they had
fought their way up in the

fall. Each of them longed
to point out the portage
where Michel had fallen, the
swamp where the bear had
almost got Jean-Paul, that
meadow where they found
the blueberries. But they
could not say a word.

The canoe flew faster
and the sights grew more
marvellous. They flew over

Lake Superior without paddling a single stroke. There lay their sleeping comrades in the trading post at Michilimackinac. In the blinking of an eye they passed over the dreadful rapids of the French River and the cabins of their friends the Nipissing people. The voyageurs gritted their teeth to keep from shouting in amazement.

The flying canoe swept down the frozen Ottawa River. Now came the most marvellous sight of all – Montreal. Home! They could see the wall around the town, the spires of the churches, the roofs of the rich merchants' houses. Smoke curled up towards them from the chimneys, and just as the scent of woodsmoke and home cooking reached them, every voyageur spotted his own home. Every mouth opened to cry out.

And with a laugh, the devil swooped in for his due . . .

There the story always changed. Around their fires, deep in the north woods, voyageurs competed to make new endings to the tale, and they whooped in glee when someone found one. Many months, many portages, and many paddle strokes lay between them and their homes, and only their songs and stories would get them through.

The Struggle for Acadia

Although most of the people of New France lived along the St. Lawrence, New France had really begun on the Atlantic coast, in the region called Acadia. Before he built his Habitation at Quebec, Champlain had spent three years in Acadia, exploring and helping to build Port-Royal. Other colony builders had followed. Charles de La Tour, Charles d'Aulnay, and Nicolas Denys established outposts along the coasts. Each swore to rule all of Acadia and control its fur trade, and their rivalries were fierce. In 1645, d'Aulnay captured La Tour's fort at Saint John. La Tour was away, and d'Aulnay hanged everyone there except La Tour's wife, who was made to watch. She died soon afterwards.

Like Champlain at Quebec, d'Aulnay wanted to build a colony, not just a trading post. He persuaded about fifty families from his family's estates in France to follow him to Port-Royal. Even after d'Aulnay drowned and La Tour moved to Port-Royal and married d'Aulnay's widow, the settlers stayed on. Eventually the king sent a governor and troops and aristocratic seigneurs to rule Acadia, but each time war broke out between England and France across the ocean, the enemies swept in to raid and loot Port-Royal. Acadia changed back and forth between French and English rule many times, and the soldiers and commanders were often driven out. The families d'Aulnay had brought to Acadia, however, went on with their lives no matter who ruled the colony. They were taking root.

The settlers of Acadia found broad salt marshes along the edge of the Bay of Fundy, but the marshes vanished under water each time the surging Fundy tides rolled in. So the Acadians built dikes, fighting the tides for land. They piled up earth walls to keep the sea out. Then they dug ditches and built ingenious sluices to drain rainwater and streams from their new fields. The marshes became rich and fertile meadows where the Acadians could plant crops and raise livestock. Over the years, a few hundred Acadians grew into several thousand. In 1710 the British conquered Acadia once more. This time France did not get it back,

Young people in eighteenth-century dress help to bring the reconstructed city of Louisbourg to life. From 1713 to 1758 the fortified city on Cape Breton Island was a busy centre of fishing and trade.

Marie-Joseph-Angélique

Marie-Joseph-Angélique may have been born in Africa, or in the Caribbean islands, where hundreds of thousands of African slaves laboured on France's sugar plantations. A few of these slaves were sent to New France. Marie-Joseph-Angélique was one of them.

In 1734, Marie lived in the house of Monsieur de Francheville in Montreal. He was a merchant, and his family and his clerks lived in a fine house at the heart of town, close by the Hôtel-Dieu hospital. Like most slaves in New France, Marie was a household servant. She worked in the kitchen, washed the clothes, cleaned the house, and ran errands. She probably ate table scraps and slept in a corner of the kitchen. Her life was miserable, and she dreamed of escaping.

One day in 1734, Marie set fire to the Francheville house. She knew everyone in the crowded town would race to fight the flames, and no one would notice what one slave was doing. She knew a young Canadian who intended to walk south towards the English colonies, and she planned to go with him.

The fire succeeded beyond anything Marie had imagined. It raged across the town of Montreal, and destroyed fifty houses and the hospital. The fire she set was Montreal's worst disaster since the Iroquois attacks, but it did Marie no good. She was caught not far from the town and hanged for her crime.

but the people remained where they were, paying little more attention to their British rulers than they had to the former French ones.

With Acadia again in British hands, France began a new colony nearby, on Ile Royale (called Cape Breton Island today). At Louisbourg, capital of the new colony, soldiers and workers laboured for twenty-five years to build massive stone walls, bristling with cannon, around the city. All along the coast of Ile Royale, fishermen in small open

Opposite:
*Backbreaking work was daily
fare at Newfoundland fishing
stations during the busy summer
season. As boatmen bring in the
catch, shore crews split, wash,
and salt the fish in the shed.
They squeeze medicinal oil from
the cod livers, and lay out the
split fish on "flakes." In a few
weeks sun and salt will make
the fish hard and dry, easy to
transport and store for months
or even years.*

boats caught great hauls of cod. The colony reeked with the smell of drying cod, and the merchants of Louisbourg grew prosperous shipping the hard-dried fish to France and Spain and the islands of the Caribbean. There were few farms on Ile Royale, so Louisbourg bought grain from Quebec City, and schooners plied the Gulf of St. Lawrence between the two ports.

The War of the Conquest

In the 1750s, New France was at the height of its power, but war loomed ahead. Britain and France were rivals in Europe, around the trading ports of India, among the sunny islands of the West Indies – and in North America. The British colonies in North America were as old as New France, and they confronted the French colony on every side. The Hudson's Bay Company struggled to take the fur trade away from Montreal's merchants and voyageurs. Irish and English fishermen of Newfoundland competed with the French ones of Ile Royale. The largest, strongest British colonies, however, lay along the Atlantic coast in what is now the United States.

These British colonies had grown faster than the French ones. In the 1700s they had thirty times as many people as all of New France. Fishermen and sailors had prospered in the New England settlements founded by religious pilgrims in 1620. New York, founded by Dutch colonists but taken over by the English, competed with Montreal for the fur trade and backed the Iroquois in their wars with New France. Pennsylvania was a rich farming community. In Virginia, wealthy planters ran vast tobacco farms with the labour of African slaves.

For all the power and wealth of Britain's colonies, New France did not fear them. Its voyageurs had out-traded, out-travelled, and out-fought the men of the Hudson's Bay Company, who "slept by the frozen sea" while Montreal traders collected all the furs they needed. Many times the soldiers of New France and their Native allies had struck

The Acadians

In 1755, the British decided to drive the Acadians from their homes around the Bay of Fundy and scatter them to the four winds. The Acadians were transported far away, and families found themselves in France, Georgia, Quebec, Louisiana (where their descendants would become the "Cajuns"), and many other places. But some of the Acadians refused to give up their homeland. A few managed to hide out in the woods. Many who had been carried away struggled back, even though it took them most of their lives.

François Cyr of Beaubassin in Acadia was just two years old in 1755 when his family was marched aboard the ship *Jolly Phillip* and taken to Georgia. In a few years François's family made its way to Boston, Massachusetts, and later to the French islands of St-Pierre and Miquelon, near Newfoundland. When the British attacked St-Pierre in 1778, 25-year-old François was exiled to France. There he married another Acadian refugee, Rosalie Boudreau. Then France recovered St-Pierre, and the Cyrs returned to the island together.

The Cyrs moved on to the Iles de la Madeleine, in the Gulf of St. Lawrence. Finally, in the 1790s, they joined other Acadians on the Gaspé Peninsula, and there they stayed. They had been refugees for almost forty years.

Many Acadians had stories like those of François and Rosalie. The British had taken the old Acadia around the diked land of the Bay of Fundy, but the people gradually built a new Acadia on the coasts and islands of the Gulf of St. Lawrence. There were about 13 000 Acadians when the British tried to get rid of them in 1755. Today there are nearly half a million in Atlantic Canada.

into New York or New England or seized outposts of the Hudson's Bay Company. Despite the British victories in Acadia, it was usually New France that carried the fight to its rival. In all its battles with the British colonies, New France rarely suffered defeat. When another war began in the 1750s, New France was confident of victory.

But this war proved different from any the soldiers of New France had ever fought. They had learned the Native way of war, racing silently through the forests to strike with lightning speed and fade away again. Now the battles were fought by armies and fleets sent from Europe, as well as by the colony's own soldiers. Fighting ranged farther across North America than ever before. This war would be fought along the voyageurs' rivers, but also over the habitants' fields, and it would come to the very heart of the colony, Champlain's city of Quebec.

In 1755, even before war was declared, the British decided to get rid of the Acadian people they had ruled since 1710. That summer, ships bearing soldiers swooped down on Acadian towns and farms all around the Bay of Fundy. A few Acadians fled into the woods, but most were rounded up and forced onto the ships. They were scattered around the American colonies to live or die in exile from their homeland, often separated forever from friends and relatives.

The war for New France raged from Acadia and Ile Royale to the colony's western frontiers. In 1758, a British army marched north from New York and met the French near a fort the French called Carillon and the English called Ticonderoga. The commander of New France's troops, Louis-Joseph de Montcalm, won a great and bloody victory that stopped one threat to New France. That same summer, though, the British besieged and captured the fortress of Louisbourg and shipped all the people of Ile Royale to France.

The French had won startling victories against the powerful invaders, but slowly they began to fall back. Many soldiers were killed or wounded, and every man and youth was away with the army, so women and children were left to bring in the harvests. Food became scarce, and hungry

Following pages:
In July 1758, the British attacked General Montcalm's French army at a place that the British called by the Iroquois name "Ticonderoga," but that the French called Carillon, "the chimes," because of the sound of the nearby rapids. Montcalm's men built an abattis *of heaped-up trees and brush. It trapped the Scottish soldiers of the Black Watch Regiment when they attacked, and they were slaughtered by the French.*

children grew sick and died. The hardworking little horses the habitants had been so proud of now went into the cooking pots. Everyone was struggling to survive. In their churches they prayed for New France to be saved.

In 1759, one British army marched on Montreal from the west while another army advanced from the south. At the same time, a seaborne invasion sailed up the St. Lawrence to deliver General James Wolfe's army to the gates of Quebec. But Montcalm defied him. All summer long, Montcalm and his army kept Wolfe's soldiers from climbing the cliffs to attack the city.

James Wolfe was a small, sickly man, but he was brave, and his way of fighting was bold and reckless. He was not used to delays, and he spent the summer in a fury of frustration. When he could not attack the city of Quebec, he ordered his gunners to destroy it, and they fired cannonballs and exploding mortar bombs from across the river. Soon the handsome cathedral, the Ursuline convent, the intendant's palace, and hundreds of homes were pounded into ruin.

Wolfe sent his soldiers out to burn and plunder all along the river. He wanted to destroy as much of the colony as he could, because he thought he had failed in his bid to take Quebec and conquer New France. As the habitants fled to the woods, the red-coated soldiers burned their homes and barns and took any cows and sheep the farmers still possessed.

Everything happens at once in this imaginary re-creation of the Battle of the Plains of Abraham: the British army sails up the river, climbs the cliffs, forms up on the Plains of Abraham, and fights the famous battle of September 13, 1759.

As the summer came to an end, Wolfe tried one last gamble. His officers had suggested they should attack upriver, beyond the city. Wolfe seized their plan and made one bold change: he would attack close to Quebec, using a narrow footpath to get his men up the cliffs under cover of night. His aides were horrified, fearing that the French defenders on the clifftops would destroy them.

Wolfe was determined – and lucky. On the night of September 12, 1759, he landed his soldiers at the foot of the cliffs, and they scrambled to the top without being seen. By dawn, James Wolfe's army stood on the Plains of Abraham.

Montcalm and his soldiers came out to face them. The French army was exhausted. The men had been fighting for four years. Every time veteran soldiers died or were wounded, untrained boys or old men had to replace them. But Montcalm had fought the invaders every step of the way, and he would not let them have Quebec without a battle. He ordered his soldiers to attack the British and, bravely, they did.

Wolfe's soldiers were ready when the lines of French soldiers came into range. They fired, and the French soldiers were cut down where they stood, or fled in retreat. Although the battle was over in minutes, both generals were fatally shot. Wolfe heard the news of his victory just before he died on the battlefield; Montcalm was helped back into the city and died early the next morning, in the ruins of the Ursuline convent.

General Montcalm, the defender of Quebec, actually died in bed the day after the Battle of the Plains of Abraham, but the artist has created a more dramatic scene.

Chapter 4
The Colonists

THE WEARY BRITISH REDCOATS TRUDGING AWAY FROM THE BATTLE
of the Plains of Abraham were 5000 kilometres from home,
but many of them were not going to see their homes for a
long time. Montcalm's body was buried in a mortar-bomb
crater, and Wolfe's body was shipped home pickled in a
barrel, but the war raged on. In 1760 the British soldiers
cheered to see the last French flags pulled down in
surrender, but even then they stayed on. Britain had
conquered half a continent. Now the soldiers and a
handful of British colonists would try to build a British
Canada among a French population of more than 60 000.

The new governor in British-ruled Canada, General
James Murray, wondered how the French and English
would live together. By the time a peace treaty was signed
in 1763, France had no lands left on the continent of
North America, and the French governors and French
soldiers were gone. But the farmers, artisans, priests, and
voyageurs remained. Their families had made Canada
their home for over a hundred years, and the British had
always been their enemies. To be able to govern French
Canada, the governor had to accept its people as they
were. Gradually Britain confirmed the right of the French
Canadians to preserve their Catholic faith, their language,
and their distinctive legal code.

To the east and south of Quebec, all the colonies
were British. In the outports of Newfoundland, English
and Irish fishermen had become "liveyers," who brought
their families and lived year-round on the island. Nova
Scotia had been a British colony since 1710, and after the
conquest of New France it included what are now New
Brunswick and Prince Edward Island. Halifax had been a
busy port since British soldiers and traders founded it in
1749. German settlers at Lunenburg were launching ships
and going fishing, and New England families were moving
north into the old Acadian lands. Only a handful of fur
traders lived in the Saint John valley, and a few fugitive
Acadians who had escaped from the deportation or had
managed to return were gathering on the shores of the
Gulf of St. Lawrence.

Previous pages:

*Perhaps as many as 10 000 New
York Loyalists were crammed into
temporary shelter at Port Rose-
way, Nova Scotia, in 1783. In
the months and years before they
all were resettled they suffered
from shortages of food, the
harshness of the weather, and the
ravages of sudden illness – as
shown in this picture of a family
seeking help for their sick child.*

Scots merchants were quick to move into Montreal, joining the fur trade and venturing into the northwest with the voyageurs. British soldiers took over the French forts strung along the rivers and lakes. Still all the land west of Montreal remained the land of the Native nations.

French-Canadian lady and priest in the early 1800s.

Refugees

On New Year's Eve, 1775, snow drifted up against the old stone walls of Quebec. Icicles hung from the eaves of the Golden Dog, the busy tavern where Governor Guy Carleton had set up his headquarters. Quebec was under siege once more. This time, American rebels were marching to attack.

That night, General Richard Montgomery and his troop of American soldiers charged through the swirling snow into Quebec's Lower Town. "Quebec is ours!" cried Montgomery. British cannon and muskets roared in reply. Montgomery fell dead in a snowbank, and the rebels fled. British Canada had won its first victory.

Massachusetts, New York, Pennsylvania, Virginia – thirteen of the old British colonies, in all – were rebelling against British rule. They said they were tired of being ruled and taxed from overseas by King George III. In 1776, these colonies' leaders signed the Declaration of Independence of the United States of America. The American Revolution had begun.

The American rebels – "patriots" they called themselves – wanted to get all of Britain's North American colonies to join their movement, by force if necessary. But Montgomery failed to capture Quebec, and the rebels failed again at Fort Cumberland in Nova Scotia. From Nova Scotia to Michilimackinac in the northwest, British redcoats fought to defend British Canada against the Americans.

There were some people in the rebellious colonies who wanted to remain subjects of the British king, and the rebels in the new United States were soon making war on these "Loyalists." Some were painted with hot tar and

"It is the roughest land I ever saw," said Loyalist Sarah Frost when she arrived at Saint John, New Brunswick, in 1783, "but this is to be the city, they say!"

John Crysler of Butler's Loyal Rangers.

rolled in feathers, and others were jailed or even hanged. Many had their property seized. Loyalists fled to Canada for safety – and many continued the fight on the British side. From Nova Scotia, sailors attacked American ships. From Canadian forts, Loyalist rangers and scouts attacked the rebels.

Young John Crysler was a Loyalist. When his father left their home in the Mohawk Valley of New York to fight for the king, a band of rebels attacked the Cryslers' farm. They smashed the family's furniture, took their food, and hounded them off their land. John's mother and his brothers and sisters joined other unhappy families trekking through the wilderness towards refugee camps near Montreal. John went to Fort Niagara and joined Major John Butler's Loyal Rangers, a band of frontiersmen who raided rebel territory alongside Iroquois warriors led by Thayendanegea. Butler made John Crysler a drummer boy. He was only seven years old.

The British, the Loyalists, and the Natives could not stop the Americans' revolution, but they kept Canada British. In 1783 the American colonies celebrated the victory of their war for independence, but both Quebec and Nova Scotia had said no to joining them. The northern colonies would stay in Britain's empire, ruled by a British

king and a British governor general. Loyalist Americans
who had not already fled were now driven into exile, and
they too came north to find new homes.

Suddenly, British North America was becoming
home to a large English-speaking population. Some 30000
homeless Loyalists sailed north up the Atlantic coast in
fleets of British ships. About 10000 landed at a place they
named Shelburne, and that quiet Nova Scotia harbour was
overnight the largest town in British North America. At
Halifax, Loyalist refugees set up tents on the Common and

*When the American colonies
rebelled against Britain, many
slaves escaped and fought on
the British side. This Black
trooper was a Loyalist in the
60th Foot, Royal American
Regiment.*

on Citadel Hill. Fourteen thousand more sailed up the Bay
of Fundy to seek new homes in the broad valley of the
Saint John River. When the border was officially drawn,
one new Loyalist village found it was still in American
territory; the people put their houses on barges and floated
them across to St. Andrews, in what is now New Brunswick.
Some of those homes still stand there today.

Edward Winslow was one of the Loyalists who settled
on the Saint John River. Winslow came from a proud old

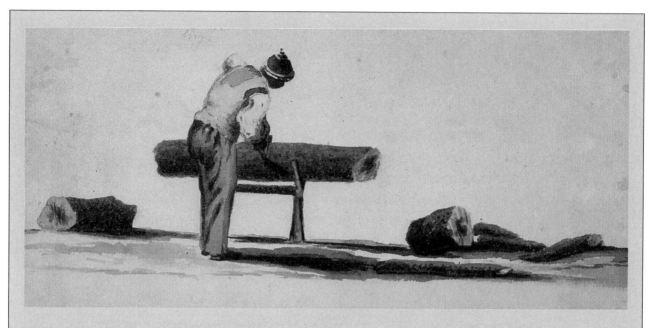

The Black Loyalists in Nova Scotia

Many Americans who fought for independence from Britain – including General George Washington, the first President of the United States – were slave owners. Many of their slaves fled to the British army for freedom, and many helped the British fight against the Americans.

Three thousand Black Loyalists came to Nova Scotia in 1784. They built homes and churches in Birchtown, near Shelburne, but they faced more hardships than other Loyalists. Few of them got the land that was promised to every Loyalist. Many white Loyalists wanted the Black Loyalists to be servants and labourers, and would not accept them as equals.

In 1792, Thomas Peters had had enough of this treatment. He had been a slave in North Carolina, and a Loyalist soldier, and he wanted real freedom. He persuaded a thousand Black Loyalists to leave Nova Scotia. They sailed to Sierra Leone, in Africa, where a community of freed or escaped slaves was growing.

Other Black Loyalists stayed on in Nova Scotia, and during the War of 1812 more slaves from the southern United States came to join them. But there were slaves in Nova Scotia, brought by Loyalists who had kept their slaves with them. Once they were in Nova Scotia, the slaves demanded freedom, and when they took their cases to court, many judges supported them. But it took over twenty years to end the practice of buying and selling slaves in Nova Scotia. Slavery was finally abolished throughout the British empire in 1834.

The descendants of the Black Loyalists, the escaped slaves of 1812, and those who won their freedom in Nova Scotia have stayed on as a permanent and important part of the Nova Scotian community.

New England family used to power and wealth. Though the rebels had won the war and seized his property, he was full of hope. When he saw the country awaiting the Loyalists in Atlantic Canada, he was excited. "By Heaven, we shall be the envy of the American states," he cried.

At Quebec, General Frederick Haldimand, a tough old soldier, was now the governor. He too had thousands of refugee Americans on his hands. He was sure there would be trouble if they settled among the French-speaking people of the lower St. Lawrence Valley, so he urged the Loyalists to go farther upriver. He made treaties with the Mississauga nation of southern Ontario, who provided land and let the refugees settle among them. Haldimand's Loyalists then went up the river to settle "Upper" Canada. Justus Sherwood, who helped survey the land along Lake Ontario, said the Loyalists who settled there would be "the happiest people in America."

John Crysler probably thought so, too. On a bright May morning in 1784, he became the proud owner of a hundred acres (about forty hectares). His father and brother got land nearby. In New York, the Cryslers had always been tenant farmers. Now they owned every acre of their new land free and clear. John was just fourteen.

Not all the Loyalists could face the challenges their new home presented them. British America was a land for pioneers, people with the strength and skill to clear land,

The Loyalist Cow

Along the Niagara River, there is a story that even a cow was loyal to British Canada. It seems that a farmer in Queenston, on the Canadian side, sold the cow to a farmer in Lewiston, on the American side. One day as the cow stood by the rushing water, chewing her cud and gazing at the green pastures on the other side, she was overcome by homesickness. In she plunged and swam home. A Loyalist cow, they called her in Queenston. No one knows what they called her in Lewiston.

Elizabeth Simcoe

When John Graves Simcoe arrived in Upper Canada as the colony's first lieutenant-governor in 1792, his wife, Elizabeth, came with him. At Niagara – far from the country houses and well-tended gardens she had known in England – she lived in the woods. With her maid, her French chef, her jewels, and her fine clothes, she made her home in a canvas house that was done up with wallpaper and paint and kept warm with stoves.

Yet Elizabeth loved the Canadian wilderness. She travelled widely, painting lovely watercolours and often being much more adventurous than her

build their own houses, and provide many of their own goods themselves. Many American Loyalists, however, had always lived in cities like New York. Some swallowed their pride and returned to the United States. Shelburne, which had grown so fast in 1784, dwindled to a village within a few years. But many Loyalist families put down roots in Canada just as enthusiastically as Edward Winslow and Justus Sherwood.

Gentlemen and Governors

Whenever Lieutenant-Governor Thomas Carleton of New Brunswick returned to Fredericton after a tour of his colony, the cavalry formed up for inspection on the parade ground. The artillery fired a thunderous salute. Ladies and gentlemen in their best linens and silks came to pay their respects, and the regimental bands played sprightly marches. Together they went to a welcoming service at the Anglican cathedral. Then Sir Thomas retired to his elegant residence, furnished with fine mahogany, crystal, and silver imported from London. Servants awaited his every wish.

The lieutenant-governor was pleased. Only a few years before, he had created Fredericton from a rustic Acadian

husband. When her husband made the village of York the colony's capital, she wanted a house high above the Don River.

"We went six miles by water," she wrote in her diary, "and landed, climbed up a series of sugar-loafed hills and approved of the highest spot from whence we looked down on the tops of large trees." She went on,

"We hope the height of the situation will secure us from mosquitoes. We dined by a large fire on wild ducks and chowder."

Elizabeth named her woodland house Castle Frank, after her son. When the Simcoes left Upper Canada in 1796, never to return, Elizabeth wrote in her diary, "I could not eat, cried all day."

village on the bank of the beautiful Saint John River. Fredericton was already a city fit to be the capital of New Brunswick, one of British North America's newest colonies. New Brunswick had been carved out of Nova Scotia when the Loyalists came in 1784. Prince Edward Island was already a separate colony (it became one in 1769, but was called the Island of Saint John until 1799), and Cape Breton Island (the old Ile Royale) became a separate colony for a time. In 1791, Quebec was divided. The older, mostly French part became Lower Canada. The newer part, up the St. Lawrence River, became Upper Canada.

Each colony had a lieutenant-governor, and over them was a governor general for all of British North America. All these governors were powerful men. They had come from Britain to rule in the name of the king, and they expected to be obeyed. In the new United States the people elected their governors, but British North America's governors wanted none of that Yankee democracy. Thomas Carleton and the other governors were confident that British rule was far better. John Graves Simcoe, who was Upper Canada's lieutenant-governor in the 1790s, invited Americans to settle in Upper Canada. Upper Canada needed settlers, and Simcoe was sure the Americans would soon see that the British way was better.

After 1792 every colony had an elected Assembly, but only men who owned land could vote to elect its members. The Assembly could pass laws and levy taxes, but it was the governors and their chosen councillors who really ran the colonies. Many councillors came from wealthy Loyalist families: men like Edward Winslow of New Brunswick, and John Beverley Robinson, whose family moved from New Brunswick to Upper Canada. Others came from England to take up important government posts. They expected to become the aristocracy of the colonies and to shape the destiny of British North America.

Most of the settlers were busy building new lives for themselves, and they were willing enough to be led by their British governors. At Williamsburgh, Upper Canada, John Crysler married Nancy Finkle, a young woman from another Loyalist family. They built a mill and opened a store and a tavern for travellers going up the St. Lawrence River. Then John Crysler started cutting timber to sell to Britain. He and Nancy built a fine stone house, and in 1804 his neighbours elected him to sit in the Assembly of Upper Canada.

British Canada was growing, but the Americans still hoped to add the northern colonies to the new United States. They were not yet finished with British Canada – or with the Crysler family.

The War of 1812

Britain and the United States went to war again in July 1812, and the Americans decided to punish Britain by invading and conquering British North America, particularly Upper Canada. Since so many Upper Canadians were newcomers from the United States, the Americans were sure they would not put up a fight. "It will be a mere matter of marching," said American Thomas Jefferson confidently. Some Upper Canadians feared he was right. Isaac Brock thought otherwise.

General Brock commanded the British troops in Upper

General Isaac Brock believed his small force of British soldiers could defeat the huge American armies. When the War of 1812 began, he went on the attack. This portrait shows Brock as one artist imagined he looked.

The Citadel of Halifax

The British knew they might have to fight for British North America. From Signal Hill in St. John's, Newfoundland, to Fort Rodd Hill near Victoria, British Columbia, British guns guarded every strategic place where an American attack might come.

Few places were more elaborately fortified than the port of Halifax. In peacetime, and even more in war, Halifax was a vital naval base. Warships went out from there to fight the French in 1759 and the Americans in 1776 and 1812. In the First World War and the Second World War, Halifax became home base for the convoys of ships that sailed between North America and Britain.

The British began to build a fort on top of the green hill at the edge of Halifax's harbour as soon as they arrived in 1749. After the War of 1812, they ringed the city and harbour with powerful batteries of cannon and thick stone ramparts. The heart of the defences was the citadel, dug into Citadel Hill until it was almost invisible from the town.

No enemy has ever attacked Citadel Hill. Today visitors drive up its grassy slopes for the best view of the city and harbour. Inside, they explore the life of "Tommy Atkins," the nickname for the ordinary British soldiers who guarded Canada for more than a century.

Canada, and he was not going to let the colony fall to the invaders. He forged an alliance with Tecumseh, war chief of the alliance of Native nations that were fighting the Americans for their land south of the Great Lakes. Together they went on the attack. In August 1812, Tecumseh and Brock terrified an American army into surrendering Detroit. The victory inspired Upper Canadians, and they began to believe their colony could be saved from the Americans.

In October 1812, the American army crossed the fast-flowing Niagara River in boats and barges. The Americans seized the heights above the village of Queenston, and Brock's regiment, the "Green Tigers," rushed to attack them. Upper-Canadian volunteers and their Native allies

Previous pages:

A surprise attack captures an American gunboat on Lake Huron. In the summer of 1814, British troops and their Native allies held the forts and trading posts north of the Great Lakes – but the Americans controlled Lake Huron. Lieutenant Miller Worsley crossed the lake in a fleet of open boats and seized the American schooner Tigress. *Soon afterwards,* Tigress *joined the unsuspecting gunboat* Scorpion. *At the last moment, Worsley (shown on the right) gave the signal, and his soldiers (of the Newfoundland Fencibles Regiment) raced from their hiding-places below decks to capture the* Scorpion. *The Americans were driven from Lake Huron, and the fur forts were saved.*

fought alongside the British soldiers. They recaptured Queenston Heights, driving the invaders back across the river.

Isaac Brock was not there to share the victory. When the Americans had first appeared on the heights, Brock had led his "Green Tigers" in a desperate charge up the hill. The Americans shot him dead. Upper Canada mourned its hero, who had shown the colony that it could defend itself.

The Americans also attacked Lower Canada, hoping French Canadians would not fight for their British rulers, but French Canada did not welcome the invaders either. The Catholic bishop and the old seigneurs of French Canada had accepted British rule once their language and religion seemed safe, and for ordinary people, life on the farms went on in much the same way, no matter who governed from the Château Saint-Louis. At the Battle of Châteauguay, near Montreal, Charles de Salaberry – a British army officer from an old French-Canadian family – led the forces that defeated the Americans heading for Montreal.

Sea fights raged along the Atlantic coast, as Nova Scotia's seamen turned their schooners into warships called "privateers" and sailed out to attack American ships. "Prize money" from captured ships made one Halifax merchant, Enos Collins, the richest man in British North America. A British warship, HMS *Shannon*, challenged an American one, the USS *Chesapeake*, to a fight. "Don't give up the ship," urged the American captain, but the *Shannon* won the battle. When she towed the captured *Chesapeake* into Halifax harbour, the whole town turned out to cheer.

The hardest fighting was in Upper Canada. The Americans attacked York, the capital of Upper Canada, and pillaged the town. In the Assembly building they found a scalp on display, and sent it to Washington as proof of British barbarity. Then they burned the building down. The British explained that the "scalp" was merely the ceremonial wig worn by the Speaker of the Assembly, and they raided Washington and burned the White House in retaliation for the damage done to York.

In November 1813, the war came to the farm John Crysler had owned since 1784. An American army of 7000 men met 700 British soldiers in the Cryslers' wheatfields. The British commander made his headquarters in the Cryslers' big stone farmhouse. John Crysler was a captain in Upper Canada's militia, and he fought in the battle, while Nancy and their children sheltered in the cellar. When it was over, John carried the news to Montreal: victory for Britain and Canada in the Battle of Crysler's Farm!

In 1814, Britain and the United States began to talk of peace. When the war ended, the Americans boasted that they had defied the mighty British empire. But from Nova Scotia to Upper Canada, the colonists thought the real victory was theirs. With the help of British troops and Native allies, they had stood up to the United States. British North America would stay British.

The settlers of Nova Scotia, including many descendants of Loyalist refugees, came forth to fight the Americans again in the War of 1812. This drum bears the insignia of the Nova Scotia Fencibles Regiment.

Newcomers

Grosse Ile is a beautiful island in the St. Lawrence River, but for tens of thousands of immigrants in the 1800s it loomed like a deadly barrier across their path to Canada.

In 1815, when the war against Napoleon of France ended, thousands of people began to leave the overcrowded British Isles to seek new lives in British North America. Crossing the ocean was still a desperate venture in the 1820s and 1830s. The voyage might take one month or four – if the ship was not sunk or shipwrecked on the way. Immigrant families crossed the ocean packed together in dark, airless holds, with their belongings crammed in around them. They were just another cargo for the sea captains who hauled timber to Britain on the return voyage.

The most terrifying danger was cholera, a disease that rampaged through Europe and North America in the 1830s. Its victims suffered sudden, violent cramps, diarrhea, and vomiting. Usually cholera victims died in a few hours, but some people carried the disease without getting sick.

Oily black smoke drifts over the city of Quebec in 1832 in this painting, Cholera Plague, Québec, *by Joseph Légaré. During the epidemic, terrified citizens lit smudge pots and hoped the smoke might drive cholera out of the air. In fact, the bacteria that caused cholera were in the water supply.*

Without knowing it, they could spread it far and wide, infecting many others.

The colonies tried desperately to keep cholera out. Lower Canada made Grosse Ile a quarantine station for immigrant ships coming up the St. Lawrence. (Nova Scotia and New Brunswick had their quarantine islands, too.) The immigrants were eager to start their lives in Canada, and they were desperate to escape the cramped, stinking ships. But first, any who showed signs of sickness had to go ashore to Grosse Ile's quarantine sheds. There they stayed until they recovered, or died.

While frightened immigrants packed Grosse Ile, thousands more waited miserably aboard ship while the cholera spread. Many children who had set out bravely across the ocean with their parents found themselves orphans in the terrifying world of the quarantine island. Five thousand unlucky immigrants lie in mass graves on Grosse Ile, along with brave Canadian doctors and nurses who tended them.

Despite the dangers, immigrants poured into British Canada like a flood. Sometimes 10 000 landed in a single week. Families laboured to clear the forests and plant new farms, to build up the cities and towns. Gangs of young men known as "navvies" slaved to cut canals around the rapids and waterfalls. They hauled timber from the Canadian woods, salted down codfish in Newfoundland, and launched trim sailing ships from Atlantic Canada's shipyards.

Most of the immigrants came from Britain. There were Scottish highlanders, driven from their glens by cruel landlords who wanted the land to raise sheep. They came to Cape Breton Island or Upper Canada's Glengarry County, singing sad Gaelic ballads of their lost homeland. Families also came from overcrowded Ireland, or to escape teeming cities in England. They settled all over British America. Some took up codfishing in Newfoundland outports or cut timber along New Brunswick's rushing

Hurlin' Down the Pine

Along the rivers of British North America – the Miramichi, Saguenay, St-Maurice, Trent, and Gatineau – winter meant woodcutting. Men tramped off to timber shanties in the pine forests. They lived on pork and beans, swinging their broadaxes and hauling the timber over the snow to the riverbanks. When the spring runoff swelled the rivers, the lumberjacks became *draveurs*, or raftsmen, riding the logs down the rapids to the sawmills and timber ships. Only the strongest stayed with it: men like Joseph Montferrand.

For thirty years of the early 1800s, Montferrand was the greatest lumberjack on the Ottawa River. People said he was so strong that no boxer could beat him, so agile that he could plant his bootmarks on a tavern ceiling and land on his feet. He was a legend, maybe the most famous man in French Canada.

The lumber camps of the Ottawa Valley were rough and rowdy places. Montferrand led French-Canadian loggers in battles against the Irish loggers. Yet even his English-speaking rivals bragged that "Joe Mufferaw" could drink a lake dry, dig out a river channel by dragging his axe, and comb his hair with a tall pine tree. Wherever lumberjacks went in the north woods, they spread his name and fame.

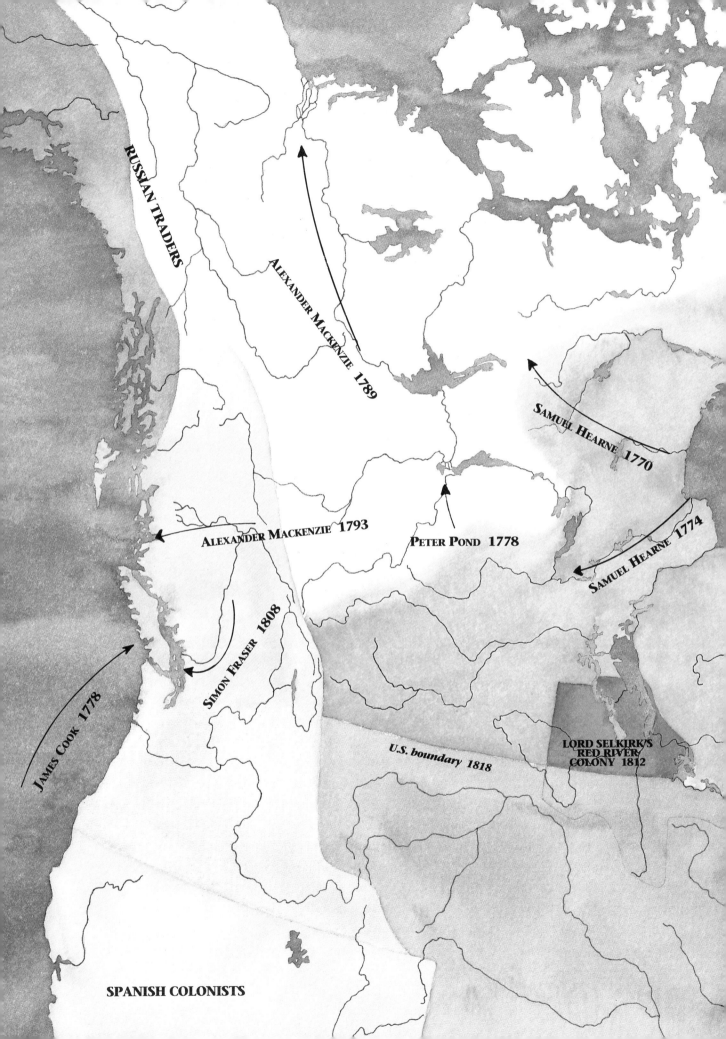

RUSSIAN TRADERS

ALEXANDER MACKENZIE 1789

SAMUEL HEARNE 1770

SAMUEL HEARNE 1774

ALEXANDER MACKENZIE 1793

PETER POND 1778

SIMON FRASER 1808

JAMES COOK 1778

LORD SELKIRK'S
RED RIVER
COLONY 1812

U.S. boundary 1818

SPANISH COLONISTS

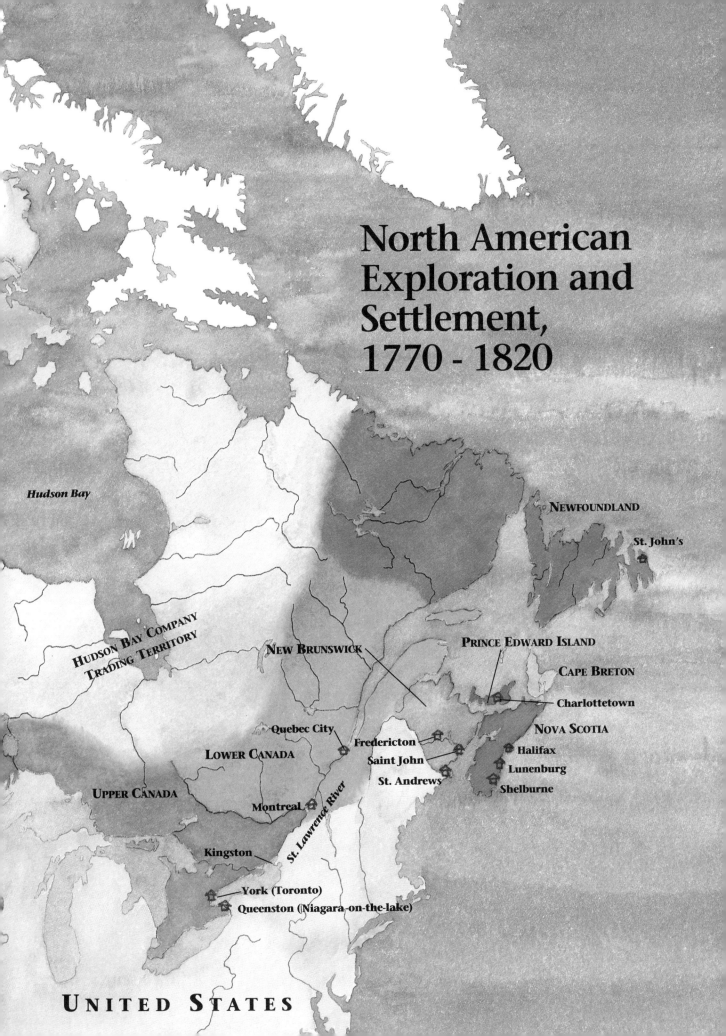

North American Exploration and Settlement, 1770 - 1820

Hudson Bay

NEWFOUNDLAND

St. John's

HUDSON BAY COMPANY TRADING TERRITORY

NEW BRUNSWICK

PRINCE EDWARD ISLAND

CAPE BRETON

Charlottetown

Quebec City

NOVA SCOTIA

LOWER CANADA

Fredericton

Halifax

Saint John

Lunenburg

UPPER CANADA

St. Andrews

Shelburne

Montreal

St. Lawrence River

Kingston

York (Toronto)

Queenston (Niagara-on-the-lake)

UNITED STATES

Restigouche River. Others settled on farms in the townships of Lower Canada or went to the backwoods of Upper Canada. Still others chose enterprising ports like Saint John or Montreal.

The newcomers called British North America "a good poor man's country," meaning that anyone willing to work hard could do well. "In England there is too many men. Here there is not enough," wrote one young man in a letter to his family. It could be a good poor woman's country, too. In those days women were still expected to have a father or a husband to take charge of them, but single women came to the colonies anyway, and worked as teachers or weavers, or often as servants.

Not all newcomers were poor. Retired army officers and ambitious "gentlefolk" dreamed of a comfortable, idle life ruling over the settlers of British North America. Mostly they were disappointed. Susanna Moodie and her elegant, cultured family found life hard when they tried pioneering near Peterborough, Upper Canada. In her book *Roughing It in the Bush*, Moodie told of a neighbour who said, "I've never know'd an English gentleman to get on in the bush." Susanna had to agree, and she was happy to move to the town of Belleville on Lake Ontario.

As immigrants braved the ocean and the children of long-established families grew up and had children of their own, the British colonies expanded and prospered. From about a hundred thousand people in the 1760s, the British North American colonies had grown to over two million by the 1850s.

With the furniture pushed back and the fire low in the iron stove, the farm families of Lower Canada are ready to dance at a wedding.

Roughing It in the Bush with Susanna Moodie

Susanna Moodie came to Upper Canada in 1832. Nothing in her life in England had prepared her for the hardships of backwoods pioneering. *Roughing It in the Bush*, her first book about her wilderness experiences, was a bestseller in Britain. Despite the snobbishness she sometimes showed, her book tells of an imaginative woman coping bravely in difficult times. In this passage from *Roughing It in the Bush*, she has to save her young family – the oldest child, Katie, is only about six – as their log cabin burns.

The house was built of cedar logs; in all probability it would be consumed before any help could arrive. There was a brisk breeze blowing up from the frozen lake, and the thermometer stood at eighteen degrees [Fahrenheit] below zero. We were placed between the two extremes of heat and cold, and there was as much danger to be apprehended from the one as the other. In the bewilderment of the moment, the direful extent of the calamity never struck me; we wanted but this to put the finishing stroke to our misfortunes, to be thrown naked, houseless, and penniless, upon the world. *"What shall I save first?"* was the thought just then uppermost in my mind. Bedding and clothing appeared the most essentially necessary, and, without another moment's pause, I set to work with a right good will to drag all that I could from my burning home.

While little Agnes, Dunbar, and baby Donald filled the air with their cries, Katie, as if fully conscious of the importance of exertion, assisted me in carrying out sheets and blankets, and dragging trunks and boxes some way up the hill, to be out of the way of the burning brands when the roof should fall in.

How many anxious looks I gave to the head of the clearing as the fire increased, and large pieces of burning pine began to fall through the boarded ceiling about the lower rooms where we were at work. The children I had kept under a large dresser in the kitchen, but it now appeared absolutely necessary to remove them to a place of safety. To expose the young, tender things to the direful cold, was almost as bad as leaving them to the mercy of the fire. At last I hit upon a plan to keep them from freezing. I emptied all the clothes out of a large, deep chest of drawers, and dragged the empty drawers up the hill; these I lined with blankets, and placed a child in each drawer, covering it well over with the bedding, giving to little Agnes the charge of the baby to hold between her knees, and keep well covered until help should arrive. Ah, how long it seemed coming!

Using snow and brine from their winter meat stores, the Moodies and their neighbours were able to put out the fire. Only the roof of their home was destroyed.

Three Native Heroes

When they conquered New France, the British generals had expected that they could rule all North America without consulting the Native nations that had been New France's allies. But Native nations all around the Great Lakes knew they had never been defeated, and Britain's claim to rule them made them angry. In 1763 they resolved to drive the redcoats from all the forts and trading posts in their territory. The Ottawa, Shawnee, Saulteaux, Sauk, Potawatomi, and other nations formed an alliance for war, and Pontiac, war chief of the Ottawas, led the attack.

At Michilimackinac, Sauk warriors distracted the sentries by playing a game of lacrosse – until the ball sailed over the palisade and the players chased the ball inside. As they entered, they grabbed their weapons from the women by the gate. In moments they had captured the fort. At Detroit, someone warned the garrison before it could be taken by surprise, but Pontiac's army besieged the fort all summer long. Other Native raiders seized a dozen other forts, and drove back soldiers who came to the rescue. The army that had conquered New France was in retreat.

The British fought for more than a year to recapture the forts. General Jeffrey Amherst, angry and desperate, ordered that blankets infected with smallpox be sent among the Native villages, and soon the sickness flared up. With the French gone, the Natives had no European ally, so they could not trade for guns and ammunition – and without weapons they could not win. In the end, they made peace and allowed the British to return to the fur trade forts.

However, the British government now realized that it could not ignore the Native nations. Later in 1763, a royal proclamation forbade British colonists to settle on Native lands unless the Native nations first gave the lands to the British king. For the first time, Britain recognized the rights and powers of the Native peoples. Pontiac, however, was killed by Native rivals a few years after.

The next leader who sought to unite Native nations

Opposite:

During the American Revolution, Thayendanegea (or Joseph Brant) of the Six Nations made a desperate gamble for his people's future. He led them into battle against the American rebels, gambling that grateful British and Loyalist allies would help defend the land and rights of the Iroquois people.

was Thayendanegea (in English, Joseph Brant) of the Iroquois or Six Nations. (By this time, the Tuscarora nation had joined the original five members of the Confederacy.) The Iroquois had been allies of Britain since the time of their wars with New France. Thayendanegea had gone to school among the colonists in New England, he had become a Christian, and he had helped translate the Bible into Mohawk. He was also a warrior and a thinker, and he wanted to use the British and their way of life to help his own people. When the American Revolution broke out, he urged the Iroquois Confederacy to help Britain against the rebels. If the Iroquois helped the British, he argued, then Britain would help to defend Iroquois land against American settlers.

All through the war, Thayendanegea's men fought alongside the Loyalist raiders. When the Americans won their independence, they took revenge on the Iroquois Confederacy, burning Iroquois towns and forcing the people to flee their homeland. Thayendanegea led his followers north to Canada, where they rebuilt a Six Nations community at Brant's Ford (now Brantford, Ontario). Like Pontiac, Thayendanegea continued to urge all the Native nations to unite to protect their lands, but the Americans and the British – and many Natives – feared his influence and worked against him. Thayendanegea died alone and bitter in 1807.

A few years later, Tecumseh of the Shawnee came forward to lead the Native peoples of the Great Lakes. With Ojibwas, Delawares, Ottawas, and other nations, he fought many battles to protect their homelands from American settlers who were moving into the land south of the lakes. In 1812, when the British were trying to keep the Americans from conquering Upper Canada, British soldiers and Tecumseh's warriors fought side by side against the invading army. But Tecumseh was killed in 1813 at the battle of Moraviantown, Upper Canada. The British preserved Upper Canada, but the Shawnees and other Native nations lost their war and much of their land.

First the French and later the British had needed the

Bytown and Ottawa

In 1826, Colonel John By and his Royal Engineers set up camp where the Rideau River falls into the Ottawa River, across from Philemon Wright's thriving lumbertown of Hull. Colonel By was there to build a canal to Lake Ontario, as a route British troops could use in case the Americans ever seized the St. Lawrence River.

In 1827, naval officer John Franklin paused while returning from one of his Arctic explorations to lay the cornerstone of the Rideau Canal. Shown positioning the stone is one of the canal's contractors, Thomas MacKay. His nearby home is now Ottawa's Rideau Hall, the residence of the Governor General of Canada.

Colonel By brought thousands of Irish-Canadian labourers to his camp to dig the canal through a swampy, fever-ridden wilderness. By the time they were done, six years later, a village called Bytown had grown by the Rideau Falls. Lumber companies moved in and harnessed the nearby Chaudière Falls for sawmills. In 1840, Nicholas Sparks sold the government two hundred acres (about eighty hectares) of farmland so it could build a soldiers' barracks on the hill overlooking the Ottawa River.

When Bytown became a city in 1855, the citizens renamed it Ottawa. Bytown or Ottawa, it was a brawling frontier lumbertown; Montrealers sneered at it and Torontonians called it "a subarctic lumbercamp." But in 1857, Queen Victoria chose Ottawa as the capital of the province of Canada. The soldiers' barracks became Parliament Hill.

friendship of the Native nations. In many wars they had been vital allies against the Americans. But by the 1830s the flood of newcomers had made the Native people a minority in their own land around the Great Lakes. The settlers no longer thought they needed the help of the Natives, and they pushed them into small reserves or into the North.

Rebellion and Reform

In the 1830s the governors of British North America felt they had much to be pleased about as they watched their colonies grow. But there was trouble ahead in both Lower and Upper Canada.

After the conquest of New France in 1763, the French Canadians had preserved their laws, language, and religion under British rule. In 1792, when Lower Canada was granted an Assembly, French Canadians quickly learned the British way of politics. They began to elect leaders who argued for the rights of their people in the new Assembly – and did so in French.

French Canada's leader in the Assembly was Louis-Joseph Papineau. He was a handsome aristocrat and an eloquent speaker in both French and English. He had fought to defend Canada from the Americans in 1812. Later, though, he grew bitter about the way the governor and a handful of English advisers – scornfully called the Château Clique – kept so much power to themselves. The Assembly could do little to control them. Papineau and his party, the Patriotes, demanded that the government obey the Assembly and the French-speaking majority. Many English-Canadian reformers supported them. They too wanted the people to have more say in how the colonies were run.

In the fall of 1837, the Patriotes held huge meetings to talk about forming a French-Canadian republic. They began to gather weapons. Papineau was reluctant to take up arms, and travelled the countryside, pleading for caution, but his

In the 1830s, thousands turned out to cheer when Louis-Joseph Papineau, leader of the Patriote Party of Lower Canada, gave fiery speeches protesting the rule of the British governors. Rebellion flared in 1837. Papineau, horrified by the violence, fled across the border.

followers were impatient. By November the British had a rebellion on their hands in Lower Canada.

Through the night of November 22, 1837, British soldiers marched from Montreal towards the village of St-Denis, on Lower Canada's Richelieu River. Colonel Charles Gore had orders to smash the Patriotes' stronghold there and arrest their traitorous leaders.

When the soldiers reached St-Denis, cold and soaked, they found the town armed for battle. The Patriotes of St-Denis had barricaded themselves behind stone walls. As Colonel Gore's men attacked, the Patriotes fired back boldly. All morning, men came rushing from the country-side to join the Patriotes' cause. In mid-afternoon Gore sounded the retreat and his soldiers fled. British troops had been beaten by armed rebels only a day's march from Montreal.

General John Colborne, Commander of the British Forces, moved quickly. He sent more troops to St-Denis and they burned it to the ground. Colborne – Old Firebrand, his men called him – then marched 2000 soldiers to St-Eustache, where Dr. Jean-Olivier Chénier

Cornelius Krieghoff, The Blacksmith's Shop. *A Dutch immigrant to British North America, Krieghoff painted thousands of scenes of life in rural Quebec. His lively pictures remain very popular today.*

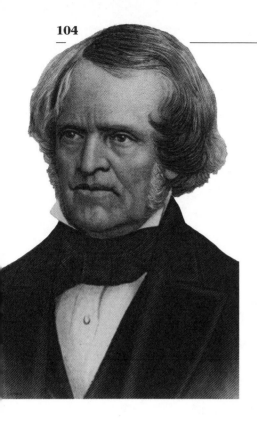

William Lyon Mackenzie, Upper Canada's stormiest politician, was a fierce critic of "the Family Compact."

and his Patriotes had fortified the parish church. Colborne blasted the church with cannonfire, killing Chénier and nearly a hundred rebels. The red-coated British troops were back in command. Papineau and the rest of the Patriote leaders fled across the border to the United States.

While British troops and Patriotes fought in the streets of St-Denis and St-Eustache, rebellion was also flaring in Upper Canada. There too, many colonists were tired of letting governors and their friends rule as they pleased.

The rebel leader in Upper Canada was William Lyon Mackenzie, a fiery little Scotsman with wild red hair. Mackenzie ran the *Colonial Advocate*, a newspaper in Toronto (York had been renamed in 1834), and he used it to argue for change. The clique that surrounded the lieutenant-governor seemed to him like one big family, with cousins and friends marrying one another's children and using the colony for their own benefit. Mackenzie dubbed them "the Family Compact," and he mocked them so fiercely that they threw his printing press into Lake Ontario. That only made him more popular with the Upper Canadians who resented the people Mackenzie criticized.

Mackenzie wanted to end the privileges enjoyed by the favoured few. He also wanted the lieutenant-governor to obey the people, not vice versa, and he wanted the elected Assembly to run the colony. Mackenzie himself had come from Britain, but now he talked of ending British rule in Upper Canada, and he looked across the border for American support. He began to talk of rebellion.

There were not many rebels in Upper Canada. Although a lot of people wanted change, few were ready for armed rebellion against the crown. But when Lieutenant-Governor Francis Bond Head sent all of Upper Canada's troops away to fight the Patriotes in Lower Canada, Mackenzie seized his chance. He mustered his followers at Montgomery's Tavern, north of Toronto, and prepared to march on the city.

It was a mistake. Upper Canada remained loyal, and thousands turned out to fight the rebels. Even old John Crysler, as fierce and loyal at seventy as at seven, marched again to defend Upper Canada. Mackenzie's little band started down Yonge Street, met the loyal defenders of Toronto, fired a few shots, and fled. Suddenly the rebellion was over, and Mackenzie had to run for the American border, disguised in women's clothing.

British North America

Again, British North America had defeated revolution. In both Upper Canada and Lower Canada, the governors ordered stern punishment for the defeated rebels. Two were hanged in Toronto and twelve in Montreal. Sixty were exiled to the prison colonies in Australia, and hundreds were jailed. The governors and their friends seemed as powerful as ever.

Britain sent a new governor general, the Earl of Durham, to investigate the rebellions and decide the fate of the colonies. Durham soon wrote a long report, and what he said shocked those who resisted change: he seemed to accept many of the ideas of the reformers! He said that the governments of the colonies should be chosen by the people's elected representatives. And that was not all he had to say.

"I found two nations warring in the bosom of a single state," Durham wrote. He had discovered a French nation and an English nation in Canada, and from his point of view the ways of the English seemed far better. If Upper and Lower Canada were joined, he declared, the French would be outnumbered and would soon begin to adopt English ways. Durham thought that would be a good thing. The French Canadians "are a people with no literature and no history," he said.

Britain accordingly decided to swallow up the French Canadians. In 1841, Lower Canada and Upper Canada became Canada East and Canada West, two halves of one colony with a single governor and a single Assembly, and with English-speakers forming the majority. But in this colony, as in the rest of British North America, the

The Rebellion of 1837 is the subject of Barbara Greenwood's popular historical novel A Question of Loyalty.

The Great Days of Sail

"There she goes!" The three-decked, three-masted *Marco Polo* roared down the slipway. She was the biggest ship ever built at James Smith's shipyard in Saint John, New Brunswick. Smith swore that she would be the fastest merchant ship in the world.

In fact, the *Marco Polo* was so big she went aground at the foot of the slipway. But once she floated free, nothing slowed her down again. On her first voyage, she crossed the Atlantic in just sixteen days. Soon after, she raced a steamship from Britain to Australia. She beat it by a week and continued around the world in record time.

It was 1851, the dawn of a great day for the ships and sailing men of Atlantic Canada. Schooners and sailors from Parrsboro and Tracadie and Twillingate were well known in all the seaports of the world. They kept busy hauling tea from Bombay, cotton from New Orleans, rice from Yokohama, or squared timber from Quebec City. Britain's trading empire spanned the globe, and every third ship in the British fleet was built in Atlantic Canada.

Maritimers were proud of their ships and sailors, and not only for the prosperity they brought Atlantic Canada. They knew that sailors around the world admired the "wooden ships with iron men."

Of course the sailors were men of flesh and blood, and the sea took its toll of lives. The fate of the Nova Scotia brigantine *Mary Celeste* became one of the great mysteries of the sea. In 1872, another ship met the *Mary Celeste* in mid-Atlantic, with her sails in order and no signs of trouble aboard. A meal waited on the table in the crew's quarters. But all the crew had vanished without a trace. No one ever discovered what happened to them.

governor remained in charge. Britain was still not ready to let the colonies govern themselves.

French Canada soon proved it was far stronger than the Earl of Durham imagined. To disprove what Durham had said, François-Xavier Garneau began writing the first history of French Canada's great deeds and proud traditions. French culture prospered along the St. Lawrence, and French continued to be heard in the Assembly of the United Canadas. New political leaders emerged to defend the French Canadians. They fought for "responsible government" – which meant a government run by the people's elected representatives, French and English – and they worked alongside English Canadians who supported the same goals.

It was Nova Scotia, however, that led the way to self-government. Nova Scotia's Assembly, founded in 1758, was the oldest in British North America. The United Canadas were larger, but the Maritimes were the wealthiest, most cultured parts of the British colonies. Samuel Cunard of Halifax ran one of the world's great shipping fleets. Judge Thomas Haliburton's funny stories of Sam Slick the Clockmaker were popular throughout the English-speaking world. Small colleges in Nova Scotia and New Brunswick trained many of the best minds in the colonies.

The statesman of self-government in Nova Scotia was Joseph Howe, a Loyalist's son with boundless energy and confidence. He argued the cause tirelessly, in the Assembly, in his newspaper, the *Novascotian*, and in rousing speeches around the province. Finally, Howe and his supporters won at the ballot box and took control of the Assembly. In 1848, Nova Scotia's lieutenant-governor agreed that the elected Assembly would choose the government and make the laws. It was all done without a blow struck or a pane of glass broken, as Howe said proudly.

Self-government in the United Canadas came soon after. The Assembly there voted to pay for damage done during the Rebellion of 1837. Even rebel families could get money: Dr. Chénier's widow in St-Eustache received a tidy sum. Many who had fought against the rebellion were dismayed and furious, but the Assembly had given its

Responsible Government – Before and After

Before Responsible Government – 1848

**The British government chooses
the governor for each colony.**

**The governor chooses the council,
which will help him run the colony.**

**The Assembly is elected by the voters.
It can give advice and raise money,
but it does not control the governor
or his council.**

**Only men can vote for the Assembly –
and not all men. To vote, a man
must be the head of a family with
a house and property.**

After Responsible Government – 1848

**The British government still chooses
the governor.**

**The governor appoints a Cabinet to run the
country. But now he must appoint the men
who are chosen for him by the Assembly.**

**The leader of the Cabinet is the prime
minister. The prime minister and
his Cabinet need the support of the
Assembly to stay in power.**

**Only men can vote – and not all men. To vote,
a man still has to be the head of a family
with a house and property.**

approval and so the governor general, Lord Elgin, decided he must sign the law. English Montrealers rioted in protest and burned the Assembly building in Montreal, but Elgin signed. Soon the elected Assembly became supreme in each of Britain's colonies.

The Assembly never again met in Montreal. The building there was in ruins, and the government began moving from place to place. First it met in Kingston, and then it moved back and forth between Toronto and Quebec City. In 1857, Queen Victoria was asked to choose a permanent home for the Assembly. She chose Ottawa. By the time new buildings were ready there, a new and larger Canada was in the making.

The day of the governors was fading, but Canada still had governors general and lieutenant-governors as representatives of the British crown. In 1760 they had

This view of Quebec was painted by George Heriot, who was deputy postmaster general of British North America. Here he has painted the officers of Britain's garrison enjoying winter sports around Quebec City, racing their sleighs along the frozen river.

been all-powerful. After 1848, they accepted the right of the colonists, including French-speaking ones, to run their own affairs. Instead of choosing their own advisers, the governors accepted the advice of whichever party dominated the Assembly. The leader of that party became the governor's primary adviser, or premier.

From the Atlantic ports to the farms of Upper Canada, these were good times for British North America. The colonies had ten times as many people as they had had fifty years earlier. They were beginning to look beyond the Great Lakes to the western plains. At Halifax, at Quebec, at Fort Henry in Kingston, the redcoats still stood on guard. The task that had seemed overwhelming in 1760 was nearly done. British Canada had survived and prospered, and it had learned to govern itself. Who knew what great things might be possible?

Chapter 5

The Great Northwest

FIVE HUNDRED YEARS AGO, 60 MILLION BISON – OR BUFFALO, AS they are more often called – roamed the grasslands of North America. They meant life itself to plains nations like the Blackfoot of what is now southern Alberta. The Blackfoot moved slowly across the land, following the herds and carrying with them everything they had. They hunted deer and antelope, they grew tobacco, and they gathered wild turnip and onion. But for centuries it was the buffalo that provided for the Blackfoot people. Buffalo hides made their tipis and their clothing. Buffalo sinews were their thread. Buffalo bones made clubs and spoons and needles. They even used dried buffalo dung as fuel for their campfires. To the Blackfoot, buffalo meat was "real" meat and nothing else tasted so good. They trusted the buffalo to keep them strong.

The Blackfoot had always gone on foot, using dogs to help carry their goods, for there were no horses in North America until Spanish colonists brought them in the 1500s. Soon after that, plains people captured animals that had gone wild, or stole them in raids. They traded the horses northward and, early in the 1700s, horses came to the northern plains. Suddenly the Blackfoot were a nation on horseback. How exciting it was, learning to ride a half-wild mustang and galloping off to the horizon!

Soon everyone on the plains could ride. Horses carried people and their belongings as they roved the plains. Horses became the proudest possessions of the Blackfoot and their neighbours. Hunters and warriors virtually lived on horseback. Now, instead of waiting for the buffalo, young men rode full gallop, bow in hand, into stampeding herds. To pick out and kill one's prey took magnificent horsemanship and cool courage.

Young men gloried in the excitement of it. They gloried in war, too, although war was even more dangerous and exciting on horseback than it had been before. The plains nations had always celebrated pride and courage, and young men had always sought to outdo each other in feats of bravery. Above all, they competed for *coups*. A coup meant coming close enough to touch an enemy,

Previous pages:
Métis cart brigades ranged the Prairies in search of buffalo herds. These families are starting the long trail back to Red River, their carts packed with pemmican after a successful hunt.

Head-Smashed-In Buffalo Jump

A "buffalo jump," like that shown here, was sometimes used in the buffalo hunt. One well-known site is Head-Smashed-In Buffalo Jump, which stands in the Porcupine Hills above the Oldman River in southern Alberta. From the top of the cliff, the plain seems to flow eastward forever. That view was the last thing ever seen by thousands and thousands of buffalo.

Archeologists say Head-Smashed-In Buffalo Jump was used by Native Canadians for more than five thousand years. In the mounds of earth at the foot of the cliffs, buffalo bones piled up ten metres deep. There people came to harvest food and to thank the spirit of the buffalo for its gift.

Today, Head-Smashed-In Buffalo Jump is a World Heritage Site. A museum stands close by the cliff's edge. Members of the Blackfoot Confederacy explain the lore of the buffalo to visitors. At the top of the cliff, in the constant wind, it is easy to feel that the spirit of the buffalo still lives.

and it was worth risking death for such glory. The bravest warriors, with many coups and many eagle feathers in their magnificent war bonnets, became honoured leaders of their people.

The Blackfoot were not beaver trappers, for there were no beaver on the plains. North of the Blackfoot and the buffalo, however, shimmering aspen forests lined the valley of the North Saskatchewan River. Still farther north, in a land dotted with lakes, stretched the dark spruce forest. This was fine country for beaver. Since Samuel de Champlain's day, beaver had meant fur traders. Peoples of the woodlands took eagerly to the fur trade. Some became hunters and trappers, while others became traders.

The Buffalo Hunt, Four Hundred Years Ago

At dawn, on a clear fall day, the Blackfoot people prayed to the spirit of the buffalo. If you had been there, you would have been shivering even in your warm deerskin shirt or shift and leggings.

Imagine you are there . . . .

Two days ago the scouts went out. Last night they came back to report that the herd was near. The best poundmakers in the band have done their work. They have chosen the strongest willow stakes and driven them into the hard ground to form the V-shaped fence of the jumping pound. At the narrow end of the pound is a small opening, right at the edge of the cliff.

Your feet in their moccasins are cold as you creep through the tall, frost-tipped grass. You have learned to read the land so well that you know the signs of prairie-dog holes, ant hills, and gullies. You go silently, as though you knew every stalk of grass.

You hear the geese honking overhead, the killdeer's shrill cry nearby. The scent of sagebrush is in your nostrils. Then you sniff buffalo.

The buffalo are coming!

Out behind the herd, three young men have wrapped themselves in grey wolf pelts. They move towards the herd, and the wolf smell makes the buffalo move away, bellowing nervously. The herd begins to flow towards you. You can feel the earth drumming under the thunder of their hoofs.

You are lying in the tall, cold grass with the women and the other children, forming two lines like beads on two strings. The beasts draw near, and one by one you stand. The buffalo move between the lines. How hot and stinking they are! The next person stands, and the next. Now it's your turn. You stand. Everyone is up. You all walk forward, closing in on the herd. Behind the herd, hunters flap pelts and fire arrows. Terror is in the buffalo, in the people, in the air itself, as the herd sweeps into the pound. Will the wooden stakes hold?

The stakes do hold and the herd is jammed together. Surging ahead, the herd drives its leaders through the opening at the narrow end of the pound. Over the cliff they go to their deaths, and the rest follow.

Now the skinning and butchering begin. Shoving frantic, barking dogs from underfoot, you work all day with your stone knives. You can feel the eyes of the hungry coyotes watching from the edge of the pound. Tonight there will be a feast. Every tipi will have a pot full of meat and wild onion. There will be singing and dancing to the music of the drum and the eagle-bone flute. There will be dice-playing and storytelling. And you will honour the spirit of the buffalo, who gave you this herd. This meat and hide and sinew and bone will keep your people strong. There will be food in the winter camp, down in a sheltered valley with a stream and a grove of trees. This year, all but the oldest and most feeble will live through to spring.

What a Buffalo Provides

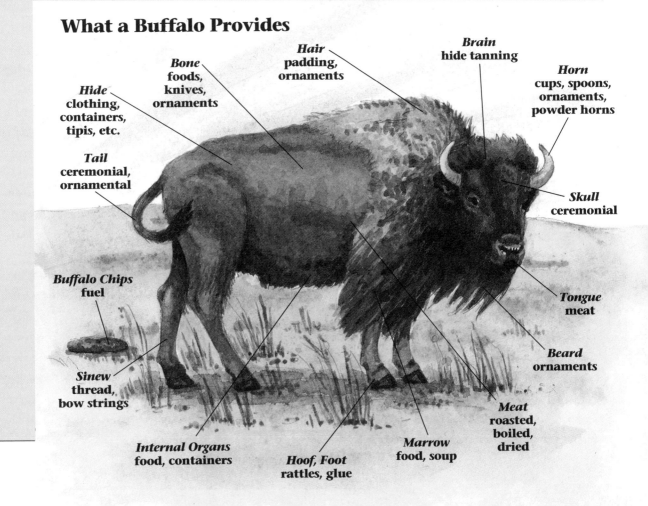

Bone foods, knives, ornaments

Hair padding, ornaments

Brain hide tanning

Horn cups, spoons, ornaments, powder horns

Hide clothing, containers, tipis, etc.

Tail ceremonial, ornamental

Skull ceremonial

Buffalo Chips fuel

Tongue meat

Beard ornaments

Sinew thread, bow strings

Meat roasted, boiled, dried

Internal Organs food, containers

Hoof, Foot rattles, glue

Marrow food, soup

Many keen traders came from the Cree nation. The Cree homeland lay in the woods, close to the trading posts on Hudson Bay, but Cree traders travelled west along the Saskatchewan River with the goods they bartered from the Baymen. Some of the traders settled along the river, and soon they were trading with the Blackfoot of the plains. The Blackfoot had horses while the Cree had muskets, and exchanging guns and horses sealed their friendship. They rode together to fight old enemies, the Sioux and the Snakes. Some of the Cree put aside their trade canoes and took to the grasslands, riding horses and hunting buffalo as the other plains people did.

The Fur Traders' Rivalry

From London, the "Company of Adventurers Trading into Hudson's Bay" sent its sailing ships through northern seas to its lonely trading posts on Hudson Bay. The most imposing was Prince of Wales's Fort, whose thick stone walls and heavy cannon guarded the mouth of the Churchill River. Few of the Hudson's Bay Company traders who manned it, and other posts like it, ever ventured farther into the country. Cree, Ojibwa, and Chipewyan traders, travelling along mysterious rivers from the heart of the continent, brought the furs to the company's trading posts by the bay.

The fur traders of Montreal did not wait for others to bring beaver pelts to them. Since the days of Radisson and Groseilliers, Montreal's adventurers had carried their trade

The rivers and lakes of Canada were highways of travel and trade for thousands of years. Every route included many portages, where canoes and goods had to be carried overland on straining shoulders.

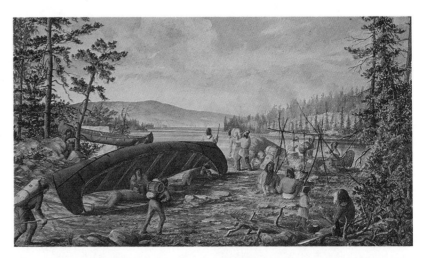

Explorer Alexander Mackenzie argues about the geography of the western rivers with tough trader Peter Pond. Alexander's cousin, the scholarly Roderick Mackenzie, who was the North West Company's factor at Fort Chipewyan, listens intently. Pond's advice sent Alexander, who was searching for the Pacific, down the Mackenzie River – to the Arctic Ocean instead.

goods up the rivers of the pays d'en haut in birchbark canoes. They wintered in the distant Northwest, always searching for new nations to trade with. With the help of their Native trading partners, they carried the fur trade almost to the Rocky Mountains. Each year, canoe brigades returned triumphantly to Montreal with bales of beaver pelts. Montreal and Hudson Bay competed for the fur trade of half a continent.

After Britain conquered New France, young Scots immigrants came to Montreal to join in the fur-trading business of the French-Canadian adventurers, and they competed with the Hudson's Bay Company as fiercely as the French merchants had. Voyageurs from farms along the St. Lawrence still paddled the trade canoes from Montreal, but they were joined now by Scots and Iroquois settled along the great river. They pushed farther west, rebuilding forts on the western plains where La Vérendrye had explored, and they scooped furs from right under the noses of the Baymen.

In the 1780s, the Scots traders of Montreal got together to create the North West Company – the Nor'Westers – one united team against the Hudson's Bay Company empire. Now began the glory days of Montreal's fur trade. The Montrealers manned trading posts on distant rivers far west of Hudson Bay. They intercepted Native traders before they

Journey to the Coppermine

Samuel Hearne was a happy young man when the governor of the Hudson's Bay Company's Prince of Wales's Fort chose him to head an expedition to the Coppermine River. He was to search for the Northwest Passage and discover whether there really was copper at the mouth of the Coppermine.

The governor chose Hearne's guides, and he chose badly. The guides deserted near the remote Dubawnt River country in "the land of little sticks."

There the party got lost, and the wind tore Hearne's compass from his hands and it broke on the ground. The guides stole everything else and deserted.

Hearne was alone in the frozen barrens without food or shelter. He began to walk, just to keep himself awake, but finally he collapsed.

Then, suddenly, a tall, imposing figure appeared. It was Matonabbee, a man Hearne knew well – a respected leader of the Chipewyans. Matonabbee knew the guides had deserted, and he had been out looking for Hearne. He had brought food and otter

robes, and when Hearne was warm and fed, the two set out. They reached the Prince of Wales's Fort in two months, stayed for just twelve days, then left again for the Coppermine River.

They reached the Coppermine to discover that there was exactly one lump of copper to be found. But the trip was not a failure. In the two years it took, from 1770 to 1772, Hearne learned to survive by dressing as the Natives did and eating what they ate. And perhaps the greatest good to come from the trip for both Hearne and Matonabbee was the friendship that lasted all their lives.

could reach Hudson Bay, and bargained for all the furs they could get. The partners of the North West Company became merchant princes. From the magnificent Beaver Club in Montreal, they ruled a trading empire that reached out across the continent.

Nor'Westers kept pushing into new territory, and Peter Pond led the way. Pond was a violent man whose rivals always seemed to die in mysterious circumstances, and no one pushed voyageurs harder than he did. Hauling their canoes and goods over long portages, Pond's men reached Lake Athabasca in Saskatchewan's far north in 1778. From there, rivers led north and west into rich beaver country. Earlier explorers had searched for a land of gold called Eldorado. Now Athabasca country, with its cold northern rivers and thousands of beaver ponds, became the fur traders' Eldorado.

From Montreal to the Athabasca country the canoe route stretched 7000 kilometres, and the Nor'Westers needed a "halfway house." In 1804 they built Fort William where the city of Thunder Bay now stands. Nor'Wester sailing ships carried trade goods through the Great Lakes to Fort William. From there, voyageurs in their canoes took the goods west and brought back the furs. Every June these "winterers" met their Montreal partners at Fort William for a month of wild celebration – and for hard-headed planning, too.

Shrewd planning was certainly needed. By 1800, the Nor'Westers and the Baymen were at each other's throats. Hudson's Bay traders no longer waited by their "frozen sea" while the Nor'Westers scooped up all the trade. The Baymen had moved inland to challenge their Montreal rivals, and soon their York boats were plying the rivers from Hudson Bay into the beaver country. Hudson's Bay Company forts began to dot the Northwest, starting with Cumberland House in Saskatchewan in 1774.

The Nor'Westers fought to keep the Baymen out. Nor'Westers undercut Bay prices for trade goods, and paid whatever they had to for furs. They destroyed Bay forts and canoes. They challenged inexperienced Baymen to fights

Blanket coats, knives, muskets – and whisky – were familiar items of the fur trade for hundreds of years. The ones shown here were Hudson's Bay Company trade goods around 1870.

and duels. They tried to starve them out. They even committed murder, sure that in that wild country no one was likely to be caught or convicted. Rival traders spent long winters thousands of kilometres from home, glaring at each other and hurling insults from tiny trading houses only a hundred metres apart. From the 1780s to 1821, a fur war raged across the West, touching many people besides the traders themselves.

The People in Between

In April 1806, Marie-Anne Gaboury married Jean-Baptiste Lagimodière in their village near Trois-Rivières on the St. Lawrence. Until then, Marie-Anne had lived a quiet life as the parish priest's housekeeper. Jean-Baptiste had just come back from five years in the pays d'en haut.

Lagimodière was a restless man, not suited to farming. He told his bride he was going west with the fur brigades. "*Bien*," she said. "If you won't stay here, I'll go with you." Friends and neighbours said she was mad. But on a warm May day, Marie-Anne set off with her new husband for the fur traders' rendezvous at Lachine, where Jean-Baptiste signed on with the North West Company as a voyageur.

The voyageurs waved their caps in the air. Then, with a flashing of paddles, four canoes loaded to the gunwales with trade goods surged into the river. In big *canots du maître* and smaller c*anots du nord*, the voyageurs were on their way to the distant beaver country around Lake Athabasca. Jean-Baptiste and Marie-Anne were not going quite so far, but it would be late summer before they reached Fort Garry, where Winnipeg now stands.

Once they were out west, Jean-Baptiste and Marie-Anne travelled the rivers by canoe and followed buffalo trails in oxcarts. In the woods they trapped beaver and traded for pelts. On the plains they hunted buffalo for the voyageurs. They wintered at forts as far apart as Fort Garry and Fort Edmonton.

Marie-Anne Lagimodière came to know the aspen

groves of the broad valley of the North Saskatchewan River and the dark forests and beaver meadows farther north. She also knew the rolling drylands of the buffalo and the buffalo hunters, where the tall prairie grass stretched away as far as the eye could see, rippling in the wind. She would spend the rest of her life in the West – and she would live to be ninety-five.

By 1810 the Lagimodières had several children, and they decided to settle along the Red River. They went to live among the French-speaking Métis people there. Métis means "mixed" in French, and the Métis were so called because they had emerged from the mixing of Europeans and Native people. At Detroit or Sault Ste. Marie on the Great Lakes, by Lake Nipigon in the north woods, or along the Churchill River near Hudson Bay, every woodland trading post became a little community. French and English traders and voyageurs married Ojibwa or Cree women. Their children and grandchildren, half Native and half European, grew up and found work around the forts. They became "the people in between," the ones who knew both Natives and newcomers. They worked with both, and

Fort Garry, at the forks of the Red and Assiniboine rivers, was the centre of the Hudson's Bay Company's fur trade at Red River. Later, the company built Lower Fort Garry, 30 kilometres away. Lower Fort Garry still stands, but it was the fort at the forks of the rivers that grew into the city of Winnipeg.

soon the fur trade could not get along without them. At first many of "the people in between" were French and Ojibwa. Later many were Scots and Cree. Whoever their ancestors were, they became a new and separate people, the Métis.

The Métis moved west with the fur trade. While the Nor'Westers and the Baymen fought, Métis families moved out onto the plains. They took to horses and buffalo hunting and became as skilled as the plains people. Buffalo meat, pounded, mixed with fat and berries, and packed into a hide bag, made a food called pemmican. Pemmican was a light and compact load in voyageur canoes, and the paddlers took long journeys on a diet of little else. As the war of Nor'Westers and Baymen raged on, both sides needed pemmican – particularly the Nor'Westers, whose voyageurs made the longest journeys.

By the early 1800s, the heart of the Métis country lay in the valleys of the Red and Assiniboine rivers, flowing down to Lake Winnipeg. And so, when they settled at Red River in 1810, the Lagimodières linked their future with that of the Métis.

Soon after the Lagimodières arrived, other pioneers came from overseas to settle at Red River. An eccentric Scottish aristocrat, the Earl of Selkirk, decided to make Red River into a colony for poor immigrants from the Scottish

This painting, Red River Settler's House and Cart, *was done by William Hind in 1870.*

highlands. Selkirk had bought control of the Hudson's Bay Company by then, so it granted him a territory of 300 000 square kilometres: Assiniboia, on the banks of the Red River. Selkirk wanted his highlanders to grow crops and raise animals. In the midst of the fur trade country, he expected them to build a little British colony.

The Red River War

Hudson's Bay Company ships dropped the first of Selkirk's settlers at Churchill in the fall of 1811, the worst possible time of the year. They struggled overland to Red River – and starvation. Only help from the Métis and from Chief Peguis of the nearby Saulteaux people saved them. Peguis's people led the settlers south, with the children riding on Saulteaux ponies, until they reached the Métis buffalo hunters. Jean-Baptiste and Marie-Anne Lagimodière advised and helped them too. More of Selkirk's settlers arrived the next year, and things were just as hard for them.

Though Métis families helped the bedraggled newcomers, they feared Lord Selkirk's plans. So did the Nor'Westers. Selkirk's colony took land that the Métis considered their own, and, as well, it lay on the route of the North West Company voyageurs. Nor'Westers feared that the Selkirk settlement was a Hudson's Bay Company plot to block their canoe brigades from reaching the Athabasca country, or to deny them the pemmican they bought from Métis hunters.

Selkirk's colony seemed doomed to disaster. Food was scarce when their first crops failed. The settlers feared the Métis and the voyageurs, and they hated the harsh winters. The Nor'Westers played on these fears. In 1815 they urged the highlanders to abandon Red River and head for Upper Canada in company canoes. The Selkirk colonists hesitated. They set out, but then they turned back. They had decided to stay and fight for Red River.

On the afternoon of June 19, 1816, a band of Métis

Lord Selkirk, with some of his settlers, is shown naming Kildonan in 1817. The settlers had survived many hardships since their arrival at Churchill in 1811.

horsemen rode past Fort Douglas, the Hudson's Bay post used by Lord Selkirk's governor, Robert Semple. Semple rode out with twenty-six men to challenge the Métis. The two parties met at a place called Seven Oaks. Both sides were armed, and both sides were angry. Semple wanted the Métis to accept the authority Lord Selkirk had given him. The Métis were furious at being ordered about by this intruder on their land. The two sides quarrelled and shots rang out. Semple and his men were no match for the Métis hunters. In a few minutes, the governor and twenty of his men lay dead. That night the Métis, who had lost only one man, sat inside Fort Douglas, chanting songs about their victory at Seven Oaks.

Lord Selkirk was far away in Montreal, but he fought back. The Baymen at Fort Douglas had already sent Jean-Baptiste Lagimodière east to warn Selkirk of the trouble brewing, and Selkirk rushed west, bringing soldiers to defend his settlers. At Fort William he arrested the partners of the North West Company, since he blamed Montreal fur traders for the killings. Then he marched on to Red River to take charge there.

Happily for Red River, there were no more massacres. Over the next few seasons, the settlers and the Métis were too busy battling locusts and floods to fight each other. And the fur trade war was finally ending. It had been ruining both companies. The Nor'Westers had more furs, more men, and more forts, but the Hudson's Bay Company had more money. In 1821 the Hudson's Bay Company bought the North West Company and hired its best men. Montreal's fur trade died away. After two hundred years, voyageurs no longer left Lachine on the long route to the pays d'en haut. Now all the furs went out through Hudson Bay.

The Bay's Empire

The Hudson's Bay Company was a century and a half old in 1821, and finally it was free of its rival from Montreal. Its trading empire stretched from Labrador to Vancouver

Métis leader Cuthbert Grant's mild, round face does not look like that of a brilliant horseman and guerrilla fighter. But the Red River settlers discovered his fearsome skills at Seven Oaks in 1816, when his Métis hunters killed twenty of the pioneers.

Island. In 1820, George Simpson had arrived from England to take charge.

Simpson was a cold, hard-hearted man but he was efficient. When he became governor of the Hudson's Bay Company and master of the fur trade, he burst upon the West like a whirlwind. He moved swiftly from post to post in a canoe paddled by specially chosen Iroquois voyageurs. After the wild times of the fur wars, George Simpson was determined that things were going to be different.

Simpson closed down trading posts that could not pay their way. He fired traders and voyageurs. He bought only as many furs as he thought the company needed, and he paid less for them. Times grew hard for Native traders and trappers. They had always had two companies fighting over their furs, but now there was only George Simpson's company and the tough terms it offered.

Everyone in the fur trade, even those who had fought the company most fiercely, now had to work with the Baymen. Jean-Baptiste Lagimodière was content to do so, but even Cuthbert Grant, who had led the Métis riflemen at Seven Oaks, found himself working for the Bay. Without the fur traders setting them apart, the Métis and the Selkirk settlers learned to live together. The Métis had their land on one side of the Red River, the Selkirk people had theirs on the other.

Every spring, the Red River carts rolled west into buffalo country. Oxen strained at the leather harnesses, while wooden wheels rumbled and shrieked on wooden axles. Hundreds of carts crowded with hunters and their families sent clouds of dust rising over the plain. The great buffalo hunt was beginning again. The skilful Métis led the way, but now settlers from Selkirk's colony went along too. After the cart brigades found a herd, the horsemen rode into a melee of dust and noise and terrified animals. Each hunter fired across his horse's neck, then rode on, jamming another ball and more powder down the muzzle of the musket as he came up to another buffalo. The hunters competed for the most kills, but when the hunt was done everyone worked to make pemmican.

A mean, tough, determined man, George Simpson made big changes to the Hudson's Bay Company, cutting prices and closing forts. But the company began making money again.

In his Assiniboine Hunting Buffalo, *artist Paul Kane captured the speed, the excitement, and the danger of the buffalo hunt.*

The spring hunt was a good time for the Métis. Men and women took pride in their riding, and the hunters boasted of their shooting, and their fearless strength. The masters of the hunt were leaders of the whole Métis nation. Before the brigades rolled back to Red River, carts piled high with pemmican bags, there was always time for a feast and a dance. Every family had its fiddler or its piper. They danced and sang inside their circle of carts, their buckskin jackets ablaze with brilliant Métis beadwork.

But trouble was looming. The plains were becoming crowded as Métis, Cree, and Ojibwa people all moved west. Since they all had horses, each prairie nation ranged over more territory. The mounted warriors of the Plains – Cree, Blackfoot, Ojibwa, Sioux, Assiniboine, and Snake – fought not just for glory, but for the buffalo that fed them all.

In the 1830s, terrible epidemics blazed across the plains. Saukamappee, a young warrior of the Plains Cree, told of riding in to attack his enemies in their tents, and finding them all dead or dying in their bedrolls. Soon after, Saukamappee's own people caught the sickness, and so did the Blackfoot. One in three died. Saukamappee never forgot those days of tears and cries of despair.

Wanderers and Artists

After the closing of Montreal's North West Company, few furs came east, but the Canadian colonies did not forget about the Northwest. Travellers and explorers who went west brought back stories of "the great lone land."

Painter Paul Kane set out from Toronto in 1845, determined to paint the West and its people. His energy impressed George Simpson, who permitted Kane to travel the Great Lakes with Hudson's Bay Company crews. Kane visited Red River and rode with the buffalo hunters. Then he pushed on across the Rockies to the Pacific, sketching and painting everywhere. When he went home and exhibited his paintings, they caused a sensation. No one back east had ever seen such images.

Other travellers, artists, and writers were also eager to explore the West. John Palliser was a cheery young Irishman who loved hunting. He wanted to dash right across the continent, hunting buffalo, grizzlies, and mountain goats as he went. But the British government decided he could do important work on the plains. Britain and the United States had agreed in 1818 that the forty-ninth parallel of latitude would be their border all the way to the Rockies. But was the land north of that line good for anything but fur trading and buffalo hunting? Fur traders, who wanted to keep out everyone else, liked to say that the West was a frozen wasteland. Americans said that a hot, dry desert stretched north to the border. If good land lay in between, the British government wanted to know. John Palliser was told to organize an expedition and find out.

Palliser's team set out from Red River in 1857. For three years his scientists studied the country. Palliser shot buffalo to keep them fed, but he had to be a diplomat as well. The land still belonged to the Cree and Blackfoot, and Palliser's men sometimes met their war parties ranging the plains on their mustangs.

Palliser told Britain's government of a huge territory too dry for farming, too dry for settlers. This triangular area in what is now southern Saskatchewan and Alberta became

A young Irishman who loved hunting, shooting, and fishing, John Palliser just wanted adventure on the Canadian plains. But in 1856 the British government gave him a bigger job. It needed to know if those distant plains were fit for farming and for settlement. Yes, said Palliser, after three years travelling the West – but not the dry part, called Palliser's Triangle.

William Hind, Bar in a Mining Camp. *In 1862, William Hind set off with the Overlanders on their arduous voyage to the Cariboo goldfields of British Columbia. The Overlanders must often have felt as weary as these men at a mining camp appear to be.*

known as Palliser's Triangle. Palliser also told of a rich "fertile belt" farther north. This was no frozen wasteland. It had fine agricultural prospects.

Interest in the West continued to grow, and not only in Britain. In Canada West, where farmland was becoming scarce, farmers who wondered where their children would find land began looking west. George Brown, a young newspaperman from Toronto, began to preach in *The Globe* that Canada must colonize and settle the West. The way Canadians talked, it was as though the entire prairie was an empty land waiting for them to come west with their ploughs.

Leaders of the West

Previous pages:
Geese wing northward as the boat builders of Fort Edmonton put the finishing touches to a new York boat. Looking on is Chief Factor John Rowand, the big, friendly, and energetic fur trader who ran Fort Edmonton for thirty years.

Red River people knew the land was not empty. Marie-Anne and Jean-Baptiste Lagimodière's children and grand-children had grown up at Red River among the Métis people. The Métis were now mainly farmers and traders, but many of their hunters had moved farther west to settle along the rivers of Saskatchewan and Alberta. They still sold pemmican to the Baymen, but they would not let George Simpson's company push them around. The Bay claimed that it controlled the fur trade of all the West, but in 1849 a Métis trader sold his furs to an American trading post across the border. Although the company took him to a Red River court, he walked out unpunished. Led by Marie-Anne's son-in-law, Louis Riel, the Métis declared they would trade their furs wherever they pleased.

French-Canadian missionaries had come from Lower Canada to serve the Catholic Métis. In 1858 one of them, Bishop Alexandre Taché, invited Louis Riel's son, also called Louis, to travel back to Montreal. Young Louis was a bright lad, and the bishop thought that, with a proper education, he might make a good priest. So young Louis, Marie-Anne Lagimodière's grandson, went east to study.

No matter what boundary lines Britain and the United States had drawn on the map, the West belonged to the Métis, Blackfoot, Cree, and Assiniboine. For generations they had ridden the plains on horseback, fighting fast, violent battles and organizing exciting buffalo hunts. They were determined that no one would drive them from their territory. If Canada and its land-hungry settlers wanted the West, Canada would have to talk to the Métis and to the people of the buffalo.

But the buffalo were being hunted out of existence. The herds began to shrink in the 1860s. Soon the Plains Cree could find none of the animals in their hunting range. They grew angry at the Métis hunters and at intruders like the English lord who came to hunt buffalo simply for sport; one chief asked why he would come so far to kill the animals that sustained the Cree people. Soon the Cree had to ride farther west in search of buffalo herds. When they entered Blackfoot land, the long friendship of Cree and Blackfoot ended.

Maskepetoon of the Plains Cree believed that his people and the Blackfoot should not fight. He was a wise and much-travelled leader; he had met an American president in Washington, D.C., and had visited Vancouver Island, where he had ridden on the Hudson's Bay Company steamship *Beaver*. Now he tried to stop the war by the bravest deed a plains warrior could perform. In 1869 he rode unarmed into a Blackfoot camp to offer peace. The Blackfoot would either accept his offer – or kill him.

Some pictographs may be thousands of years old, while others come from more recent times. This one of a buffalo hunt on horseback was drawn in 1897.

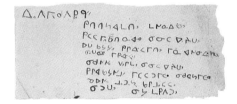

Cree traders and Protestant missionaries developed syllabics as a way to write the Cree language. This letter from Maskepetoon, the Cree grand chief, says: "He-who-speaks-from-above, I send you a letter. I shake hands with you. I want you to be here, to see you, I and the Assiniboines. There are twenty lodges. My son Benjamin, I want him to speak English. There are 164 buffalo. I tell you the news, my friend. I am Maskepetoon."

Trapped in the ice at Mercy Bay in the High Arctic while searching for Franklin, Captain Robert McClure abandoned HMS Investigator *in the winter of 1852.*

John Franklin's Tragic Quest

Was there really a Northwest Passage over the top of North America? By 1845, sailors and mapmakers knew that, if there was, it must be locked in ice most of the year, and thus quite useless to sailors. But no one actually knew what straits and passages might lie in Canada's frozen North. That year, Captain John Franklin set out to solve the last great mystery of northern exploration.

The British navy gave him 134 men and two ships, *Erebus* and *Terror*. They carried the best the navy could provide. There was steam heat and canned food (a new invention). The officers dined off fine china and drank from crystal goblets. They even had a grand piano. In July,

Maskepetoon knew that the Blackfoot and the Cree had been good friends. In past times, Cree warriors had helped the Blackfoot drive their enemies out of their hunting territories. But now both nations were desperate for buffalo. When Maskepetoon came in unarmed, the Blackfoot refused his offer of peace. One of their chiefs killed him, and the war went on.

The next year, 700 Cree warriors rode west to hunt buffalo on Blackfoot territory and to avenge their chief. By the Oldman River they met the Blackfoot. The Cree outnumbered the Blackfoot, and they spurred their horses forward to attack. The Blackfoot, however, had rifles, and they shot down the Cree horsemen. When the Cree fell back, the Blackfoot rushed across the river and surrounded them in a grove of trees. Hundreds of Cree died that day, and the Cree nation asked for peace.

The Battle of the Oldman was the last clash of the

Franklin and his men waved goodbye to whaling ships in Davis Strait. Then they sailed into the Northwest Passage – and never came out again.

It took years before the world learned Franklin's fate. As the British navy searched for him, it mapped most of the straits and islands of the Arctic Sea. There was indeed a passage between the islands, they learned – and Franklin had nearly found it when his ships had become trapped in the ice.

In 1854, Dr. John Rae, who travelled light and lived as the Inuit did, finally learned how and why Franklin's men had perished. Inuit hunters told him that Franklin's men had died, cold and starving, trying desperately to walk south to safety, until they had fallen in their tracks.

In Britain, Franklin and his men were mourned as tragic heroes of Arctic exploration. But John Rae realized that Franklin had tried to defeat the Arctic instead of living with it. To survive in the Arctic, explorers had to learn from the Inuit, who had been prospering there for a thousand years.

Young sailor John Torrington, just twenty, died on New Year's Day 1846, before the ill-fated Franklin expedition really got started. His shipmates buried him on Beechey Island. In 1984, 138 years later, scientists dug up his body, to see if lead poisoning from canned food had helped to doom the expedition. They found enough lead in Torrington to kill anyone.

plains warriors. The horseback nations had been weakened by epidemics, by the wars, and above all by the scarcity of the buffalo. Among the Blackfoot and the Cree, new leaders came forward to make peace. Crowfoot of the Blackfoot adopted Poundmaker of the Cree, and the two men urged the plains nations to stand together. They knew they must unite to face the power of the settlers who were moving into their land.

The Métis also suffered. The buffalo were disappearing, and at the same time English-speaking settlers were starting to arrive at Red River from the East. To face these challenges, the Métis needed strong leaders. The Métis council turned to young Louis Riel, Marie-Anne Lagimodière's grandson, who was just back from his schooldays in Montreal, and to master-hunter Gabriel Dumont. A new generation of leaders was stepping forth in the West.

Chapter 6

Mountains and Oceans

Between the mountains and the ocean, long green streamers of kelp floated in a cove called Yuquot, on the northwest coast of North America. Families of sea otters swam in the kelp. The sea otters were strong, lively swimmers, and the cold water never penetrated their thick, velvety-black fur. When the people of Yuquot needed winter cloaks, they hunted the sea otters. Their chief, Maquinna, wore handsome robes of sea-otter pelts.

In about 1740, Russian fur traders sailed across the narrow strait from Siberia to Alaska. Their leader, a Danish sailor named Vitus Bering, died miserably of scurvy on a bleak Alaskan island. The czars soon sent more expeditions across the strait, however, and the coast of Alaska became a Russian colony. From a forlorn outpost called New Archangel, Russian traders sent back sea-otter pelts gathered by the Aleut and Tlingit people. Rumours of these Russian traders reached the Spanish colony in Mexico, and in 1774 Juan Pérez Hernández sailed north to investigate. He landed and met the Native people of the northwest coast.

Four years later a British naval officer, Captain James Cook, came to the coast. In 1759, as an unknown young navigator, Cook had guided the British invasion fleet up the St. Lawrence to Quebec. Since then he had explored the world on sea voyages that had lasted years. Cook had already been to Australia, New Zealand, the islands of the Pacific, and the Antarctic seas. Now he was following the Russians and the Spanish to the northwest coast. He was chasing the old dream of a Northwest Passage, but looking for it from the opposite side. If a western entrance to such a passage lay on the misty northwest coast, Britain wanted to find it.

In the spring of 1778, James Cook stood on the quarterdeck as his ship, HMS *Resolution*, approached the coast near Yuquot Cove. The people who lived there sped out in their canoes to greet this strange, white-winged ship, and Cook spent a month at Yuquot. He gave Yuquot Cove the name Nootka, thinking that was what the local people called it. As his men repaired their ships, they talked and traded with the people. The Yuquot people admired the

Previous pages:
Enterprising seaman John Meares bought sea otter pelts in the Pacific Northwest and sold them in China. Sensing a good business, Meares brought back Chinese labourers, who built the ship North West America.
In the picture, Meares launches the ship at Nootka, on September 20, 1789, while Maquinna watches from the shore.

iron tools the sailors carried, and in exchange for them they offered their gleaming sea-otter cloaks.

That summer Cook sailed north from Yuquot to Bering Strait, but he found no Northwest Passage. HMS *Resolution* sailed back to Hawaii for the winter months, and there Cook got into a fight with the local people and was killed. Cook's crew sailed on across the Pacific, and at Canton (now renamed Guangzhou), in China, they discovered that Chinese dignitaries would pay huge sums to have their robes trimmed with sea-otter fur. Sailors who had brought a few pelts along to use as blankets were suddenly rich.

Whalers return from the hunt.

The seashore at low tide was the food store of British Columbia's coastal nations. Along the shore at Nootka, a woman is gathering mussels; others fish or dig for clams. Details: *a rain hat woven from cedar bark, a halibut hook, and a soul-catcher – used to cure those plagued by evil spirits.*

The Nootka Traders

Nootka soon appeared on the maps of the world, as merchant ships from London, Boston, and Canton set course for the northwest coast. Among them was the *Imperial Eagle*, which carried a seventeen-year-old English-woman, Frances Barkley. She had just married the ship's captain, a globe-trotting merchant sailor named Charles William Barkley, and the seven-month voyage from Europe to Nootka was to be their honeymoon.

The Barkleys visited Nootka in 1787 and gave their names to nearby Barkley Sound and Frances Island. Frances loved the mild climate, and she admired the people there and the power and dignity of their chiefs. At Nootka the Barkleys met Maquinna, who received them wearing his magnificent cloak. Maquinna and his people were accustomed to trading ships by this time, and Captain Barkley was able to carry away a cargo of sea-otter pelts. The *Imperial Eagle* sailed to China and on around the world to Britain. The next time Captain Barkley sailed for Nootka, friends told Frances it was not proper for a wife and mother to go on sea voyages, but she refused to be left behind. She visited Nootka again in 1792, on her second trip around the world.

Many other European ships and sailors visited the northwest coast. In 1789, Captain John Meares brought thirty Chinese labourers who built a ship for him at Nootka – perhaps the first Chinese to visit North America since the time of Hwui Shin, who, some believe, came 1300 years before. Though men like Meares and Barkley came to trade, they did not always come peacefully. Sailors who distrusted the Native people attacked or abused them. Sometimes they turned their cannon on Native villages. The people of the coast struck back.

The Voyage to Fu Sang

Fu Sang was a land far from China. To go there meant a voyage of 20 000 *li*, in the direction of the rising sun. Yet Hwui Shin set out to teach the people of Fu Sang about the Buddha.

In the year named Everlasting Origin – 499 by our calendar – Hwui Shin returned from Fu Sang and told amazing stories. The people of Fu Sang lived in houses made of planks, he said. They made their clothing from the bark of trees and were led by kings who ruled with great ceremony. Hwui Shin had travelled and preached among them before returning to China.

Perhaps Hwui Shin only sailed to Japan or to eastern Asia and found Fu Sang there. The story of Fu Sang may even have been a fable about the home from which the sun rose each morning. But Fu Sang may also have been the northwest coast of Canada. Chinese navigators may have crossed the Pacific Ocean fifteen centuries ago.

Age-old ties join the two continents of the North Pacific. In their seagoing canoes, the skilled sailors of British Columbia visited Alaska. Alaskan peoples, in turn, visited their neighbours in the Aleutian Islands, and the Aleutian people travelled across to Siberia. Everywhere they went, people traded goods and ideas and even styles of dress. The people of the northwest coast could have known about China even if Hwui Shin never reached them.

Still, it is exciting to imagine a Chinese junk with a crew of Buddhists threading its way through the misty islands and fiords and finding a welcome in the cedar villages.

Paul Kane is most famous for his paintings of buffalo hunters on the plains, but the wandering artist travelled on to the north-west coast, where he painted Clal-lum Women Weaving Blankets.

People of the Salmon

The people of the northwest coast were like no others in North America. They lived in a world of mountains, and rivers that cut deep channels through them – a world of islands and inlets and steep-sided fiords. Rainclouds rolled in from the Pacific Ocean to nurture a lush green rain-forest. Colossal cedar and fir trees, a thousand years old, grew a hundred metres tall, towering over a thick undergrowth of ferns, salal, and broom.

The bays and rivers were rich with life. Halibut and whales, seals and otters swam in the sea, and each falling tide revealed shellfish on every rock and reef. Fat salmon swam up the rivers in summer. Returning from the ocean to spawn and die in the streams where they had been born, they came in such numbers that it seemed you could walk across the rivers on their backs.

The people of the coast lived on the wealth of the rainforest and the ocean. They felled the giant red cedars and split them into timbers and planks for their strong wooden houses. They carved totem poles over their doorways to honour the family's guardian spirits. Skilled carvers made many useful items – boxes and baskets and bowls and spoons – from cedar wood. Weavers and clothmakers made cedar branches into rope, and they pounded cedar bark into a kind of cloth. Hides and leather soon grew soft and rotted in the rainforest, but cedar-bark clothes and hats kept out the rain.

The west-coast people hollowed out cedar logs to make graceful canoes with high prows carved with intricate designs. In the biggest ones, which could carry fifty paddlers, they hunted whales in the open ocean. They also used the canoes to travel the twisting waterways from winter villages to summer fishing camps, and for trading and fishing.

Men went to war in these canoes, too. There were many nations living along the coast, speaking seventeen different languages, and wars among them were common. The Gitksan warrior Nekt lived in a hilltop fortress above the Skeena River. The Haida of the Queen Charlotte Islands went raiding far to the north and south, and distant people feared the sight of their long, sleek canoes.

The rainforest people lived from the salmon, as the plains people lived from the buffalo and the corngrowers from their fertile fields. Where the rivers roared through the steep mountain passes, they harpooned, netted, and

Terrible epidemics stalked the Haida people of the Queen Charlotte Islands in the 1860s. The few survivors had to abandon many of their ancient towns. Skidegate was one of only two towns that remained. Scientist George M. Dawson photographed it in 1878.

Ninstints

Out beyond the British Columbia coast lie the misty Queen Charlotte Islands. They are the homeland of the Haida nation, who call these islands Haida Gwaii.

The war canoes of the Haida once cut through the waters of the Pacific Northwest. The Haida villages were in protected coves close to fishing grounds and reefs rich with shellfish. At Kiusta, Skedans, Tanu, and the other villages, large houses built of cedar planks stood in a row facing the beach. Over the doorways or standing in front of the houses rose forests of totem poles.

One of the Haida's most important villages was Ninstints, on Anthony Island ("Skungwai" to the Haida), near the southern end of the Queen Charlottes. Ninstints was a busy place for thousands of years. But Ninstints, along with most of the Haida villages, was abandoned in the late 1800s.

Today Anthony Island is quiet, and only the totem poles remain. Ninstints has the finest array of totem poles still standing anywhere on the west coast. The United Nations has proclaimed Ninstints a World Heritage Site, one of the treasures of world civilization.

trapped enough salmon in a few frenzied weeks to feed themselves for a year. And because they were skilled at smoking salmon until it was hard and dry, their catch would keep all year round.

Salmon made the rainforest people wealthy. The wealthiest among them were the families of the chiefs, who commanded the best fishing spots. A chief had great power. He was richly dressed. He rode in a spectacular canoe, and he lived in a magnificent cedar house whose house poles boasted of great ancestors and guardian spirits. But chieftainship was a great burden. A chief had to guide his people, lead them in war, keep them well fed, and protect them from their enemies.

A chief proved his wealth and his generosity in a *potlatch*, a feast and ceremony where he gave gifts to all those who honoured and followed him, to prove his greatness. His family and all those close to him shared his honour and held high rank. The lowest-ranked people were merely slaves, for on this coast chiefs had slaves to serve them. The people of the woodlands and the plains owned little and believed all were equal, but the rainforest people owned much and knew just what rank they held in their society.

A chief like Maquinna would tolerate no insult to his people, or to himself. When visitors came to Yuquot in their big ships, he demanded respect. The arrogance of the traders often infuriated him. In 1803, after Captain Salter of the *Boston* insulted him, Maquinna seized the brig and chopped off the heads of the captain and his crew. He spared only John Jewitt, a young armourer on his first voyage, and an older man, John Thompson. He made them his slaves. Jewitt could repair tools and forge steel harpoons for Maquinna's whaling voyages. He became a valued member of the chief's household, and he saved Thompson's life by pretending that the old sailor was his father. The prisoners spent two years among the Yuquot people. By the time they were finally ransomed, Jewitt had learned to admire Maquinna, and he understood the chief's pride and anger. Still, he was glad to be going home!

Despite the skirmishes and even the killings, sea captains and the coastal people continued to trade sea-otter pelts for copper and iron. Traders grew rich, Chinese mandarins luxuriated in furs, and rainforest villages acquired new tools. Only the sea otters lost out. In a few years they vanished from the coves and kelp beds of the northwest coast, driven almost to extinction by the trade in their pelts.

Not all the quarrels on the coast were between traders and Native chiefs. The Spanish and English empires clashed there. For centuries Spain, which had colonies from Chile and Mexico to the Philippines, had considered the Pacific Ocean its private ocean. After Captain Cook sailed to

This secret-society mask representing the sun was carved in the early 1900s by a Southern Kwakiutl artist. The tradition of carving these beautiful masks reaches back thousands of years and still continues. Today Native societies are recovering some of them from museums and collectors.

Nootka, the Spanish governor in Mexico sent many expeditions to lay claim to the northwest coast. Estevan, Alberni, Galiano, Langara, and many other Spanish captains left their names scattered over the maps of the coasts they explored. But when they built a fort at Nootka in 1789 and began seizing British ships, the British talked of war.

In the end, Spain and Britain agreed not to fight over Nootka, and the British sent Captain George Vancouver to Nootka in HMS *Discovery.* In 1792, Vancouver met Spain's Captain Quadra there, and they settled the Nootka dispute. Then Vancouver – who had been part of Cook's crew in 1778 – set out to complete Cook's explorations of the northwest coast.

Vancouver wanted to settle whether the Northwest Passage really existed. For three summers his ships and boats crawled in and out of the passages and inlets of the coast, charting and mapping, but found no channel that opened up to lead them through the continent. The notion of a Northwest Passage had tantalized navigators for nearly three hundred years, but Vancouver proved that, if any sea route around North America existed, it surely lay in the far and frozen North.

In 1789, Britain's Royal Navy chose an officer named Roberts to lead its expedition to the Pacific Northwest. At the last moment he could not go, and Captain George Vancouver was sent instead. Nearly a century later, William Van Horne of the CPR named the railway's western terminus after Vancouver. Might the city have been called Roberts or Robertsville?

From Canada, by Land

In June 1793, Captain Vancouver's boat crews explored an inlet they named Dean Channel, near Bella Coola. If they had lingered just six weeks longer, they might have made a spectacular rendezvous. For another explorer visited Bella Coola and the Dean Channel in July. Alexander Mackenzie reached there by canoe and on foot, from far-distant Montreal.

Mackenzie was one of the North West Company trailblazers who had peppered the woodlands with trading forts all the way to the Rocky Mountains, until the western ocean seemed within reach. Alexander Mackenzie decided to strike for the Pacific.

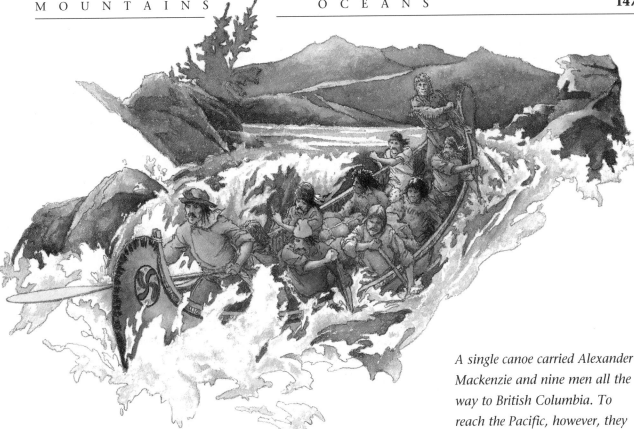

A single canoe carried Alexander Mackenzie and nine men all the way to British Columbia. To reach the Pacific, however, they had to leave the canoe and walk through the mountains to the sea.

His first venture mistakenly led him north to the Arctic Ocean, not west to the Pacific. The river he discovered was later named for him, but Mackenzie was disappointed. He went to Britain to learn more about surveying and mapmaking, and in 1793 he was ready to start again. He crammed ten men with all their gear and weapons into a single trading canoe and headed for the mountains.

Mackenzie and his voyageurs fought their way up and down wild rivers and through canyons, and hauled their boat and all their supplies across portages. Mackenzie wanted to stay on the rivers, but the Carrier people he met persuaded him to change his plans. They warned him that the rivers were murderous, and told him they had a good overland trail they used to bring fish oil up from the coast. Mackenzie and his men left their canoe behind and set off to walk this "Grease Trail" down to the ocean. On July 22, 1793, on a flat rock on the edge of Dean Channel, he wrote a message in red dye mixed with grease: "Alexander Mackenzie, from Canada, by land." With the ghosts of Champlain, La Salle, and La Vérendrye looking over his shoulders, he had reached the western ocean.

Alexander Mackenzie used fish grease and red dye to leave this message on the rocks at Bella Coola in 1793. Today, the words are carved and painted, a permanent monument to his journey.

David Thompson: Mapmaker of the West

Because British Columbia's rugged mountains block the horizon, David Thompson sights his sextant on an "artificial horizon" to measure his position. Pouring liquid mercury from an iron bottle into a flat tray, he produces an absolutely level surface, and sights on it.

"I have fully completed the survey of this part of North America from sea to sea," he wrote later, "and by almost innumerable astronomical observations have determined the positions of the mountains, lakes and rivers, and other remarkable places on the northern part of this continent."

Thompson never performed one single great feat of exploration like those of Alexander Mackenzie or Simon Fraser. Instead, he explored the mountain labyrinths of British Columbia for years, and while others simply travelled through the mountain passes, Thompson made sense of them.

Thompson began as a poor boy from England, apprenticed to the Hudson's Bay Company at the age of fourteen. He roamed the Prairies and learned Cree and Peigan. He admired the Native people, and he lived happily with his Métis wife, Charlotte, for sixty years. But he was an unusual fur trader, because he was devoutly religious and he wouldn't drink alcohol.

In 1790, laid up at the Hudson's Bay post of Cumberland House with a broken leg (and going blind in one eye), the twenty-year-old Thompson learned both mapmaking and geographical surveying. After doing surveys for the Hudson's Bay Company, he joined the Nor'Westers, who set him to exploring

and mapping the vast territory from Lake Superior to the Pacific. He would be a mapmaker for the rest of his working life.

Thompson died in 1857, old, blind, and forgotten. In his later years he had laboured over a narrative of his western journeys, based on the careful journals he had kept wherever he travelled. This is his description of how his expedition got caught in a blizzard in what is now southwestern Manitoba, in December 1797.

At 7½ AM our bit of a caravan set off; as the Dogs were fresh, we walked at a good pace for some time; a gentle south wind arose; and kept increasing; by 10 AM it was a heavy Gale, with high drift and dark weather, so much so that I had to keep the Compass in my hand, for I could not trust to the Wind. By Noon, it was a perfect Storm, we had no alternative but to proceed, which we did slowly and with great labour, for the Storm was ahead, and the snow drift in our faces. Night came on, I could no longer see the Compass, and had to trust to the Wind; the weather became mild with small rain, but the Storm continued with darkness; some of the foremost called to lie down where we were, but as it was evident we were ascending a gentle rising ground, we continued and soon, thank good Providence, my face struck against some Oak saplings, and I passed the word that we were in the Woods, a fire was quickly made, and as it was on an elevated place it was seen afar off. As yet the only one with me, was my servant who led the Horse and we anxiously awaited the others; they came hardly able to move, one, and then another, and in something more than half an hour, nine had arrived; each with Dogs, and Sleds, but one Man, and a Sled with the Dogs were missing; to search for the latter was useless; but how to find the former, we were at a loss: and remained so for another half an hour, when we thought we heard his voice, the Storm was still rageing, we extended ourselves within call of each other, the most distant man heard him plainly, went to him, raised him up, and with assistance brought him to the fire, and we all thanked the Almighty for our preservation. He told us he became weak, fell several times, and at length he could not get up, and resigned himself to perish in the storm, when by chance lifting up his head he saw the fire, this gave him courage; stand he could not but [he] shuffled away on hands and knees through the snow, bawling with all his might until we fortunately heard him. We threw the Tent over some Oak sapplings and got under shelter from showers of rain, hail and sleet: at 7½ PM Ther 36 being four degrees above the freezing point; by a south wind making in little more than twelve hours a difference of temperature of fifty six degrees. I had weathered many a hard gale, but this was the most distressing day I had ever seen.

The people by the ocean told Mackenzie they had recently been visited by a sailor they called Macubah – George Vancouver. But Mackenzie went home discouraged, even though he wrote a wonderful book about his travels and was knighted by the British king. Furs were Mackenzie's business, and the North West Company was not interested in the western ocean unless their voyageurs and canoes could follow a river to it.

The Nor'Westers returned to the western mountains in 1805. Simon Fraser was a tough young explorer whose Loyalist father had died in a rebel prison during the American Revolution. Deep in the mountain country west of the Rockies, which he named New Caledonia (from an old Latin name for Scotland), he built Fort George. Soon he began sending canoes laden with furs on the long haul back to Montreal. Like Mackenzie before him, Fraser hungered for the glory of finding a river route to the Pacific. Already sailors on the northwest coast had visited the mouth of a river they called the Columbia. Fraser hoped his Fort George stood on the banks of the same river. In May 1808, he launched his canoes to find out.

Soon Fraser and his men were plunged into terrifying rapids. The Native people of the valley urged him to take the footpath across the heights instead. But Fraser stayed on his river, even though the voyage became a nightmare. "I have been for a long time among the Rocky Mountains," he wrote in his diary, "but have never seen anything equal to this country. We had to pass where no human being should venture."

The men finally cached their canoes in a safe place and followed the river on "a kind of beaten path used by the natives, and made passable by means of scaffolds, bridges, and ladders." Fraser's Native guides climbed nimbly along swaying ladders, like sailors in the rigging of a tall ship. The explorers had no choice but to follow, and after a hundred close calls they got through the canyon. On July 2, 1808, Fraser reached the Pacific Ocean.

Like Mackenzie, Simon Fraser went home disappointed. His river – it was named for him later – was too

"We had to pass where no human being should venture," noted Simon Fraser about his struggle through the Fraser canyon. "We would never have got through if the Natives had not aided us," declared Jules Quesnel, who went with him.

wild and treacherous for fur traders, and it reached the ocean too far north to be the Columbia. Fraser said he would never have made the voyage if he had known how it would turn out. For another fifty years, the northwest coast turned its face only to the sea.

The Father of British Columbia

After Mackenzie and Fraser, few voyageurs made the long canoe trip from Montreal to New Caledonia. Although there were furs to be had there, it was easier to send them out by sea. Both Nor'Westers and Baymen began building trading posts along the coast. The Hudson's Bay Company put a fort near the mouth of the Columbia River and sent sailing ships up and down the coast. From the Columbia, the ships sailed across the oceans to Canton or London.

Spain no longer challenged British trade on the northwest coast, but the United States did. American settlers began moving into the Oregon country nearby. They were eager to drive the Hudson's Bay Company forts from the Columbia River, and they looked north, all the way to the Russian traders in Alaska. Perhaps the United States and the Russians would meet at latitude 54°40'N, squeezing out the Hudson's Bay Company and its British colony.

In 1843, James Douglas rode the Hudson's Bay

Opposite:

At Fort Victoria in 1843, James Douglas supervises as the Hudson's Bay Company steamship Beaver *unloads a horse along with other supplies.*

Company steamship *Beaver* into a sheltered harbour on the southern tip of Vancouver Island. It seemed to him "a perfect Eden," and he set about building a trading post there. He named it Victoria in honour of the young queen. A few years later, Britain yielded the Oregon country to the United States, but the coast from the forty-ninth parallel north to Russian Alaska remained British. Fort Victoria, which replaced the Columbia River trading posts, became the capital of the little colony called Vancouver Island. By 1851, James Douglas, chief factor of the Hudson's Bay Company on Vancouver Island, was also the queen's royal governor there.

"Old Squaretoes" was cold, formal, and aloof, and he made few friends. But everyone respected him. He had been a fur trader since his teens. Now he was almost fifty, a tall, powerful man with a grim stare. Like most of the settlers of his new colony, he came from far away. He had been born in the West Indies. His Scots father was a plantation owner; his mother's African ancestors had been slaves. After joining the Hudson's Bay Company, Douglas had married a half-Native woman, Amelia Connolly. Unlike

Steaming Up the Silent Fiords

In July 1836, the steamship *Beaver* came churning and rattling through the steep-sided channels of the northwest coast. Its paddle wheels streamed a broad wake behind the ship, and its smokestack billowed a tall white plume overhead. A team of axemen needed two days to cut enough wood to fuel the *Beaver's* boilers for a day, but, for the first time, the beat of an engine echoed along the coast.

Unlike the sailing ships that had come before, the *Beaver* could slip in and out of every narrow creek and sheltered cove, in contrary winds or no winds at all. It made the northwest coast a little outpost of the Hudson's Bay Company and the British empire. The Baymen drove all competition from the coast, and the *Beaver* helped them do it.

Barely fifty years before the *Beaver*, the first sailing ships had appeared on the coast. By the time the steamship was wrecked at the entrance to Vancouver's harbour in 1888, the Hudson's Bay Company's Pacific outpost had grown into a proud province of Canada.

Lady Amelia and Sir James Douglas.

many fur traders, he did not disown her when he became wealthy and important. Douglas dared any British-born people to insult his origins or his wife's.

Douglas intended to see a colony grow around the little outpost at Victoria. He encouraged sawmilling, salmon fishing, and mining, and tried to attract farmers. People came from all directions. Some came from England and sailed round South America's Cape Horn, and others came up the coast from California. Chinese labourers and Hawaiian Islanders came across the Pacific. There were even a few settlers from distant Canada.

The Native people of the rainforest were still powerful and independent, and their fleets of war canoes still sailed the coastal waters. They far outnumbered the handful of settlers on Vancouver Island. When a settler at Barkley Sound told the Nootka chiefs that "King George's men" – as the British were still called, even after Victoria became queen – would pay the Native people for their land and take care of them, the chiefs replied, "We do not wish to sell our land nor our water. Let your friends stay in their own country."

But British settlers continued to arrive. Once more, disease travelled with the newcomers, and dreadful epidemics swept along the coast, killing thousands of Native people. Villages that had been bustling communities for centuries suddenly stood empty, and the forest crept over them. The power that chiefs like Maquinna had wielded so proudly began to shift to the newcomers. Governor Douglas demanded that the Native nations accept British law. Once, armed with only a cutlass, he sat all day facing 200 angry Cowichans, until they surrendered a man who had killed a settler.

All the same, Douglas's colony was still a very small place on the edge of the world. Victoria had only 700 people in 1858. Then something changed the northwest coast for ever. It was gold.

The Gold Fields

In the 1850s, gold fever was making the world seem a smaller place. Gold seekers had rushed to California in 1849 and to Australia in 1851. A few who were early or lucky got rich fast. The rest never found enough gold to pay for their shovels and pans, and they moved on, looking for a new strike. In 1849 the "Forty-Niners" had transformed California from a faraway outpost of Spain into a state of the United States. Within a few years, many of them were broke and looking for new goldfields.

Then bright flakes of gold turned up in sluices and pans along the sandbars where the Thompson River runs into the Fraser. In April 1858, the paddle-wheel steamship *Commodore* arrived in Victoria from California, its decks crowded with excited men wearing the trademark red flannel shirts of gold-rush miners. By the end of the year, some 20000 miners had passed through Victoria to seek their fortune on the Fraser. Soon prospectors had staked every sandbar on the Fraser.

The gold rush gave James Douglas a new challenge, and he acted swiftly. Though he was governor of only Vancouver Island, he took charge of the mainland too, imposing British rule and British law. When the distant government in London heard of his action, they approved. The mainland became the colony of British Columbia,

The Hudson's Bay trading post at Nanaimo on Vancouver Island became a busy place after coal was discovered there in 1852. The coal miners' labour made a fortune for mine-owner Robert Dunsmuir, who moved to Victoria and built a castle for his family.

named by Queen Victoria herself, and James Douglas became governor of British Columbia as well.

Douglas imposed order on the goldfields and the miners, and soon even bewildered Californians were giving three cheers for Queen Victoria by the banks of the Fraser. Judge Matthew Begbie arrived from England to administer stern British justice in the wild gold-rush shantytowns. Once, when a jury acquitted a man accused of murder, Judge Begbie called the jurymen a pack of horse thieves and said he wished he could hang *them*. When a tough miner named Ned McGowan declared that he was the king of Hills' Bar and told Governor Douglas to leave him alone, Colonel Richard Moody's Royal Engineers marched in and persuaded him to salute the Union Jack.

In 1859, Colonel Moody began clearing the forest for a town called New Westminster, to be the capital of the mainland colony. The Royal Engineers also built roads and trails along the rivers and through the mountain passes. Their greatest project was the Great North Road to the Cariboo country. The miners knew that the Fraser River gold had washed down from somewhere else, and they kept pushing north in search of the mother lode. In 1861 a Cornish sailor named Billy Barker struck gold in the Cariboo country, and the fading excitement of the Fraser River rush revived. Douglas sent the Royal Engineers scrambling through the mountain passes to build a road 650 kilometres long, much of it blasted out of solid rock, from Yale on the Fraser River to the heart of the Cariboo.

In Montreal, Toronto, and a hundred other eastern towns, news of the Fraser River gold strikes reminded people of Simon Fraser and his epic voyage. Now that Canada was looking west again, the old fur trader, who was living quietly near Cornwall in Canada West, became famous again as "the first discoverer of that golden stream." Young men from eastern farms and towns, including Fraser's own son, headed for the B.C. goldfields by land or sea.

The Overlanders, a group of men and one woman, Catherine Schubert (who joined the group with her husband and children), set out to cross the continent to

Someone had the bright idea that camels would be the perfect pack animals in the dry Cariboo country. Some of the camels escaped and went wild, but they could not survive the winters.

the Cariboo. They chose Thomas McMicking, a young shopkeeper from Niagara, as their leader. The Overlanders faced a thousand perils and hardships as they crossed the Prairies in carts, but McMicking got the whole party to British Columbia. The day after they reached Kamloops, Catherine Schubert gave birth to a baby girl, Rose.

One man who earned a nickname and became a legend in the Cariboo was John Cameron, from Glengarry, Canada West. In 1861, when news of the Cariboo gold strike reached Glengarry, Cameron and his wife, Margaret, set off by sea to Victoria, then hiked up the Cariboo road to Barkerville. Cameron staked a claim on Williams Creek and kept a crew digging all summer and fall. In December came the bonanza: gold, in fabulous amounts! A town called Camerontown sprang up overnight. Cariboo Cameron found himself rich.

Catherine Schubert, the only woman to travel overland across western Canada to the British Columbia goldfields, gave birth to a baby the day after she arrived at Kamloops, B.C.

Rich but broken-hearted, because Margaret Cameron had died of typhoid fever in October. Cariboo had sworn then that he would take her back to Glengarry. A month after the big strike, he carried her sealed coffin to Victoria. Before the year was out, he had taken her home and buried her in the family plot.

Cameron settled in Glengarry with his money and married again, but jealous neighbours claimed he had brought home a coffin filled with gold, not his wife's body. To stop the rumours, Cariboo Cameron had to dig up Margaret and open her coffin. Then, disgusted with his neighbours, he moved back to British Columbia. By the time he died in Barkerville, his fortune was gone, and no one sent *his* body back home.

The gold miners had expanded the territory of British Columbia inland from the edge of the ocean. Already railways were spreading across the eastern half of the continent. Indeed, when John Palliser's exploring party had made its way into the Rocky Mountains in 1857, one of Palliser's scientists had actually spent some time calculating how a railway might run through the passes. One day it might be possible to cross the continent without the hardships of the voyageurs or the Overlanders.

Mister Deas Cans Fish

John Sullivan Deas's parents had been slaves in South Carolina. Young John learned the tinsmithing trade and went to the California gold rush of 1849, but then drifted north with other Black adventurers and began tinsmithing in Victoria in about 1861.

Captain Edward Stamp had started a salmon cannery on the Fraser River not far from New Westminster. The river ran thick with salmon every summer, and Stamp knew that, if he canned them, he could sell salmon all over the world. He hired John Deas to make tin cans. When Stamp suddenly died, Deas took over the cannery. Soon he was running the largest salmon canning business in the colony. Thousands of cases of John Deas's Fraser River salmon went off to Britain every year.

With a Black owner, Native fishermen supplying the salmon, and Chinese immigrants doing most of the labour, it was a remarkable multicultural business. But Deas was mocked and abused for the colour of his skin. The Natives were soon driven out of the fishing business, and the Chinese labourers suffered cruel discrimination. John Deas moved back to the United States and died young, probably poisoned by the mercury that tinsmiths used. Newer, bigger canneries replaced his, but his name lives on in Deas Island, at the mouth of the Fraser River.

Mountains and Oceans

Gold fever drew tens of thousands of people to British Columbia in the late 1850s and early 1860s. Within a few years the gold rush was over, but the colony continued to grow. In less than a lifetime, the rush of settlers and the cruel scourge of epidemics left the Native nations a dispossessed minority in their own land. In 1866, British Columbia and Vancouver Island united to form one colony. To the disgust of the mainlanders, Victoria became the capital, but the united colony took the name British Columbia.

The "father" of the colony, James Douglas, had retired,

honoured by Queen Victoria with a knighthood, in 1864. By the time he died in Victoria in 1877, the threat from the Americans seemed almost as faint as that from the Russians or the Spanish. The governor and his colonists had turned a land once known only to the Native nations and a few lonely traders into a thriving British colony.

Victoria had 6000 people and Barkerville nearly as many. There were newspapers in the towns, and a legislature full of squabbling politicians at Victoria. (The most colourful of the politicians was William Smith, who had come from Nova Scotia by way of California, and changed his name to Amor De Cosmos, "lover of the universe.") British naval vessels cruised the British Columbia waters, and merchant vessels from all over the world came and went. A tough Scots coal miner named Robert Dunsmuir was amassing a fortune from the coal mines of Nanaimo, while the miners, who risked life and limb for a meagre wage, cursed his name and went on strike whenever they could, for more money and more safety.

On Burrard Inlet, near New Westminster, Sewell Moody's sawmills cut lumber for California, Chile, and Australia, and a little community called Gastown sprouted around talkative "Gassy" Jack Deighton's hotel. On the Fraser River, John Deas's cannery was packing salmon for sale in England. Steamships churned up the Fraser to Yale, and stagecoaches and wagons rumbled along the road to Barkerville – where, in 1867, the Canadians cheered for Dominion Day on July first and the Americans celebrated Independence Day on July fourth. British Columbia was part of neither country; it was still a British colony.

"Who can see what the next ten years may bring forth?" wrote James Douglas in 1863. "A railroad on British territory, probably, from the Gulf of Georgia to the Atlantic." British Columbia had rooted itself on the shores of the ocean, and it still looked out to the sea. But it had pushed into inland valleys and was beginning to look eastward over the Rockies. From the other side of the mountains, Canada was looking west with new interest.

Susan Allison

Susan Moir was born in Ceylon and arrived in British Columbia with her family in 1860, when she was fifteen. In 1868 she married John Allison, a gold-rush miner who had turned to ranching. Long before other settlers moved inland, Susan went with him over the Allison Pass to the lovely Similkameen valley. She lived there for thirty years, confronting fires, rattlesnakes, outlaws, and wolves, and she raised fourteen children.

Later, in Vancouver, she wrote about that "wild, free life" and the Native people's stories of mysterious Bigmen in the mountains and the dangerous monster that swam in Lake Okanagan.

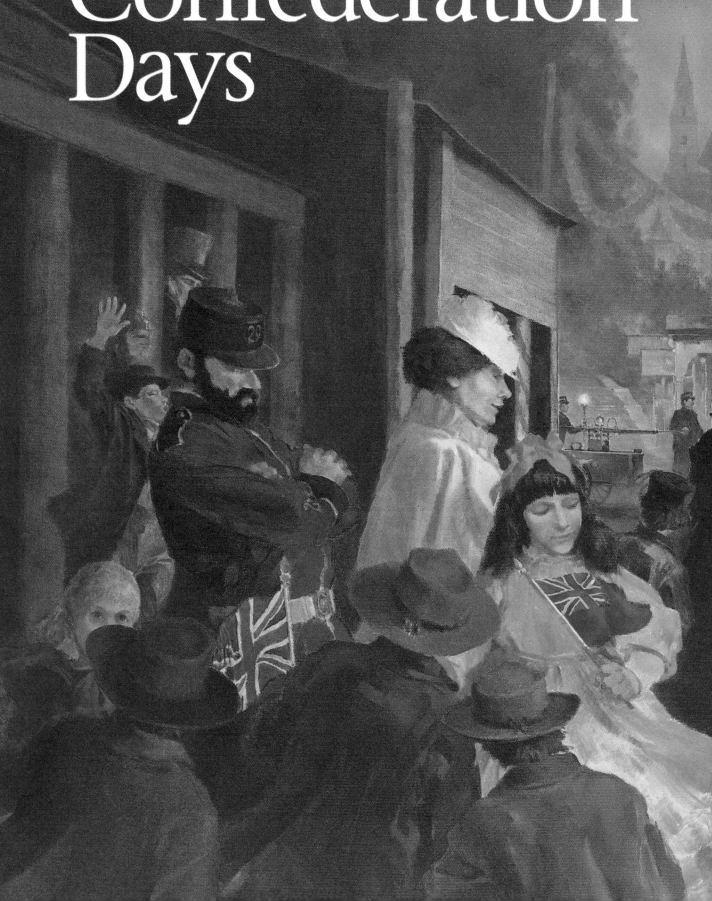

Chapter 7
Confederation Days

THE 1860S WERE BUSY, EXCITING YEARS IN BRITISH NORTH AMERICA. Queen Victoria, who ruled Britain and its colonies, had been just eighteen when she had ascended the throne in 1837, but by the 1860s she seemed as permanent as the empire itself. After her beloved husband, Prince Albert, died in 1861, she always wore black, and she insisted that her courtiers at Windsor Castle wear black armbands. But the empire of "the widow of Windsor" was bigger and richer than ever, and British North America was proud to be part of it.

You could feel the excitement in the daily newspapers. There were 300 newspapers in British North America, and most towns had several. Halifax had nearly a dozen. For a penny or two a day, men and women could sit down in their comfortable parlours and keep up with the news. The news probably included some horrible crime or maybe a hanging, for newspaper writers, like some of their readers, could be bloodthirsty.

There was sure to be something about railways in the newspaper. Railway mania had possessed British North America ever since Canada's first train began running on flimsy wooden tracks laid near Montreal in 1836. By the 1860s, iron tracks crisscrossed the colonies. Belching smoke and showering sparks, steam locomotives roared through the night, drawing towns and colonies closer together. Newspapers were full of stories about new railway lines, new iron bridges, and new telegraph lines humming with news.

In the 1860s, many people still farmed. Others worked at dangerous jobs such as mining and earned barely enough to live. Even scrawny, underfed children worked twelve hours a day, with no laws to protect them. When the work was done, men and women – and sometimes children, too – drank raw whisky and played rowdy games to forget their troubles.

But other people in British North America had a different, more enjoyable life. They lived in comfortable houses, worshipped in handsome stone churches with soaring spires, and attended concert halls to hear a reading

Previous pages:

On July 1, 1867, the great Dominion Day torchlight parade marches past the intersections of King and Queen in Berlin (now Kitchener), Ontario. The New Hamburg militia lieutenant (left) *who is watching the volunteer firemen roll their new pumper has already marched in the military parade, held earlier in the day.*

by Charles Dickens, the English novelist, or a concert by Jenny Lind, "the Swedish nightingale." For them, British North America was a place of religion, proper manners, and temperance.

There was always news of politics in the papers. Britain still ruled its colonies, but on local matters the elected governments ran the affairs of each colony. In each one, the leader of the party with the most support in the elected Assembly became premier, and so the parties battled furiously for votes. In most of the colonies, voters had to stand up in public and declare which candidate they wanted. Supporters of other candidates shouted, threatened, and often stopped rivals from voting. Only men could vote, and most of them declared that women were represented by their fathers or husbands and had no need of their own votes. In fact, many men did not have a vote either; only those who owned enough property could qualify.

Many newspaper editors were also politicians – and an editor who wasn't in politics himself probably worked for an owner who was. George Brown, a tall, loud, redheaded

When the Prince of Wales visited Ottawa in 1860, one of the amusements that was arranged for him was a ride down a timber slide.

Follow the Drinking Gourd

Josiah and Charlotte Henson were slaves who laboured on the cotton plantations of Kentucky. One dark night in 1830, they gathered a small parcel of food and twenty-five cents (all the money they had), and fled north with their children. Josiah Henson carried his youngest children in a sack on his back.

The Henson family hid from slave-catchers by day and walked through woods and swamps at night. They were following the "drinking gourd," the Big Dipper. It pointed the way north to Canada, which had abolished slavery. The Hensons sang:

So long, old master,
Don't come after me,
I'm heading north to Canada
Where everyone is free.

Soon the Hensons got aboard the underground railroad. This wasn't really a railroad, just a network of people who hated slavery so much that they sheltered escaped slaves and helped them to reach Canada – often at great risk to themselves. When he crossed the Niagara River, Josiah Henson fell on his knees and kissed the earth.

The drinking gourd and the underground railroad led thousands of escaped slaves to Canada. Near Dresden, Upper Canada, Josiah and Charlotte Henson founded a Black community named Dawn. Mary Ann Shadd ran a newspaper and fought against the discrimination that Blacks suffered. Jack Little and his wife went into the woods "where any people might go, coloured or poor, and have a chance to settle the land." After fifteen years, the Littles were the proud owners of a thriving hundred-acre (forty-hectare) farm.

In 1861 a civil war broke out in the United States, between the northerners, who had now abolished slavery, and the southerners, who still depended on slaves. Many Blacks went back to fight on the northern side. When the North won the war, slavery was abolished throughout the United States.

Scotsman from Toronto, was one of those newspapermen-politicians. He was the publisher of *The Globe*, the most widely read paper in British North America, and he was also the leader of the Reformers of Canada West. He was a passionate, outspoken man, and his loves and hates helped bring a group of Canadian politicians to Charlottetown on a sunny day in 1864.

Breaking the Deadlock

George Brown loved his newspaper, his new wife, Anne, and their baby daughter, his Presbyterian church, and his political party, the reforming "Grits" of Canada West. He did not like Catholics or anything that struck him as anti-British, and he hated the way the people of Canada West were bound in union with the French Catholics of Canada East. In the Parliament of the United Canadas, the two halves of Canada had vetoed each other's plans and blocked each other's ambitions for years. This squabbling made Brown so angry that he talked of quitting politics.

Most of all, George Brown hated John A. Macdonald of the "Tories." Their two political parties had been rivals for years, but this was a personal battle too. They flung insults at each other in the Assembly of the United Canadas in Quebec City, and they opposed each other at every step. Brown could hardly stand to be in the same room as the slim, jaunty man everyone called "John A." To Brown's fury, John A. usually won their battles. With his ally George-Etienne Cartier, the leader of the "Bleu" party of Canada East, Macdonald kept George Brown out of power for years.

One steaming, humid day in June 1864, George Brown stood up in the Assembly of the United Canadas to make a startling offer. His Grits would join Macdonald's Tories and Cartier's Bleus, he announced. His Protestant followers from Canada West would work alongside the Catholic French of Canada East. He would even work with John A. Macdonald. There was one condition. No more petty politics! No more squabbling over Canada East and

In the 1860s, being photographed meant you had to sit absolutely still for several minutes, often with a brace holding your head steady. Perhaps that is why George Brown always looks long-faced and solemn in his photographs. In real life he was full of energy, brimming with enthusiasm one moment, fury the next.

Sir John A. Macdonald.

Canada West! They must work for a common cause, said Brown – the transformation of all of British North America into one nation.

Macdonald and Cartier agreed to work with Brown. But to achieve anything, the Canadians had to talk to the Maritimers as well. Barely two months after Brown's offer, the Canadian leaders set sail for Charlottetown, Prince Edward Island, where the Maritime politicians were meeting. So few of the Canadians had ever been to the Maritimes that one of them asked, "What kind of people are they?"

The Idea of Confederation

September 1, 1864, was a warm, sunny Thursday in Prince Edward Island. In those days Charlottetown was a pretty little town of barely 7000 people, but it was no sleepy backwater. It and all the other seaports of Atlantic Canada were busy places. Maritimers built and sailed a fleet of beautiful ships and schooners that hauled freight around the globe. In summer, Charlottetown harbour was a forest of masts, where trim sailing vessels loaded and unloaded and sailors caroused on shore.

This week, every hotel and boarding-house was crammed. The Olympic Circus was in town for a four-day

A four-horse team pulls a load of logs out of the woods. All through the nineteenth century, lumbering was the greatest industry in many parts of eastern Canada. Logs were dragged to the rivers in winter, and floated down to sawmills or seaports in the spring.

run, and at the same time the leaders of the three Maritime colonies were holding a conference. Down on the dock, William Henry Pope was rushing about, trying to find a boat. Pope was a Cabinet minister in the government of Prince Edward Island, and he had distinguished guests to greet. Out in the bay, the steamship *Queen Victoria* had just anchored. The leading politicians from Canada were aboard – among them John A. Macdonald, George-Etienne Cartier, D'Arcy McGee, and George Brown. Finally, in desperation, Pope seized a filthy flat-bottomed scow, and an old fisherman rowed him out to meet his visitors.

The Canadians had not originally been expected at the Charlottetown Conference, which was supposed to discuss Maritime union – the joining of Prince Edward Island, Nova Scotia, and New Brunswick into a single colony. But that idea was going nowhere. The island's

A man rakes oysters through the ice at Shediac, New Brunswick, in this painting by William Hind. Atlantic Canada's shellfish, today a gourmet specialty, were once harvested mostly as poor people's food.

premier, John Hamilton Gray, had said he did not mind adding New Brunswick and Nova Scotia to Prince Edward Island, but he certainly did not want Prince Edward Island added to the mainland!

Just when the chance for Maritime union seemed about to die, the Canadians arrived with a different suggestion: Why not unite *all* of British North America? It was a big, bold idea, and the Maritimers liked it. They put aside the plan of Maritime union and began to discuss the Canadian proposal. As the two groups worked together and got to know each other, the idea of Confederation seized them all.

Let us found a nation on the northern half of this continent, the men at Charlottetown said eagerly. From the Great Lakes to Newfoundland, Britain's North American

colonies were thriving and prosperous communities. Now the time seemed right for these colonies, each with its own traditions and dreams, to become provinces of a new nation. Because they would form a federal union, each province would run its own affairs – but there were many great things they could do together. There were railways to build, trade links to expand, bonds to forge against the American hunger to expand northward. The colonists felt ready to build a country.

The seed of Confederation was sown in those sunny September days at Charlottetown. But there were still a thousand details of this new nation to thrash out. The Charlottetown delegates agreed to meet again a month later, at Quebec.

Many of the Fathers of Confederation can be seen in this painting of a ball at Province House in Charlottetown. Making Confederation was not all meetings and work. At Charlottetown and Quebec, the politicians and their families and guests dined and danced whenever they could.

From Charlottetown to Quebec

Poor Mercy Ann Coles! All the way by ship and train from Charlottetown, she had been looking forward to the excitement of Quebec City. Her father, George Coles, was one of Prince Edward Island's delegates to the great Confederation conference, and dinners, dances, and sight-seeing tours were planned for the delegates and their families. Mercy Ann, who was seventeen, had brought her beautiful blue silk ballgown with her. But no sooner had they all arrived and the dances begun than Mercy Ann caught a fever.

For ten days she lay miserably in her bed, gazing out at the October rain. "I am sure I shall know the shape of every shingle on the roof of the old house opposite," she told her diary bitterly. Charles Tupper, who was a doctor as well as the Premier of Nova Scotia, came to check on her health every day. John A. Macdonald sent get-well wishes. Soon Mercy had a collection of the statesmen's visiting cards, each with a photograph. (Photography was still a new and thrilling process.) "The gentlemen have all been having their likenesses taken," she wrote. "Papa's is only tolerable."

At last she was well enough to dine downstairs, and she sat beside John A. Macdonald. "What an old humbug he is," she wrote mischievously in her diary that night. But she liked him better than George Brown, who did not dance and never knew what to say to young ladies.

Brown had too much on his mind for chit-chat, but behind closed doors he had a lot to say. Each day the thirty-three delegates – from Canada East and West, New Brunswick, Nova Scotia, Prince Edward Island, and Newfoundland – met to plan the new nation. They made speeches and posed questions. Sometimes they shouted and pounded the table. They argued over which powers should be given to the national government and which to the provinces. They planned a House of Commons and a Senate. They debated how to protect minorities. They agreed to build a railway from Halifax to Quebec.

They even looked ahead to the day when the new nation would expand west across the plains to British Columbia.

The delegates wrote out seventy-two resolutions which were to be the foundation for the new nation. George Brown scribbled a happy note to his wife in Toronto: "All right! Constitution adopted – a most creditable document. Is it not wonderful?" The delegates and their families began a triumphal tour through the Canadas, and Mercy Ann Coles finally got to wear her blue silk gown. She even went to Niagara Falls, and was speechless with admiration.

Before the end of 1864, barely five months after George Brown's amazing proposal, it seemed that Confederation was almost a reality. But many obstacles lay ahead. George Coles, Mercy Ann's father, would help to create some of them.

After drafting the details of Confederation at Quebec in 1864, the Fathers of Confederation travelled to Montreal and Toronto – and to Niagara Falls.

The Battle for Confederation

There would be no Confederation in 1865, or in 1866 either. George Coles did not support the seventy-two resolutions, and he went home to Prince Edward Island to fight them. The plan might be good for Canada East and

Robert Harris's painting of the Fathers of Confederation at Quebec was lost when the Parliament Buildings in Ottawa burned down in 1916. Artist Rex Woods painted this re-creation of it.

Canada West, he had decided, but the Maritime colonies would be dwarfed and left powerless. William Henry Pope fought for Confederation, but most Prince Edward Islanders shared George Coles's feelings, and they made him premier. Soon the idea of Confederation was near death throughout Atlantic Canada. The excitement of Charlottetown was gone, and Maritimers were asking why they should be pulled into Confederation just to solve the problems of Canada East and Canada West. When New Brunswick held an election, the supporters of Confederation were driven from office.

Ambrose Shea and Frederick Carter had gone to the Quebec Conference on behalf of the colony of Newfoundland. Both men liked the Confederation plan, and they went home to urge Newfoundlanders to join Canada. However, most Newfoundlanders had always felt closer to Britain than to North America. Canada seemed remote and foreign and threatening. "Your sons will all be conscripted into Canada's armies and sent to leave their bones in the deserts of the west," cried one opponent.

Frederick Carter, who was the Premier of Newfoundland, decided the people must make the final decision. The election was furiously fought, but Newfoundland's choice was clear. The islanders rejected Confederation.

"We are sold for the price of a sheepskin," thundered Joseph Howe in Halifax when he learned that the seventy-two resolutions (written on sheepskin parchment) included Canada's offer to pay some of Nova Scotia's debts. Nova Scotia's great statesman did not want his beloved colony to become one small part of Canada. Some Nova Scotians, including its premier, Charles Tupper, did argue in favour of Confederation and the railway to the Canadas it would bring. But so many Nova Scotians opposed the idea that Dr. Tupper did not dare call a vote on Confederation.

In Canada East, George-Etienne Cartier, leader of the Bleu party, led the fight for Confederation. In 1837, Cartier had been a Patriote rebel at St-Denis, but later he grew to admire the British empire so much that he said a French Canadian was an Englishman who spoke French! Cartier and other French-Canadian leaders were confident that Confederation would serve French Canada well. Twenty years earlier, they had defeated Lord Durham's plans to swallow up the French, and now they were playing important roles in shaping the new nation. French Canadians would have their own province, Quebec, and they would share a vast country with English Canada. Cartier had a powerful personality and a beautiful speaking voice. His arguments for Confederation did much to win French Canada's support.

When photography was new, William Notman of Montreal was Canada's greatest photographer, and he took pictures of many famous people. This is George-Etienne Cartier, who led Quebec into Confederation.

In Canada West, Confederation was popular. Canada West would become a province named Ontario, instead of being yoked together with Canada East. It already had more people than any other colony in British North America, and Confederation appealed to its ambitions. And the old rivals, John A. Macdonald and George Brown, made an unstoppable team in their home province – although working together for Confederation had not made them friends.

Slowly the tide turned in some of the Maritime colonies. Prince Edward Island and Newfoundland held to their refusal to join Confederation, but in 1866, supporters of Confederation returned to power in New Brunswick.

The battle was fiercest in Nova Scotia. Arguments flared in every household from Yarmouth to Sydney. Joseph Howe

The fashion of pressing suits and pant legs smooth and flat came in after Confederation. But Joseph Howe, the great orator, politician, and newspaperman of Nova Scotia, would probably have been rough-edged and rumpled in any age.

inspired the "antis"; the proposal should not be called Confederation but "Botheration," he wrote scornfully. When Nova Scotia newspaperman Jonathan McCully came home from Quebec to argue for Confederation, the owner of his newspaper fired him. McCully had to start a new paper, while in his old one Howe tore the Confederation idea to shreds.

If Nova Scotia had held an election, the opponents of Confederation would surely have won. But the British government wanted Nova Scotia to agree, and at last the wily premier, Charles Tupper, devised a plan. He suggested that the Nova Scotia Assembly should vote in favour of the general idea of Confederation, then attend another conference that might produce better terms than the ones settled on at Quebec. The debate in the Assembly raged late into the night, but when the vote was held, Tupper and his supporters won. It was done "at black midnight," Joseph Howe said furiously.

Late in 1866, delegates from Canada East, Canada West, New Brunswick, and Nova Scotia sailed to London, England, to work out the last details of the Confederation plan. At the Westminster Conference, John A. Macdonald emerged as the star of Confederation. He was a master political fixer – as well as being a man of vision. He could charm almost anyone, and even George Brown admitted that his old enemy was "steady as a rock." With Cartier's help, Macdonald guided Confederation through every crisis. As Britain's Parliament prepared to pass the British North America Act, creating the new nation, the delegates agreed that John A. would be its first prime minister.

But what would the nation be called? The delegates settled on "Canada" – although people had proposed "Acadia," "British North America," and even "Hochelaga." Leonard Tilley, the Premier of New Brunswick, looked in his Bible and found a psalm that read, "He shall have dominion from sea to sea and from the river to the ends of the earth." The Dominion of Canada was born.

July 1, 1867, was a Monday. The weather was fine across the new nation. At dawn, the cannon of every fort

Creating Canada

The British North America Act made Canada a "federation" in 1867. There was a government in Ottawa for the whole country, but there was also a government in each province to administer local affairs. The problem in a federation is: who runs what?

John A. Macdonald wanted to keep as much power in Ottawa as possible. He wanted the provinces kept under Ottawa's control. The BNA Act listed certain things the provinces could do – and all the powers that were left over belonged to Ottawa. But John A. could not keep all these powers in his hands for ever. Soon the provinces would gain more rights and powers, and become equal partners in Confederation.

The Fathers of Confederation created the House of Commons. Everyone who could vote could help choose the members of Parliament who sat in the House of Commons. Every part of the country had members of Parliament – how many depending on its population. The leader of the party with the most members of Parliament became prime minister.

The Fathers of Confederation also created the Senate. Senators were appointed by the prime minister, not elected by the people. John A. Macdonald believed the Senate should restrain the House of Commons. He wanted to make sure that ordinary people did not have too much say in running the country. Each region (not each province) had the same number of senators.

The governor general still had a lot of influence over how Canada was governed in 1867. The governor general represented the British government as well as the queen. Because Canadians respected and honoured the queen's representative, he was able to disagree with Canadian leaders. Over the years, governors general gradually agreed to leave decisions to the Senate and the House of Commons, but it would be many decades before a Canadian became governor general.

In 1869, Newfoundland fought an election to decide whether or not to join Confederation. "Come near at your peril, Canadian wolf," sang the "antis." Their leader, Charles Fox Bennett, claimed that Newfoundlanders would be taken into Canada's army and would "leave their bones in the deserts of the west." Newfoundland elected him as premier, and it was eighty more years before Newfoundland joined Canada.

and naval ship roared out salutes. Religious services were held and parades began in hundreds of towns. Brass bands, militia companies, and local clubs marched proudly through Halifax, Saint John, Ste-Hyacinthe, and Sarnia. In Kingston they played cricket, in Barrie they had sailing competitions, in Dunnville there was horse racing. Homes were decorated with bunting and flowers. Bonfires blazed, fireworks exploded, picnics were organized, and speeches were given in honour of Confederation.

Not everyone was ready to celebrate. Diehard opponents of Confederation hung out black wreaths. Young Quebecker Wilfrid Laurier denounced Confederation as a threat to French Canada. (He would change his mind one day and go on to become prime minister.) Joseph Howe was still opposed to Confederation in 1867, but later he would join John A.'s government, still fighting for better terms for Nova Scotia. Newfoundland would not join Confederation until 1949, but in 1873 Prince Edward

Thomas D'Arcy McGee

Irish immigrants had been coming to Canada for decades. Some were prosperous farmers and merchants. Others were starving refugees who staggered from the immigrant ships after Ireland's terrible Potato Famine of 1848. And a few had to flee Ireland after fighting against British rule there. Thomas D'Arcy McGee was one of these. But after he settled in Montreal, McGee decided Canada could be a good home for the Catholic Irish. He became their spokesman, and they elected him to Parliament in Ottawa.

A politician, journalist, and poet, McGee dreamed of a Canadian nation where Protestant and Catholic, French, Irish, English, and all others could share a proud new country. "I see in the not remote distance, one great nationality bound by the blue rim of ocean," he cried, and he became the prophet of a Canadian nation under Confederation.

McGee's silvery words swayed many to the cause of Confederation. But the Fenians hated him. The Fenians were Irishmen who fought for rebellion against Britain, and they attacked Canada as a way to attack Britain. But D'Arcy McGee rallied Irish Canadians against the Fenians, and they found little support here. Canada drove back the small bands of Fenians who made several raids from the United States in 1866.

Less than a year after Confederation, as McGee walked to his boarding-house after a late-night session in Parliament, a gunman put a pistol to his head and shot him. McGee fell dead on the wooden sidewalk of Sparks Street. Pat Whelan, a Fenian, was tried and convicted for the murder of Confederation's first martyr. Whelan protested his innocence to the last, but he was hanged on Nicholas Street in Ottawa – the last man to be publicly hanged in Canada.

Island agreed to become a province, and Mercy Ann Coles became a Canadian at last.

In the streets of Toronto, people sang and let off firecrackers on the eve of that first Dominion Day. George Brown sat all night at his desk in the office of *The Globe*. He had left politics more than a year before, confident that, with Confederation coming, his work in politics was done. Now he was writing the whole Confederation story for his newspaper. "We hail the birthday of a new nationality," he finished triumphantly, just as dawn broke.

In Ottawa, Governor General Lord Monck swore in the Cabinet ministers of the first government of Canada. Then the governor general and the prime minister, who had been knighted by Queen Victoria and was now Sir John A. Macdonald, went out together to review the troops and greet the cheering crowds.

Into the West

Louis Riel (centre) *sits among the members of the Manitoba Provisional Government he formed in 1869. When British and Canadian forces arrived in 1870, its leaders had to flee across the border.*

The makers of Confederation intended to extend Canada from sea to sea. Ontario's farmers wanted the new country to include the vast western prairie; if Canada did not move west, the Americans might move in, and Canada would be unable to grow. Barely a year after Confederation, George-Etienne Cartier went to London on behalf of Canada and arranged for the new nation to buy the rights to Rupert's Land, the vast fur-trading territory which the Hudson's Bay Company had held since 1670. In 1869, William McDougall set out for Red River to become the first lieutenant-governor of Canada's Northwest Territories,

which in those days meant the old Hudson's Bay territory.

McDougall never reached his destination. The Métis of Red River had not been consulted in the negotiations over Rupert's Land, but they did not intend their land to be overrun by governors from Ottawa and settlers from Ontario. Louis Riel and the newly formed Red River Council took charge. Métis horsemen galloped down from Red River to Pembina to stop McDougall before he could enter Métis territory. Next they seized the Hudson's Bay Company's Fort Garry, in the heart of the Red River country. The council declared it wanted to negotiate with Canada on behalf of all the people of Red River, and it won the support of many of the English-speaking "mixed-blood" settlers of Red River.

Riel was twenty-five years old, a dark, stocky man with a thick black beard. He had returned from school in Montreal with a passion to lead his people. He sent the demands of the Red River Council to Ottawa. Red River must enter Confederation as a province, the council declared. The settlers must be consulted, and the rights of the Métis to their language and religion must be guaranteed.

Riel's decisive actions forced Prime Minister Macdonald to halt the Canadian takeover of Red River. Soon he agreed that Red River would enter Confederation as a province, not as a territory to be run from Ottawa. The Métis seemed to have won. But in Red River, a handful of English-speaking, Protestant settlers from Ontario refused to accept the rule of the French-speaking, Catholic Métis. They defied the Red River Council and fought Riel's authority. Riel had one of them, young Thomas Scott, shot by a firing squad.

English-speaking Canada was shocked by the news that Louis Riel's Métis government at Red River had executed Thomas Scott, a young troublemaker from Ontario. This engraving, which appeared in the Canadian Illustrated News, *shows the execution as a cold-blooded murder. The picture probably helped to make readers even more determined to avenge Scott and destroy Riel.*

Hunters with rifles killed thousands of buffalo for their pelts, or simply for sport, leaving the bones to litter the prairie. For years after the herds had been destroyed, buffalo bones were loaded into boxcars and hauled east to be made into fertilizer.

Ontario erupted in fury when Scott was executed, and the government of Canada decided to send troops to take control of Red River. While the soldiers struggled on the long trek across what is now northern Ontario by boat and canoe, Louis Riel fled south to the United States. Manitoba became a province of Canada on May 2, 1870 (exactly 200 years after the founding of the Hudson's Bay Company), and half a million hectares of land were promised to the Métis and their descendants. But instead of being saluted as a maker of Confederation, Riel was an exile.

The Métis of Red River were not the only people Canada had to deal with when it tried to take over the lands where the Hudson's Bay Company had traded. In the early 1870s, the great Cree, Assiniboine, and Blackfoot confederacies still commanded the plains. With the buffalo herds being hunted almost to extinction, the tribes were hungry, but the land was still theirs. If Canada wanted the West, Canada would have to talk to them. During the 1870s, Canadian officials talked.

The government's Indian agents sat under the hot sun and the broad sky with the tribes, bands, and nations of the plains. Canada intended to take most of the land, but Native leaders resisted. The Cree chief Pitikwahanapiwiyan,

The Man Who Saved the Buffalo

Michel Pablo's ancestors had been buffalo hunters for ten thousand years. But in the 1880s, rifles, railways, and relentless slaughter destroyed North America's buffalo herds. All over the plains, the buffalo-hunting nations fell from greatness to poverty in barely a decade.

Michel Pablo lived on the Flathead reserve in Montana. He rounded up a few buffalo calves and kept them on the reserve. By the early 1900s, he had the largest herd in the world. But Michel Pablo's people lost their reserve to settlers in 1906. There would be no room left for the wild buffalo.

At that time, Canada was creating national parks in the West, and the Canadian government offered to buy Michel Pablo's herd – if he would drive them to Buffalo National Park, near Wainwright, Alberta. Pablo agreed to do the job for $250 a head, and the great buffalo drive was on.

They called it "the longest, costliest, most frustrating roundup ever." In the heat and dust of an Alberta summer, Native cowboys drove 400 buffalo north from Montana. The drive brought a great animal back from the edge of extinction. Today, descendants of Michel Pablo's herd make up roughly half of all the buffalo in the world. They roam wild in Wood Buffalo National Park, in northern Alberta.

The dignity and wisdom of Crowfoot, seen here with his family in 1884, were admired by all who dealt with him, but rarely captured by photographers. Crowfoot was widely mourned when he died.

called Poundmaker, said, "This is our land. It is not a piece of pemmican to be cut off and given in little pieces back to us." Another Cree, Piapot, was against making treaties. He did not trust the government's agents, even though the Canadians claimed to give their word "for as long as the rivers ran, as long as the grass grew, as long as men walked on two legs."

The government was determined to get its way. Government agents bullied, threatened, and offered money, and one by one most of the chiefs gave in. They felt they had to. "If left to ourselves we are gone," declared Isapo-muxika, or Crowfoot, who was chief of the Blackfoot. Smallpox had ravaged his people, settlers were coming from the west and the south, and the buffalo herds were all but gone. He hoped that, if they signed the treaties, his people would get help to settle down and turn from hunting to farming. The treaties promised that kind of help, so in September 1877 Crowfoot signed a treaty at Blackfoot Crossing on the Bow River and led his people to a reserve near Calgary. Most of the other prairie nations signed treaties. The great prairie West was becoming part of settled Canada.

Policing the plains became the job of the North-West Mounted Police. In midsummer 1874, the new force rode out of Dufferin, Manitoba, and headed west, 300 strong, with their wagon train stretched out behind them. They looked like an army, dressed in their scarlet tunics and tall white helmets. Even their horses matched – greys for one company, blacks for the next. That summer the Mounted Police crossed 1500 kilometres of hot, dry plain. Men and horses were staggering and weak before they reached the safety of the foothills of the Rockies, where water and fodder were plentiful. Yet the American whisky traders of "Whoop-Up Country" (as the territory north of Montana was called), who had been selling illegal whisky to the Native people, fled before them. Canadian law had come to the Canadian plains.

To keep order across Canada's vast new territories seemed an impossible task for 300 Mounted Police. But the Mounties earned the respect of angry Native bands and land-hungry settlers alike. Ta-tanka I-yotank, called Sitting Bull, and 5000 Sioux crossed the border in 1877, with the

In their early years in the West, Mountie patrols not only caught the criminals and tried them, they also did all kinds of small jobs. In this picture, a Mountie delivers mail to a homesick settler from Ontario.

Massacre in the Cypress Hills

The Cypress Hills rise only a few hundred metres above the dry prairie of what is now southern Alberta and Saskatchewan, but that is enough to make them the highest ground between the Rockies and Labrador. Wolves and deer, hunters and whisky traders were all drawn to their forested slopes.

In 1872, an Assiniboine band built its winter lodges in the Cypress Hills. The Assiniboine had just made peace with the Blackfoot Confederacy. Now that the fighting was over, they hoped for prosperous hunting in the hills. Instead, they found American hunters spreading poison to kill wolves for their pelts, and American traders offering the poison of liquor to the Native bands. Both hunters and traders moved back and forth across the unmarked border, evading the law on both sides, and they were well armed. They disrupted the Assiniboine people's own hunting, but no one could control them.

In May 1873, after the whisky traders and the Natives quarrelled over horses, the traders attacked the Assiniboine lodges. Thirty-six Natives were shot down in the raid, and the traders burned the village.

News of the Cypress Hills Massacre helped to convince the government in Ottawa that it needed a police force to keep order in the new prairie territories, and so the North-West Mounted Police was created. When the Mounties marched in, outlaw traders retreated from Canada. Although the killings in the Cypress Hills went unpunished, they were not repeated across the plains.

United States Cavalry not far behind. South of the border the Sioux had been at war, but Inspector James Walsh met them with just a handful of Mounties. He promised that if they kept the peace while they were in Canada there would be no trouble. The Sioux stayed in Canada for four years, and the American soldiers stayed out.

The Mounted Police helped to keep the peace, but Canada paid little attention to the promises it had made to the Native nations in the treaties it had forced them to sign. In 1876 Parliament passed the Indian Act. Canada's Indian agents took control of the reserves, and Native children began to be sent away to school, so they would not learn Native ways. Canada wanted to turn the Native peoples into ordinary Canadians as quickly as it could. It wanted them to give up their languages, their beliefs, and their treaty rights as free people. Few Native people wanted to do that. They resisted, but it would be a long time before they began to recover the power and the freedom they had once had.

The Whole Nation Minus One

On the Pacific coast, British Columbians were watching as the new nation marched west. In 1870, British Columbia sent delegates east to talk to the Canadian government about joining Confederation. British Columbia was a long way from Ottawa, they pointed out, and a long way even from Manitoba. British Columbians were independent-minded people who had not ruled out joining the United States, which was closer to them than Canada. If they were to join Confederation, they declared, Canada would have to build a road across the Prairies and the mountains to the Pacific. A railway would have to follow later.

George-Etienne Cartier, who was acting prime minister because Macdonald was ill, scorned this talk of roads. Join Confederation, he promised exuberantly, and we will build a railway to the Pacific in ten years. The delighted British Columbians could hardly believe their ears. They shook

*J.W. Bengough was Canada's
most successful cartoonist in the
years after Confederation. His
favourite target was Sir John A.
Macdonald, here seen at the time
of his resignation, talking to
Opposition leader Alexander
Mackenzie.*

"WE IN CANADA SEEM TO HAVE LOST ALL IDEA OF JUSTICE, HONOR
AND INTEGRITY."—THE MAIL, 26TH SEPTEMBER.

hands with the Canadians, and British Columbia became
the sixth province of Canada in 1871.

Two years later, the American-Canadian International
Boundary Commission completed the survey that marked
out the border between Canada and the United States.
That same year, 1873, James Pope (William Henry Pope's
brother) led Prince Edward Island into Confederation as
Canada's seventh province. Since 1870 the plains west of
Manitoba had been Canadian territories, although Alberta
and Saskatchewan did not become provinces until 1905.
In 1880, Canada acquired the Arctic Islands from Britain.
Even though most of the North was still unknown to all
but the Inuit, no one consulted them about this transfer.

Newfoundland still had not joined Confederation, but,
from the Atlantic to the Pacific to the Arctic, the territory
of the Dominion of Canada now truly stretched from sea to
sea to sea. It was time for the railway to pull it together.

The Great Railway

Ten years after George-Etienne Cartier's rash promise, work on the railway had barely begun. During the election of 1872, Sir John A. accepted money from the "railway barons," businessmen who wanted the contract to build the new line. When he was found out, he had to resign in disgrace. The second Prime Minister of Canada, Alexander Mackenzie, called the railway to the Pacific "an act of insane recklessness." It looked as if he was right.

The Canadian Pacific Railway was the most ambitious railway project in the world. It was going to cost a fortune. Tracks had to be pushed through the rock and muskeg of northern Ontario, across the prairie, and through the mountains. No one even knew if passes suitable for railway lines existed in British Columbia's mountain ranges. For years, surveyors had scrambled up and down the slopes and valleys in search of a route. The obstacles seemed insurmountable.

About 15 000 Chinese workers, nearly all men, came to work on the British Columbia section of the Canadian Pacific Railway. The work was gruelling and dangerous, and many died.

The Mennonite Pioneers

Mennonites began coming to Canada from the United States soon after the American Revolution. Their religion forbade them to fight or to serve in armies, and they came seeking a homeland where their young men would not have to be soldiers. Canada's first Mennonite communities grew up along the Grand River of southern Ontario in the late 1700s.

Almost a hundred years later, Canada wanted immigrants to settle in its new province of Manitoba. Mennonite Jacob Shantz of Berlin, Ontario, visited Manitoba. He thought it would make a good home for his Mennonite brethren of southern Russia. In 1874, Russian Mennonites travelled by boat, train, and oxcart to Manitoba.

Soon almost 7000 more Mennonites came from Russia to join them. In a few decades, there were prosperous Mennonite communities across the West.

Then an American "railway general" called William Van Horne became manager of the Canadian Pacific Railway. Van Horne said he liked things "big and bulgy like myself," and the CPR was the kind of challenge he loved. Soon he had his work crews racing west over the Prairies and conquering the "bottomless bogs" of northern Ontario. By then the surveyors had found a route through the mountains, and workers began fighting inch by inch into British Columbia's rugged terrain. "Fix it up," Van Horne would cry whenever a problem slowed the pace of construction. "Fix it up!"

Thousands of men laboured to build the Canadian Pacific Railway. There were Canadians, Americans, Germans, Swedes, Finns, and Italians laying track. Six thousand workers came from China to drive the line east through the canyons and passes of British Columbia towards the work crews moving west from the plains. Rock falls, dynamite explosions, winter cold, and summer heat took hundreds of lives, but the work went on.

In 1885, the railway was nearly completed – and nearly bankrupt. The costs were enormous and the debts mountainous. Van Horne's cashbox was empty. Then a new rebellion flared suddenly on the Prairies – and the railway was in the middle of it.

Canada had never fulfilled its promises to the Métis of the Northwest, and new settlers were taking the land. The Métis turned to Louis Riel again. He returned from exile, older now and more bitter (some claimed he was insane), and more than ever determined to lead his people. When he raised the Métis flag at Batoche in 1885, the North-West Rebellion was under way. The Mounted Police marched a hundred men to the Métis camp at Duck Lake. Métis general Gabriel Dumont and his men sent them flying in retreat, and soon the Mounties abandoned their base at Fort Carleton. The Métis fighters had won every skirmish.

The Native nations might have joined the Métis, for few of them were content. Those who had signed treaties were poor and hungry, and Canada was not giving them the help it had promised. Plains Cree bands led by Big Bear and Poundmaker still resisted the treaties, and Riel urged them to join him. Some bitter and angry young warriors led raids and ambushes when the Métis began to fight. But the chiefs were skilled war leaders and they could see the power that Canada now had. They urged their people to stay out of the conflict.

John A. Macdonald, who had been back in office since 1878, moved to smash the rising, and the new railway was there to help. Within a few days, troops were boarding trains in Ottawa and Toronto. A few days more, and they were on the plains and marching out to fight. Despite the

When the Mounties sleighed into Duck Lake early in 1885 to control the rebellious Métis, Gabriel Dumont and his men easily defeated them. Twelve Mounties and volunteers were killed. If Louis Riel had not held back Dumont's men, few of the rest would have escaped.

Photographing the Last Spike

The photographer sets up the most famous photograph in Canadian history – the driving of the last spike at Craigellachie, B.C., on November 7, 1885. Young Edward Mallandaine peers from behind Donald Smith, who raises his hammer. In the background, William Van Horne's young son shouts out in excitement.

Despite the skill of the Métis cavalry, Riel's rebellion was doomed once the new railway rushed troops to the plains. The last battle was fought at Batoche in Saskatchewan, on May 12, 1885.

Pitikwahanapiwiyan, called Poundmaker, did not want to join Louis Riel's rebellion, but many of the young Cree did. After Riel's defeat, Poundmaker decided to surrender. "You did not catch me," he told General Middleton. "You have got me because I wanted justice."

skill and courage of Gabriel Dumont's Métis fighters, the Canadian troops overwhelmed the rising. Dumont fled to the United States, but Louis Riel was captured and put on trial. In November 1885 he was hanged in Regina. Big Bear and Poundmaker were thrown in jail, even though only a handful of their young men had gone to war – and against their urging, at that.

As a reward for its help during the North-West Rebellion, the Canadian Pacific Railway got the money it

Climbing the Rockies.

When the prime minister and his wife rode the CPR in 1886, Agnes Macdonald decided the front of the locomotive was the best place from which to see the Rockies. Sir John preferred the comfortable passenger cars. Soon, riding the cowcatcher became a fad, and CPR photographs like this one helped promote it.

needed, and construction workers closed the last gaps in the railway line. The tracks from east and west met in the British Columbia mountains, and William Van Horne rode west to see the last spike driven at Craigellachie. He insisted on a plain iron spike just like all the others. "All I can say is that the work has been well done in every way," he said when the spike was hammered into place. "All aboard for the Pacific," cried the conductor.

In barely twenty years, the Dominion of Canada had been dreamed of, begun, and almost completed. Great deeds had been accomplished, great hardships endured, great injustices suffered. Many complained or grumbled about Confederation, and they had cause, but a new nation had been created.

In 1886, John A. Macdonald and his wife rode the great railway to the Pacific. Agnes Macdonald was determined to see every spectacular view of the mountains. She had a chair mounted on the cowcatcher at the front of the loco-motive, and there she sat. Back in a comfortable coach, John A. had much to be proud of as the train puffed on towards the booming new railway town called Vancouver. His friends had said that he would be in heaven looking down by the time the CPR was completed. His enemies had predicted that he would be looking up from hell. "Now I am taking the horizontal view," joked the man who had once described his goal as "one people, great in territory, great in resources, great in enterprise."

This poster announced the opening of the Canadian Pacific Railway to passengers travelling from coast to coast.

Sunny Ways

W

Always elegant, well-dressed, and charming, Wilfrid Laurier seemed unbeatable on the campaign trail from 1896 until 1911. That year, opposition to his plan for free trade with the United States drove him from office.

Previous pages:
Despite the rough, muddy roads, a brand-new Stanley Steamer makes a wonderful toy for a well-to-do family. Meanwhile, most people still make do with a horse and wagon, and children from poor families still gather coal along the railway tracks.

ILFRID LAURIER STROLLED DOWN THE STEPS OF PARLIAMENT IN Ottawa. In his days as a young lawyer and newspaper editor, he had written passionate articles against Confederation. Now, in 1896, he was leader of the Liberal Party in Parliament, and he was as committed to Confederation as John A. Macdonald had been. He was the first French Canadian to lead one of Canada's national political parties, and as leader of the Opposition he was just one step from being prime minister. He was considered the best-dressed man in Ottawa, and everyone agreed that he was charming and graceful. But what kind of leader was he? people wanted to know. Where did he stand on the great issues of the day?

In 1896, Canada seemed to be adrift. Macdonald, "the old chieftain," had died in 1891. In the five years that had followed, Canada had had four prime ministers, but no real leader had come forth to fill the shoes of Sir John A. In Ottawa, politicians argued with each other and fought with the provincial leaders. Across the country, people seemed unable to settle their differences. There was tension and distrust between the French and the English, and between East and West.

The Manitoba Schools Question was the great issue of the day, and it drew angry words from all sides. Manitoba's French-speaking Catholic children had had their own schools until 1890. Then the government of Manitoba had stopped paying for them. It said the French-speaking population had become so small that the schools were no longer needed. French Canadians were furious over the loss of their rights.

Everything the Conservative prime ministers tried to do only seemed to make things worse. As an election campaign loomed, someone challenged Wilfrid Laurier: how would he and his Liberals solve this terrible problem when everyone else had failed?

Laurier replied with one of Aesop's fables, a story he had learned as a child in St-Lin, Quebec. In this fable, the sun and the wind made a bet to see who could get the coat off a man's back. The wind howled and shrieked around

the man, but the harder it blew, the more tightly he clutched his coat around him. Then it was the sun's turn. With a warm smile, the sun beamed upon the man, and soon he was so warm that he pulled off his coat himself. There had been enough windy threats about the Manitoba Schools Question, Laurier said. If he were prime minister, he would try the sunny way.

It seemed like a reassuring answer, and in mid-summer of 1896 Wilfrid Laurier became prime minister. The man of the sunny ways would be Canada's leader for fifteen years. His times were not sunny for everyone, of course. There were neither health-care plans nor unemployment insurance for workers. Punishments were harsh, even for children, and prisons were hellish places. But for many Canadians, Laurier's years brought good times and prosperity. The gold horseshoe tiepin he liked to wear for good luck seemed to promise a bright future for a growing country.

A one-room school in Ontario's Muskoka District in 1887. The children vary widely in age.

A wedding in Dartmouth, Nova Scotia, in the late 1800s. In Victorian times, formal behaviour spread from the rich and powerful to the middle and working classes. Top hats, canes, and elaborate lace dresses became the proper attire for weddings.

In 1897, Laurier and his wife, Zoë, went to London, England, for Queen Victoria's Diamond Jubilee, a celebration of her sixty years on the throne. The British empire was at its peak of might and power, and the Jubilee brought together imperial leaders from India, Africa, Australia, and all the rest of Britain's empire. None shone brighter than Laurier, who became Sir Wilfrid when the aged queen knighted her Canadian prime minister.

Gold Fever

During the same summer that Wilfrid Laurier became prime minister, George Carmack and his Native brothers-in-law, Skookum Jim and Tagish Charlie, went prospecting for gold in the Klondike River Valley of the Yukon country. A fellow prospector had said they should try Rabbit Creek, so they headed that way. There, on August 17, 1896, they found gold "lying thick between the flaky slabs of rock like cheese in a sandwich." Rabbit Creek has been called Bonanza Creek ever since. It took nearly a year for the news to get out, but then stories about "a ton of gold" flashed around the world by telegraph.

Every miner heading for the Yukon had to take a year's worth of goods with him. To cross the Chilkoot Pass, a miner had to go up and down that steep slope many times, until his whole stock was at the other side.

In Canada, the United States, Europe, and Australia, 100 000 people (mostly men) dropped what they were doing and headed for Bonanza Creek. Some went to Edmonton and spent months struggling overland to the North. Most sailed to Skagway, Alaska, and took "The Trail of '98." First they hiked over the White Pass or the fearsome Chilkoot Pass. At the foot of the thousand-metre Chilkoot, Mounties would let them go on only if they had a year's supplies with them. Gold-seekers struggled up and down the snow steps of the pass, bent double under load after load, until all their precious supplies were across. If they made it, they built rafts and floated down the Yukon River to the goldfields.

Where the Klondike flows into the Yukon River, Dawson City was born. Hotelkeepers, storekeepers, clerks, gamblers, entertainers, and prospectors poured in from all over the globe. In a month, Dawson became the largest Canadian city west of Winnipeg, and it was bursting with people frantic to get rich. A few did, for at least fifty million dollars' worth of gold came out of the Klondike. But the miners spent about as much as they found, and

Officers of the North-West Mounted Police keep law and order during Canada's first gold rush, on the Yukon River near Dawson, in 1898.

Naturalist Martha Louise Munger left fashionable society in Chicago in 1898 to join the Klondike gold rush. There she married George Black, commissioner of the Yukon Territory. She was seventy when her husband retired from the House of Commons in 1935, but she campaigned for and won his seat, becoming the second woman ever elected to the Canadian Parliament.

many left poorer than when they arrived. A young bank clerk named Robert Service got rich by writing about the miners. His poems about "the strange things done in the midnight sun, by the men who moil for gold" made him famous and popular all over the world.

The Yukon was a rough, wild place during the gold rush, but it was not lawless. Canada created a special military unit, the Yukon Field Force, to protect the border and discourage the many American prospectors from trying to add the Yukon to the United States. Meanwhile, the Mounties kept order among the miners. Because of the gold rush, the Yukon became a territory of Canada, with Dawson its first capital. In a couple of years there was a railway to carry miners over White Pass, and paddle-wheelers, rather than rafts, took them down the Yukon to the goldfields. But by then the Klondike boom was already fading.

The Last Best West

"The twentieth century will belong to Canada," said Wilfrid Laurier boldly in 1904. All the country needed was people, and more people were coming to Canada than ever before. To bring jobs to Canada, John A. Macdonald had created the National Policy, and Laurier maintained that policy. Under the National Policy, Canada collected fees (called tariffs) on foreign goods coming to Canada. The fees made imported goods more costly, and farmers complained about the high prices they paid. But enterprising Canadians became manufacturers, and American businessmen came here to build "branch plants." The factories made work for Canadians, and also for the immigrants who came to join them. Laurier predicted that Canada's six million people would soon be sixty million.

Hundreds of thousands of settlers also headed for the prairie West so recently claimed from the Native nations. At first, the most successful were not farmers but ranchers. As soon as the railway opened, cattle barons began stocking the southwestern Alberta plains with beef cattle. Grizzled cowpunchers, with only a saddle, a rifle, and a Navajo blanket to their names, guided the herds from the dry shortgrass prairie to winter shelter in the Rocky Mountain foothills. Canadian Pacific trains and ships hauled the "beef bonanza" away to market in Chicago and London.

Immigrants from eastern Canada, the United States, Britain, and Europe began to stream into the Canadian plains, drawn by advertisements which called the region "the last best west" – the last part of North America that was not yet crowded with farms and towns. In 1913, Canada welcomed over 400000 immigrants – more than in any single year before or since. Most of them were heading for the Prairies.

Isaac Barr, an English clergyman, led 2000 English settlers to Saskatchewan. Barr wanted to create a little corner of England on the plains, but his followers were city folk, not farmers. Barr had no idea how to organize or lead them, and the Barr colonists' first years were desperate ones. Thousands more immigrants came in family groups or on their own, as did the "remittance men." These were young men whose wealthy families shipped them off and "remitted" money to them so long as they stayed away. Remittance men were famous on the Prairies for lounging about and organizing foxhunts, but almost never for breaking the tough prairie sod.

Many Ontario farmers went west to find farmlands on the plains, but only a few French-speakers moved there.

Wheat and wildlife still seemed to be what Canada was known for when this truck was driving through Britain, urging immigration to Canada.

Despite Laurier's sunny ways, Manitoba had not reversed its decision to close its French-language schools. Although Manitoba, with its Métis traditions, had joined Confederation as a bilingual society, there were so many newcomers from Ontario, the United States, and Britain that English became the main language, not only in Manitoba but throughout the West.

Only a few Maritimers joined in the western migration. The age of sailing ships, of "wood, wind, and water," was ending, and the great Maritime sailing fleet had nearly vanished. For a while, it seemed that factories might bring new prosperity. Canada's first steelplant opened in Trenton, Nova Scotia, in 1883 and soon there was another one in Sydney, near the Cape Breton coalfields. But most of the new factories were built in central Canada, not the Maritimes. Maritimers began leaving their homes to look for work, but they went south to "the Boston states" more often than "up to Canada."

Canada had always preferred white, English-speaking immigrants. When the SS *Komagata Maru* tried to bring 400 East Indians to Vancouver in 1913, the passengers were prevented from landing, and Canada's first naval ship, HMCS *Rainbow*, helped drive them away again. But some Asians did reach Canada. Japanese settlers built up a thriving fishing fleet in Steveston, B.C., and Chinese immigrants continued to come in spite of the "head tax" they were obliged to pay.

In Eastern Europe, word of the last best west was spreading. Two Ukrainian farmers, Wasyl Eleniak and Ivan Pylypiw, settled in Alberta in 1891. They wrote home that Canada was a great country where farmers could find *vilni zemli* – free land – and live free from persecution. Slowly families from Poland and the empires of Russia and Austria set off for Canada and vilni zemli.

Many Canadians claimed that letting in settlers who were not British would create a "mongrel Canada." But Clifford Sifton, Laurier's Minister of Immigration, decided western Canada needed these farmers. "A stalwart peasant in a sheepskin coat, with a stout wife and a half-dozen

Poster for "Western Canada's Greatest Fair," which later became the Calgary Exhibition and Stampede. The first Stampede was held in 1912.

children, is good quality," said Sifton. (These were times when Canadian leaders felt comfortable describing people of non-British origin as if they were part of the livestock.) Sifton sent immigration agents to recruit farmers from Eastern Europe, and the flow became a torrent.

Whole communities that had suffered persecution or hardship began to move from Europe to the Prairies. In 1875, Icelanders had founded New Iceland around the community of Gimli ("Paradise") in Manitoba. The Doukhobours ("spirit wrestlers"), a religious sect from Russia, settled in Saskatchewan in 1898, but after disputes with their neighbours they trekked west to settle in the Kootenays of British Columbia. German-speaking Mennonites also came from Russia seeking religious freedom, and they settled in Manitoba and Saskatchewan. Many other European ethnic and religious groups settled in Canadian towns or founded their own communities.

In those days, Canada offered a quarter-section (160 acres, which is 65 hectares) of land to "homesteaders" who could pay ten dollars and who promised to live on the land and to build a house and barn on it within three years. The homesteaders "busted sod," ploughing under the tough cover of prairie grasses. In summer they had to endure 35°C heat, and they worried about drought and fire. For

The Old Mill, painted by Homer Watson in 1886. When Watson was a boy, his father was a miller on the Grand River in Canada West. Watson became one of the first important artists of Canada in the years after Confederation, and mills were among his favourite subjects.

Maryanne Caswell's Journey

"Amid waving of hankies and promises to write we left our pretty town, the only home we had ever known." Fourteen-year-old Maryanne Caswell wrote those words to her grand-mother back in Ontario when the Caswells left to pioneer in the West in 1887.

"A long slow train . . . the seats and backs are wooden slats that can be pulled out, and the two facing and joining are used for a bed which mother used. Then, above, a large shelf is pulled down, and hangs by rods and hinges. This was our bed. . . . Then there is a room at the end of the car with a stove to cook on and water. At the other end are the washrooms."

The train trip from Toronto to Moose Jaw – a journey that had taken the old *voyageurs* three months by canoe – took the Caswells only three days. For another weary week they walked with the cows and sheep following along behind, to reach Saskatoon. "How tired we were of walk, walk!" wrote Maryanne. And when they finally arrived in Saskatoon there were only fourteen houses. "Where is the city?" Maryanne wanted to know. "On the map in the surveyor's office," was the answer.

safety from fast-moving grassfires, they had to plough a cleared circle around the homestead. In winter they put up with 40°-below cold and wild blizzards, with only the sod walls of their shanties for insulation. In a generation, the homesteaders turned the unbroken prairie grasslands into a sea of bright golden wheat fields that swayed like ocean waves in the prairie wind.

Imagine what it was like around 1905 for a Ukrainian girl new to western Canada. She had crossed the sea in the stinking hold of a steamship, crowded in with hundreds of others. In the new country, almost the only people who spoke her language were those who had travelled with her. After the long train journey from Montreal, the prairie made her heart sing: it looked like a fresh, new version of her old country. Perhaps her family had brought enough money to buy farm machinery, so her father did not have to go away to work on the railway or in the mines. Before the year was out, the family might have a real house to replace the sod shanty.

The girl walked down the concession road to the one-room school. She found, however, that the children called her stupid because she couldn't read English or even speak it very well. Some of them made fun of the clothes her mother made her, because they were different from theirs. However, the Ukrainian families had already begun their own church, and they were determined to have a school soon. They intended to preserve the Ukrainian language in this new land.

Meanwhile, what a relief to hurry home to the farmhouse. Mother would have good familiar borscht and perogies waiting, and Grandmother would be ready with stories about the old country. The family was glad to escape poverty and oppression in Europe, but in the safety and promise of the new land, the good memories could be cherished.

Another family, with barely enough money for its fare, would not be so lucky. If the land agent considered them poor prospects, he would send them to poor land at the far end of his district. They might spend their first winter in a hut dug into the ground, with only planks for a roof. The father probably had to go away from home to find work, and big comforting meals would be few and far between.

These prairie settlers were doing well. Instead of living in a sod hut, they had a solid house with an attic and a thatched roof.

Many families failed and were forced to move on to new districts or to the slums of cities. Enough remained, however, that in 1905 two new provinces, Alberta and Saskatchewan, were created.

What made it possible for these western settlements to grow so quickly? The railway. The train was as important to pioneering on the Prairies as the canoe had been in the fur trade. The big steam engines puffed through the forests, across the plains, and over the mountain passes, hauling long trains crowded with passengers, goods, and mail.

Marquis Wheat

It takes a special kind of wheat to produce good crops in western Canada's short summers and frigid winters. By 1903, the Central Experimental Farm in Ottawa had developed a strain of wheat tough enough for the prairie cold. It was called Marquis, and when it was ready to test, the scientists in Ottawa sent a sackful to a government farm in Indian Head, Saskatchewan.

When the boss, Angus Mackay, was ready to plant the wheat, he couldn't find it. He searched frantically. Finally he put a sign up in the barn, saying, "Please, whoever took the sackful of wheat marked Marquis for testing, return it at once. Urgent. No questions asked." The wheat came back – one of the men had taken it to feed his chickens! The Marquis wheat was planted and harvested and proved perfect for prairie farming, and its flour made good bread.

A few years later, an American railway offered a $1000 prize for the world's best wheat. The railway officials were expecting American wheat to win but, when a Saskatchewan farmer named Seager Wheeler took a sample of Marquis to the competition, he won the prize – and Marquis wheat became world-famous.

Trains brought the people to the land and took wheat, beef, or timber back to faraway customers.

Prairie towns grew up around the railway stations, and by the grain elevators where the wheat crop was weighed and stored until the boxcars arrived to haul it away. Soon there would be a church – with an Anglican steeple in a British-settled area, an onion-shaped dome in a Ukrainian one. There might be a Chinese restaurant and a Jewish family's general store along Main Street. If the district prospered, there would soon be a newspaper and a bank, a Knights of Pythias Lodge for the gentlemen, a Women's Christian Temperance Hall for the ladies, and for the children a baseball diamond beside the school. The towns were like islands. Beyond their last houses, the wide prairie rolled on for ever.

This 1897 view of Winnipeg shows Main Street south of City Hall.

Dreams and Struggles

Canada's cities were developing as fast as the prairie farms. Soon there were factories and factory towns along the rail lines from Halifax to Vancouver. Cities seemed exciting places, with their street lights, electric streetcars, glamorous theatres, and amusement parks. Young people left family farms to find jobs in the factories, and not all immigrants headed to the Prairies. Thousands settled in the cities. Soon there were synagogues in Winnipeg, Sikh temples in Vancouver, Greek and Italian newspapers in Toronto, and Lebanese grocery stores in Halifax.

Cities were not as wonderful as young farmers and immigrants dreamed they would be. Big factories were putting local enterprises and craft workshops out of business. Brewers and blacksmiths in every town found their wares replaced by factory-made products that the trains brought from the cities. Shopkeepers found their customers ordering from the Simpson's or Eaton's catalogues instead. Big manufacturers could make goods more quickly and cheaply, partly because they used powerful new machines run on electricity, but also because their employees worked long shifts six days a week, for low wages.

For most of the nineteenth century, unions were small,

This ice castle was the star attraction of the Montreal Winter Carnival of 1887. Today Quebec City's Carnaval is the unchallenged champion for elaborate ice castles, but Montreal and Quebec City competed for years.

The Wishing Books

For rural Canadians around the turn of the century, department store catalogues were a glimpse of another world, a world of glamorous clothes, marvellous household furnishings, stoves, books, games, and toys, as well as more practical items. There was in them everything the heart could desire – if the purse could afford it.

The day a catalogue reached a rural mailbox

was a great day. At home it would be pored over and kept in a special place while family members debated what they would buy.

When the next season's catalogue arrived, children were sometimes allowed to cut the old one up for scrapbooks or paper dolls. What was left often went to the outhouse as toilet paper. From start to finish the catalogues served their customers well!

local organizations of workers trying to improve their lives. In 1872, workers in Ontario towns and in Montreal campaigned to reduce the working day to nine hours. The printers struck at George Brown's newspaper, *The Globe*, and 1500 workers marched through the streets of Hamilton. In 1883, unions formed the first truly national organization, the Trades and Labor Congress of Canada, and by 1910 more than 100000 Canadian workers belonged to unions. Factory owners fought against unions and their demands for better pay and better working conditions. There would be violence and lockouts and setbacks for workers, but the union movement continued to grow.

A Voice for Women

There were always some workers who gave up the struggle and turned to drink for comfort. Rye whisky was cheap, and for a few hours poor people could forget their woes in a bottle. But if a man spent his wages on liquor, there was no welfare system and no protection for his family. Women had few legal rights, and so a drunken husband meant dire hardship, as well as abuse, for his wife and children. For that reason, women, along with religious and political leaders who cared about working people, preached the value of temperance. At first they simply wanted people to be careful – "temperate" – about how they drank, but soon temperance societies began to demand total bans on alcohol.

There were temperance societies throughout the country, and politicians won office on the temperance platform. Women could neither vote nor hold public office, but they became leaders in the movement for temperance. In Winnipeg, a teacher and writer named Nellie McClung fought for temperance – and began a lifelong battle for the rights of women. Women should have the same opportunities as men to make decisions about their lives and their children's lives, she argued. She insisted that women must

Nellie McClung

Nellie Mooney McClung was a writer and a champion of human rights. She was born in Ontario in 1873 and moved with her family to the Souris Valley in Manitoba when she was seven. She didn't begin school until she was ten.

At sixteen, Nellie McClung became a teacher. She wrote sixteen books, including her autobiography, *Clearing the West*, and many magazine articles. She began her political life fighting for temperance, and fought for the right of women to vote and own property. She also fought for laws to bring safety practices into factories.

Nellie McClung is remembered for her books and her devotion to human rights, but in her own time she was just as famous for her quick wit and sense of humour. Once when she was giving a speech during a Manitoba election campaign, a heckler yelled from the audience, "The prime minister would quit politics if a woman were ever elected."

"That proves what a purifying effect women would have on politics," retorted Nellie.

---

have the vote. It was no good pretending their fathers and husbands could be trusted to represent them.

In rural Ontario, Adelaide Hoodless began working for better education for women after her baby son died from drinking impure milk. In 1897 she founded the Women's Institute, in Stoney Creek, Ontario, as a place where women could share their knowledge of household management, health, and family nutrition. Women's Institutes were an instant success, and spread across the country and around the world. Mrs. Hoodless went on to help found the National Council of Women of Canada and the Victorian Order of Nurses. At first her organizations focussed on the traditional "women's sphere." Gradually their successes encouraged more women to campaign for votes and other rights that had been restricted to men.

Christian churches were the backbone of turn-of-the-century Canadian society. Most Canadians were Christians and churchgoers, and the churches were at the centre of most people's lives. Women got together in the Christian Temperance Union or the Dorcas Society, where they made

When Lucy Maud Montgomery wrote Anne of Green Gables *she probably didn't realize it would become the most popular Canadian book ever. First published in 1908, the famous story of red-haired Anne was enjoyed by so many people that Montgomery wrote sequel after sequel to please them.*

Emily Howard Stowe was the first woman to practise medicine in Canada.

clothes for missionary work. In the countryside, families often went to church with a packed lunch in the wagon. They shared a picnic, played games and heard a temperance speech with their neighbours after the morning service, and stayed for evening services before returning home. The family and the church were still the centres of life.

A Turn-of-the-Century Time Trip

Travel back in time and see what life was like for Canadian children around 1900. First imagine a boy, ten or twelve years old, who lives in a great stone house on Jarvis Street in Toronto. The house has a wide, curved drive in front, a coach house and stables in back. It has polished mahogany furniture, huge gilt-framed paintings on the walls, and thick Turkish carpets on the floors. Gas heat is piped into all the rooms through ornate vents with marble overmantels, and the rooms are bright with electric light. Hot and cold water runs from the taps in the kitchen and several bathrooms and there are indoor flush toilets.

Artist and photographer William Notman created this tobogganing scene in his studio. The scenery and the snow are all special effects, and the young models have been carefully posed. Notman created hundreds of scenes like this and hired talented artists to work on them.

Home Children

They were called "home children" but they were far from home. They came from orphanages in Britain, unwanted children or children whose parents couldn't feed them any more. Some of the people in charge of those orphanages thought the children would be better off where they could have fresh air and farm food, and so they advertised in Canada and Australia for people who would take a child.

There were willing people. Some took children out of the kindness of their hearts. But too many wanted them only as workers.

One man remembered his life many years later. "I was beat up with pieces of harness, pitchforks, anything that came in handy to hit me with, I got it. I didn't get enough to eat. . . . I used to swipe flour and sugar. . . . I never had a coat if it was raining. Just a grain sack over my shoulders and no shoes. I was supposed to go to school six months of the year, and in the seven years I only got to grade three. . . . They would buy me shoes that wouldn't fit. I used to cry with the pain."

Some of the children were actually starved. Some died. All in all the idea turned out to be a poor one. But between the 1860s and the 1930s, thousands of children were brought to Canada that way.

The boy goes to a private school where he learns English literature, composition, and spelling, British history, geography, mathematics, penmanship, Latin, and ancient Greek. His sisters' lessons are nearly the same, but their school teaches embroidery and piano playing instead of Greek. After school, the boys play cricket and lacrosse against teams from other boys' schools, while the girls practise archery and field hockey. In the evenings there are several hours of homework.

Saturdays bring him freedom. Perhaps the boy rides the trolley across town to meet a "chum." His sisters, however, are not allowed to travel on their own, and their Saturdays are often taken up with hairdressers or seamstresses who come to the house. Sometimes they have social calls to make with their mother.

The father of the family goes to his office every day but Sunday, and the mother manages the household. She sees that the cook, the housekeeper, the maids, and the houseboy all do their work properly. She organizes the family's social life, keeping track of invitations to dinner, mission society meetings at the church, and plays at the Royal Opera House that would be suitable for her children.

The thirteen-year-old maid who lives in the attic is not nearly so well off. She is up before dawn seven days a week (with just one day off a month) to help the cook with breakfast. Her bed is hard, the gas heat does not reach the third floor, and the small allowance of coal for her stove never really warms her room.

At least she has enough to eat, and she is glad to have her job, for her family could not afford to let her stay in school. Her father has a steady job in the brickyard. Her young brother makes a few cents a week selling *The Globe* on the street, and her older brother, a soldier in South Africa, sends home his pay. With the money their mother earns taking in washing and mending, the family manages to pay the rent and buy the coal for the two-room house on Sumach Street.

Some people are not so lucky. When their earnings do not pay the rent, they are turned out of their homes. The children live on the street, begging or stealing, and they may die of cold or malnutrition. Children are no longer hanged for stealing twenty-five cents (as one was in Saint John, New Brunswick, in 1824), but they can be whipped or jailed for minor offences. The first Children's Aid societies have just been started.

By this time Jewish immigrants from Poland, Russia, and Romania have settled in many parts of Canada. In Montreal or Winnipeg, the new arrivals have formed tightly knit groups, partly because Jewish law requires them to live close to their synagogue. Many live in walk-up apartments, often two families together. Mothers and aunts work on sewing machines, making clothes for the department

The Poor Children's Clinic at Toronto's Hospital for Sick Children in 1916. The sign is written in English and Yiddish, for Toronto's Jewish community was clustered around nearby Kensington Market.

Choosing sides for a hockey game in Sarnia, Ontario, in 1908.

stores. Fathers and uncles work in grocery or tailor shops or push peddler's carts around the city. The community is crowded and noisy, but it is hard to be lonely.

It is a very different life in a French-Canadian farm-house a hundred kilometres east of Montreal. As in other rural areas, where many hands are needed about the farm, families are large, even though some of the children – and some of the mothers – are likely to die in childbirth. The children are up at four in the morning to milk the cows, feed the animals, and shovel out the barn. In summer, the older girls preserve vegetables, and the boys work in the long narrow fields with the men and horses.

Winter is easier. In the parish school, the nuns teach catechism, reading and writing in French, and a lot of the history of French Canada. The brightest children in the school go on to colleges, and many will become priests or nuns. A few of the boys have a piece of family-owned farmland waiting for them. Others will head to Montreal or the factory towns in New England, or off to lumber camps in the north woods.

The best times are midwinter Saturdays when the neighbours gather in the parlour. They sing and dance to the fiddle and hear the storytellers. Late in the evening

Many boys needed to work in the coal mines of Cape Breton to help support their families, and the mine owners liked the way they could fit into cramped tunnels deep underground.

they share sandwiches and sugar pie before everyone scrambles into the cutters for the ride home, still singing.

In a Cape Breton Island coal-mining town, a boy works underground, crouching in a mine shaft that runs out under the bottom of the ocean. Since the working day starts before dawn and ends after dusk, he sees the sun only on Sundays or during the few short weeks of summer. His lunch, a bit of bread and cheese called a "piece," always tastes of coal dust. Coal dust has gotten into his skin so deeply that it seems he cannot get it out, no matter how hard he scrubs in the big tin tub in front of the fireplace.

Many Canadian children, neither rich nor poor, were able to complete their schooling, though few went on to university. They lived in homes that were warm and comfortable, though they might not have electricity and the toilet was an outhouse at the back of the garden. Growing up in Canada around 1900 was so different for rich and poor, for settled families and immigrants, for city children and country children, that it was almost like living in different countries.

Into the North

There were no factories, schools, or churches in the Far North. Inuit had lived there, almost undisturbed, for a thousand years. Without consulting them, Canada had claimed all the land up to the North Pole in 1880, although no one knew what land was there. Between 1903 and 1906, Norwegian explorer Roald Amundsen manoeuvred his small ship, *Gjoa*, through the twisting, icy channels from the Arctic to the Pacific – through the long-sought North-west Passage. During his voyage, Amundsen met many American, British, and Norwegian whalers pushing in from both east and west. They brought trade goods to the Inuit, but they also brought disease. In 1900 one whaling ship carried sickness to the Sadlermiut Inuit of Hudson Bay – and they all died.

Far to the south, in Ottawa, Wilfrid Laurier's government began to think that Canada had to take charge of the North. If it did not, the Americans surely would. On July 1, 1909, Captain Joseph Bernier planted Canada's flag at Winter Harbour on Melville Island in the heart of the Arctic Islands. His ship, the *Arctic*, was still frozen in the ice, but Bernier was a master sailor and an Arctic veteran, and he was confident. Boldly he laid claim to every inch of the Arctic for Canada.

A swimming class in the Don River at Toronto, 1909.

In 1913, Vilhjalmur Stefansson led another Canadian expedition to the Arctic. Stef, as he liked to be called, had been born in Manitoba's Icelandic settlement and raised in the United States. He loved the North. He called it "the friendly Arctic," and said it was a wonderful place for those willing to adapt to it as he did.

Stef had lived among the Inuit, learning their language and how they were able to live in harmony with the North. He travelled by dogsled instead of taking large ships into the ice. He hunted as he went, trusting the land and sea instead of hauling huge stocks of food. Ranging across the North, he added a whole group of islands to the map of Canada. When he found his first uncharted island in June 1915, Stef and his men put aside their usual raw sealmeat and shared the only treat they had – some biscuit crumbs and malted milk. Before he headed south in 1918, Stefansson filled in the last large blank on the map of Canada.

Billy Stark bought a Curtiss biplane in 1912 and brought it home to Vancouver, where crowds gathered to watch him fly. A herd of cattle complicated his landing at Hastings Park on May 4. Fortunately, Stark (and the cows) survived, and his airplane was soon repaired.

The Canadians and the Empire

As Canada grew, differences among Canadians seemed to become greater, not less. Those who dreamed of building a new nationality from ocean to ocean regretted these differences, and Canada's diversity made life hard for its political leaders. "This is a difficult country to govern," Wilfrid Laurier said ruefully.

In Laurier's time, many Canadians of British descent looked as much to London as to Ottawa for leadership. They called themselves "imperialists." Britain governed the most powerful empire in the world. Canadian imperialists did not want to be independent, but to share in running the whole empire. In 1899, when Britain went to war against the Dutch-speaking Boer settlers of South Africa, the imperialists wanted Canadians to fight alongside the British. Later they argued that Canada should buy ships for the British navy instead of building a Canadian navy.

Hundreds of Torontonians flooded the streets on Pretoria Day, June 5, 1901, to celebrate the end of the South African War.

A young Montreal newspaperman named Henri Bourassa fought the ideas of the imperialists. He hoped that French Canadians and English Canadians would build an independent Canada together. Quebeckers cheered when he asked if the English Canadians intended to be colonials forever. In the Boer War, he sympathized with the Boers more than with the British.

Wilfrid Laurier had to steer a careful course, for he needed the support of both English Canada and Quebec. During the Boer War, his government supported Canadian volunteers who went to South Africa, and many did. But he also began building a Canadian navy – which the imperialists sneered at as "the tin-pot navy."

Britain eventually won the South African war, but the tough resistance of the Boer forces embarrassed the mighty British army. Queen Victoria, the symbol of imperial might and glory for over sixty years, died in 1901. As the world moved into the twentieth century, Canada's interests

Silver Dart, *piloted by J.A.D. McCurdy, took off from the frozen surface of Baddeck Bay, Nova Scotia, on February 23, 1909. It was the first aircraft flight in Canada. Within a few years, planes were buzzing through the skies all over Canada.*

Stephen Leacock

"Lord Ronald said nothing; he flung himself from the room, flung himself upon his horse and rode madly off in all directions." Stephen Leacock wrote that in 1911, and people all over the world laughed. Leacock was a professor at McGill University who wrote serious books about economics, but he became much more famous for his funny books. When people said being funny must be easy, he half-agreed. "You just jot down ideas as they occur to you," he said. "The jotting is simplicity itself – it is the occurring which is difficult."

Some of Leacock's best stories are set in the imaginary town of Mariposa. He based Mariposa on Orillia, Ontario, where his summer home still stands.

moved more and more towards the United States.

Canada's relations with the United States were almost as complicated as those with Britain and its empire. Laurier had continued Macdonald's National Policy of tariffs to protect Canadian factories. Then, in 1911, he proposed to switch paths completely – free trade with the Americans became the new policy.

"Follow my white plume," cried Laurier, whose hair had gone white while he was prime minister. But few did. Bourassa had challenged his popularity in Quebec, and imperialists rejected him in English Canada. An American politician made matters worse for Laurier by predicting that free trade would be only the first step. Soon, he boasted, "the American flag will float over every square foot of the British North American possessions clear to the North Pole."

In the Canada of 1911, that was enough to kill the notion of free trade with the Americans. Laurier's luck had run out. Canadians threw out the Liberal Party, and Laurier was back to being leader of the Opposition. His sunny days were ending, and stormy times were coming to Canada.

Chapter 9

Stormy Times

W

Mr. Gus Gabert and his students in Bruderheim, Alberta, in 1915. During the First World War, many towns with German-sounding names changed them, but Bruderheim never did.

Previous pages:
At the end of the First World War, hundreds of thousands of Canadians came home. They were welcomed by big-city parades and, like this soldier at a small-town station, by their wives and children – children who sometimes barely knew their father.

AR CLOUDS GATHERED IN EUROPE IN THE SUMMER OF 1914, BUT Canadians were not very concerned about the rumble of that far-away storm. The prime minister, Sir Robert Borden, had gone away to his summer home to play golf. Across the country, boys and girls were going to summer camp with the Boy Scouts or the Girl Guides, new movements which had recently become popular. In Carlstadt, Alberta, known as "the star of the Prairies," farmers spent the summer of 1914 praying for rain. They even hired rainmakers, who roamed the dry plains of southeastern Alberta with mysterious instruments, promising to create downpours on demand.

No rain came to Carlstadt, but war came to Europe. In a town called Sarajevo, an assassin shot Franz Ferdinand, the archduke of Austria-Hungary. Tensions between the states of Europe had been building for years, and they had bound themselves together in tangled alliances. When Austria-Hungary declared war on Serbia, blaming it for the killing, the alliances drew in one country after another. On August 4, 1914, after Germany attacked France and Belgium, King George V declared war on behalf of all the British empire. Canada, as part of the empire, was now at war.

"When the call comes, our answer goes at once," declared Sir Wilfrid Laurier. "Ready, aye, ready!" Canada may not have been prepared, but it marched into the war enthusiastically. In Toronto, thousands cheered in support of Britain and sang "God Save the King." In Montreal they sang France's national anthem, "La Marseillaise," as well. Carlstadt, meanwhile, boasted of being the first village in Canada to form a Home Guard to help defend the country.

In small towns and big cities, men rushed to join the army. By September, 30 000 Canadian soldiers were marching on the dusty drill fields at Camp Valcartier, near Quebec City. On October 1, the First Contingent of Canada's Expeditionary Force sailed for England, where they endured three cold, dull months of training. Some soldiers worried that the war might end before they could win glory. But it would last longer than the excited young Canadian soldiers could imagine.

A few weeks at the front washed away the Canadians' naive notions about a quick, clean war full of heroism and romance. By April 1915 the Canadians were defending a Belgian town called Ypres, when the Germans attacked with something new in the history of war – poison gas. Gagging and choking, the Canadians managed to hold their positions, but they paid a terrible price. In two savage weeks of fighting over a few hectares of Flanders, 6000 Canadian soldiers died or were wounded. Four Canadians at Ypres won the Victoria Cross, the British empire's highest medal for bravery, and two of them died winning it.

Trench Warfare

Across the rolling plain of Belgium and the north of France, the rival armies lay locked together, unable to advance or retreat, battling over a narrow strip of ground called "no-man's-land." The generals said they must fight on, suffering in their trenches and dying in no-man's-land, until the other side gave in. Instead of marching gloriously into Germany, the Canadians began to dig.

The soldiers lived like moles in a maze of trenches and underground shelters, pounded by shells and bombs. To

H.J. Mowat, Stretcher Bearers. *During the First World War, Canada sent "war artists" to capture the experience of Canadians at war. Paintings often did this more poignantly than photographs could.*

Damp, dirty, cold, and crowded, the trenches were also dangerous. The soldier looking out of the trench knew he might be in the gunsights of a sniper.

Canadian troops cross "no-man's-land" under fire during the Battle of Vimy Ridge, in April 1917.

advance against the enemy, they had to worm forward among water-filled shell holes and tangles of barbed wire, while snipers and machine-gunners tried to kill them. Between battles, they had to live in the wet, filthy trenches. Their feet, never dry, became infected, and their mud-soaked uniforms teemed with what they called "seam squirrels": itchy, biting lice. Spirits ebbed.

The Newfoundland Regiment discovered the horrors of trench warfare at a place in France called Beaumont-Hamel during the Battle of the Somme, on July 1, 1916. That morning, hundreds of thousands of soldiers of the British empire stormed the enemy lines. The first wave of attackers was slaughtered in no-man's-land. The Newfoundlanders' turn came next. As soon as they left their trenches, the enemy's machine-gunners cut them down in hundreds. In half an hour, the regiment was destroyed, leaving every outpost on the island with someone to mourn. Even after Newfoundland joined Canada in 1949, most Newfound-landers thought of July first as the anniversary of their tragic losses at Beaumont-Hamel.

At Easter of 1917, the Canadians won a victory. Fighting for the first time as a Canadian corps, they attacked a hill called Vimy Ridge, near Arras, France. They took the ridge in the morning and held it against fierce counterattacks. More than 3000 Canadians died and many more were wounded, but Vimy was a rare victory in the endless trench warfare, and those who survived felt great pride in the Canadian success.

"The Canadians were brought along to head the assault in one great battle after another," wrote the British prime minister. That fall, at Passchendaele, in Belgium, thousands of Canadians died or drowned in the mud while the enemy rained shellfire down on them. The following spring, two field hospitals in France were hit by shellfire, and four Canadian nurses were killed as they tended their patients. There was not much glory in trench warfare.

More than 22 000 Canadians fought a different war – the war in the air. Canada did not yet have its own air

In Flanders Fields

Dr. John McCrae of Guelph, Ontario, sailed off to the First World War as a medical officer with the First Contingent of the Canadian Expeditionary Force, and he went to the front early in 1915. After the terrible battle and poison-gas attack at Ypres that year, he wrote a few lines in memory of a friend who had been killed. The British magazine *Punch* published the poem "In Flanders Fields," and it became the best known of all war poems. But by the end of the war its author was dead. McCrae had died of pneumonia earlier in the year, while still in the army. McCrae's poem expressed what later generations saw as the most important aspect of the First World War: not the glory of victory, but the millions of deaths.

In Flanders fields the poppies blow
Between the crosses, row on row,
    That mark our place; and in the sky
    The larks, still bravely singing, fly
Scarce heard amid the guns below.

We are the Dead. Short days ago
We lived, felt dawn, saw sunset glow,
    Loved, and were loved, and now we lie
            In Flanders fields.

Take up our quarrel with the foe:
To you from failing hands we throw
    The torch; be yours to hold it high.
    If ye break faith with us who die
We shall not sleep, though poppies grow
            In Flanders fields.

Celebrated First World War flying ace Billy Bishop was awarded the Victoria Cross for one of his most daring exploits. Bishop was credited with shooting down seventy-two enemy planes in all.

When Berlin, Ontario, changed its name to Kitchener and heaved a statue of Germany's Kaiser Wilhelm into the lake, not everyone approved. These citizens pulled the Kaiser out again.

force. In 1914, when flyer J.A.D. McCurdy had offered to start an air service, Canada's Minister of Defence had declared, "The aeroplane will never play any part in such a serious business as the defence of a nation, my boy!" But soon Canadian flyers were fighting in biplanes and triplanes that swooped like butterflies high above the horrors of the battlefields below. Eleven of the top twenty-seven "aces" who downed more than thirty aircraft for Britain's Royal Flying Corps hailed from Canada.

Billy Bishop, of Owen Sound, Ontario, had been in continuous trouble at military college before the war, but in aerial combat he found his niche. He was blessed with "the courage of the early morning," always ready to take off at dawn to launch reckless, desperate, close-range attacks on enemy pilots. He emerged from the war with a Victoria Cross and credit for seventy-two victories. His feats inspired other flyers, but few led his charmed life. In 1917, a new pilot could expect to be shot down within about ten days – and there were no parachutes.

Struggles at Home

On the home front in Canada, civilians put their backs into the war effort. They shipped tons of wheat and beef overseas to feed the soldiers. In hurriedly built factories, they churned out bullets and shells, aircraft and ships. People sang patriotic songs, bought war bonds, and donated cigarettes and candy for the troops "over there." Many Canadians became intolerant of anything German, and Canadians of German ancestry felt obliged to show that they were loyal to the British side in the war. In Ontario, the town of Berlin changed its name to Kitchener, after the British war minister, and a statue of the German kaiser was dumped into the lake. "Carlstadt" was a German name, so the people of the Alberta town renamed it Alderson, after the British commander of the Canadians at Ypres.

With so many men off to war, women kept the country going. They gathered in church halls to make

bandages and to knit socks, sweaters, and scarves from endless skeins of khaki-coloured wool. They also took over many jobs once held by men. Before the war was over, 30 000 women were working ten-hour days in munitions factories and other war industries. Women were farming, too. In Ontario alone, 2000 female high school and college students, billeted in camps and hostels, helped bring in the harvest each summer.

As soon as the war began, many Canadian women volunteered to work overseas as nurses. More than 3000 white-veiled nursing sisters served as officers in the Canadian forces. They worked in dangerous field hospitals just behind the trenches, or in base hospitals in France and Britain. Because of the colours of the uniforms they wore, the soldiers called them bluebirds.

Since women were doing so much, they wanted a share in making decisions about the country. Women's groups demanded better government, prohibition (the banning of alcohol), and votes for women. Before the war ended, women could vote in federal and most provincial elections. The support women gave to the war effort helped them in their campaign to participate fully in public life. But women were also the backbone of pacifist movements.

During the First World War, posters preached that every conservation effort was important for the war effort.

In wartime there were few men left to help on the farm, and city women were recruited to help bring in the harvests.

Canadian nurses tending wounded soldiers at the Canadian hospital in Paris, in 1917. The patients here are French soldiers.

The sentimental "When Your Boy Comes Back to You" was only one of many songs written and sung during the First World War.

"War is a crime committed by men," wrote feminist Nellie McClung. Laura Hughes campaigned tirelessly against the war, to the fury of her uncle, Sir Sam Hughes, the Minister of Militia.

By 1917, Canadian soldiers were dying in thousands, but fewer young men were now coming forward to join the army. Prime Minister Robert Borden decided that Canada would have to start conscripting men, which meant taking them into the army whether they wanted to join or not. In Alderson, the farmers protested. They were struggling to bring in crops for the war effort, and they could not spare their sons for the army. In Cumberland, British Columbia, a policeman shot fiery labour leader Ginger Goodwin dead when he refused to go into the army. But it was Quebec that exploded in the largest protest over conscription.

Some Quebeckers did join the fighting forces, and distinguished themselves by their bravery. Quebec's 22nd Battalion performed heroic service. Many young soldiers and most of the regiment's officers died in the trenches. One who survived but lost a leg was Georges Vanier, who would one day be Governor General of Canada. Major Talbot Papineau, who was a descendant of the 1837 Rebellion leader Louis-Joseph Papineau, argued that the war could unite French and English in one noble cause.

Papineau's cousin Henri Bourassa disagreed. Bourassa ran Montreal's influential newspaper *Le Devoir*. For years he had written that French and English Canadians should build a new Canadian nationality together. But the way English Canadians went off to fight for Britain convinced him that English Canadians were British first and Canadian second. He felt betrayed. Canada was not in danger, Bourassa told Papineau, and he argued against conscripting unwilling soldiers. Since Ontario was at that time passing new laws to close down French-language schools, Bourassa said that "the Prussians across the Ottawa River" were as dangerous to French Canada as the Prussians who ruled Germany.

Most French Canadians agreed with Bourassa. They did not think this was their war, and they hated the thought of their sons being forced to fight for *les anglais*. Nor were they

persuaded by the fact that France was also under attack.
Young French Canadians fled to the woods or chopped their
fingers off to avoid being dragged into the king's army. But
the Conservative Party's plan for conscription was approved
by most English-Canadian Liberals. In 1917 a Union government of Conservatives and Liberals, nearly all from English
Canada, rammed conscription through Parliament. Some
Quebeckers lost faith in Confederation for ever.

The battle over conscription split Wilfrid Laurier's
Liberal Party and destroyed his vision of sunny ways and
Canadian harmony. "I am branded in Quebec as a traitor to
the French," he mourned, "and in Ontario as a traitor to
the English. I am neither. I am Canadian." Talbot Papineau,
in despair over the hatreds the war had caused, asked to
be sent back to the front lines. He was killed at the battle of
Passchendaele.

Canada gave all it could to the war effort, including
more than 600 000 soldiers from a country of eight million
people. Yet Prime Minister Robert Borden discovered that
British leaders still treated him as a mere underling, and
British commanders threw away Canadian lives without
even consulting him. Borden successfully demanded that
Canadian leaders sit as equals at the imperial conference
table where policy was decided. On the battlefields of
France and back home, Canadians were learning to think
of themselves as a nation.

Borden feared the war would last into the 1920s,
but victory came at last, at 11:00 a.m. on November 11,
1918. In the town of Mons, Belgium, five minutes before
11:00 that morning, a sniper killed an unlucky soldier
named George Price, the last Canadian to die in the First
World War.

The end of the war brought joy and relief, but the
scars left were deep. There were 60 000 dead to mourn,
thousands of wounded to care for, and half a million
veterans to bring back home. Everyone prayed that these
sacrifices had been made in fighting "a war to end wars."
Now that it was over, they swore to build a peacetime
world worthy of the wartime heroes.

*Not many French Canadians
were persuaded by recruiting
posters like these. Across
Canada, but particularly in
Quebec, many farmers preferred
to keep their sons at home to
bring in bumper crops.*

The Halifax Explosion

Canada's war effort kept the port of Halifax busier than ever. Early in the morning of December 6, 1917, a Belgian ship named the *Imo* was hurrying through the narrows in front of the town when it collided with a French ship, the *Mont Blanc*. The *Mont Blanc* was loaded with ammunition, and it caught fire.

At six minutes after nine the *Mont Blanc* blew up, and in an instant much of Halifax was destroyed. The blast flattened the city, and fires roared through the ruins. A tidal wave flung broken ships ashore. Sixteen hundred people were killed, and ten thousand – one person in five – lay injured. To make things worse, snow began to fall, and a blizzard raged for days.

For months, the people of Halifax struggled to rebuild their city, while help poured in from the rest of the country and the New England states. Until the atom bomb fell on Hiroshima in 1945, the Halifax explosion was the biggest manmade explosion ever.

The Heartbreaking Twenties

Instead of glory, peace, and prosperity, the postwar years began in hardship and bitterness for many Canadians. In 1918 and 1919, an epidemic of influenza killed 50000, many of them young people. Soldiers coming home found the factories that had boomed in wartime were now out of work and closing their doors. Unemployment went up while wages went down. Even millionaires felt the pinch. Sir Henry Pellatt went broke and had to move out of Casa Loma, his Toronto castle with towers and battlements and secret passages. Prices kept on climbing. Many manufacturers had made fortunes in the war; now workers and soldiers wanted their share of prosperity. To get better wages, they joined unions. In the coal and steel towns of Cape Breton Island, the factories of central Canada, and the west-coast lumber camps, workers organized strikes.

In Winnipeg, workers organized a general strike in May 1919, shutting down the whole city in support of their demands. No factory could open. No trains or buses could run. Even police and firefighters joined the 30000 strikers. Prime Minister Borden sent Mounties and soldiers to fight Canadian workers in the streets. On "Bloody Saturday," police on horseback charged a parade, and one striker was killed. Scores were arrested, and strikers who had been born outside Canada were expelled and sent home. The

Casa Loma was millionaire Sir Henry Pellatt's fantasy castle, built on a bluff overlooking Toronto. After he lost his money, he moved to an apartment.

In 1919, when Winnipeg metal workers struck for better pay and union rights, 30 000 working men and women joined them in a general strike. City leaders called it a conspiracy led by "alien scum." On Bloody Saturday, police on horseback charged crowds of strikers. Strikers retaliated by overturning and burning one of the town's streetcars.

Nobody seemed to be able to beat the world champion "Grads" from Edmonton. They were the best team in women's basketball from 1915 until 1940.

strike was broken, but one of its leaders, a Methodist minister named James S. Woodsworth, began talking about the need for a political party to speak for workers.

There were good times in the 1920s, too, and new inventions that brought excitement and fun. Cars had been rattling around since before the turn of the century, but until after war they were still new and strange. For a while, Prince Edward Island allowed them on the road only three days a week. By the 1920s, quite a few Canadians owned cars. Canadian cars – McLaughlins, Russells, Fossmobiles, and Bourassa Sixes – clanked and clattered down rough Canadian roads. Often they chased horses and buggies off the road, but sometimes a bolting horse would frighten a driver and leave the car upturned in a ditch, its wheels spinning wildly.

In 1919 two British pilots took off from Newfoundland and crossed the Atlantic in a plane, and in that same year several paper companies hired a pilot just back from the war to fly on forest-fire patrols. But for most people aircraft were still mainly for thrills. Pilots "barnstormed" the country in fragile aircraft, flying Tiger Moths or Curtiss Jennies to a farmer's field or large park and charging

Dozens of small machine shops blossomed into carmakers in the early 1900s. Sam McLaughlin's Carriage Works in Oshawa, Ontario, eventually became the giant General Motors plant that is there today.

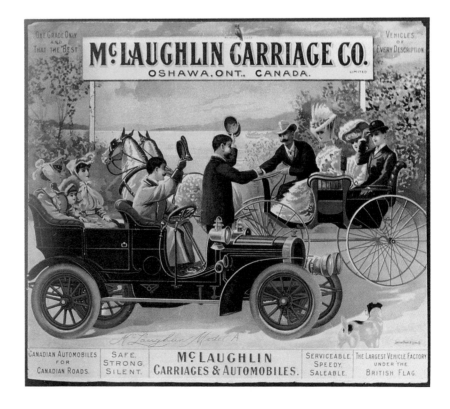

people for rides or for watching a stunt show.

Canadians continued to develop the wild places of their country. Electric companies dammed the rivers to supply hydro-electric power. Electricity was still new in many Canadian homes, and so were all the wonderful inventions that promised an easier life: vacuum cleaners, electric irons, and radios. The American economy was booming – these years were called "the Roaring Twenties" there – and Americans came north to open pulp mills, mines, and smelters. Prospectors and foresters now roamed the northern "bush" where, in the past, only fur traders and missionaries had visited the Native peoples.

Flying was the best way to get to these regions, and the 1920s became the heyday of the bush pilot. Pilots like "Wop" May came back from the war to fly small planes off lakes and clearings across the North. Flying "by the seat of their pants," they braved snow squalls, half-frozen lakes, and the constant risk of breakdown far from help. In Regina, Roland Groome and Ed Clarke started an air transport service in a field near the Saskatchewan Legislative Building. They carried mail, freight, and even passengers around the country. For a while, Canadian bush planes carried more freight than all the aircraft in the rest of the world combined.

In October 1929, Andy Cruickshank, of Western Canada Airways, joined the search for a party of explorers lost on the Arctic coast. But Cruickshank's ski-equipped Fokker airplane crashed on the ice at Bathurst Inlet. The pilot of another airplane engaged in the search saw the mishap and landed a short distance away. After desperate work in the brief daylight hours, Cruickshank and the other fliers managed to repair the plane and fly out. Soon after, they heard by radio that Inuit hunters had guided the lost explorers to safety.

Tom Thomson, West Wind.
*The paintings of Tom Thomson
and the Group of Seven gave
Canadians a whole new way
of looking at the northern land.
The paintings became so popular
they were hung in schools,
banks, and public buildings
everywhere.*

The adventures of the bush pilots encouraged
Canadians to look to the North. So did the work of new
young artists. Even before the war, Tom Thomson had
begun sketching and painting in the Ontario woods.
Whenever he could, he left the city to go canoeing and
exploring. The rocks, waters, skies, and blazing autumn
leaves inspired Thomson, and he began to paint them.
Thomson drowned in Algonquin Park in 1917, and his
overturned canoe was found floating nearby. Three years
later, Thomson's friends founded the Group of Seven. They
no longer wanted to paint in traditional, imitative styles.
They developed a bold new way to paint, and their subject
was often the lonely northland. Some people hated their

dramatic paintings – one critic called them the Hot Mush School – but in a few years the Group of Seven taught Canadians to see the savage beauty of their landscape.

One friend of the Group of Seven, an awkward young doctor and amateur painter named Frederick Banting, would become famous for something quite different. In 1921 he persuaded the University of Toronto to let him spend the summer studying diabetes, a disease that condemned thousands of young people to a slow, wasting death. With luck and skill, Banting and his team discovered the lifesaving insulin treatment. Banting and one of his colleagues won the Nobel Prize for Medicine in 1923.

In 1918 all female citizens over twenty-one had gained the right to vote in federal elections, and one province after another was granting them provincial rights as well. In 1921 Agnes Macphail became the first woman elected to the House of Commons, and in 1929, after a decade-long campaign, women were recognized as "persons" and therefore eligible to be senators and judges. The next year Cairine Wilson became Canada's first woman senator.

The Dirty Thirties

By 1929, stock-market prices were sky high. A stock represents an investment in a business, and it is worth whatever people will pay for it – which means whatever people think the business is worth. In the 1920s many people thought prosperity was just around the corner, and they wanted to put their money into stocks, so prices soared higher and higher. Then, on October 29, 1929, the market "crashed." St. James Street in Montreal was then the financial capital of Canada, and business tycoons and their brokers watched in horror as the value of their investments plunged to almost nothing. Everyone claimed to know some ruined investor who had jumped out of a window in despair. The crash sent the entire Western world into an economic crisis. Nobody wanted to buy Canada's wheat, timber, or minerals any more. The Great Depression settled over the country.

Emily Murphy

Emily Murphy was a writer, reformer, and politician at a time when few Canadian women had even one of those occupations. She was born in Ontario in 1868, and moved to Edmonton, Alberta, in 1903, with her husband, an Anglican minister. Emily Murphy wrote popular books under the pen name "Janey Canuck." She worked for women's causes, and she was appointed police magistrate for Edmonton – the first woman in the British Commonwealth to be named a judge.

On her first day on the magistrate's bench, a defence lawyer challenged her. As a woman, he said, she had no right to sit as a judge, since a woman was not legally a person. Judge Murphy and four other women, including writer Nellie McClung, spent ten years fighting the "Persons Case." In 1928, after the Supreme Court of Canada agreed that women were not legally "persons," the women appealed to England. In 1929 the British Privy Council declared that the ruling was "a relic of days more barbarous than ours," and women were finally recognized as persons.

City people lucky enough still to have jobs saw their wages cut and cut again. One family in three had neither work nor wages. There was no unemployment insurance in those years, and not much welfare. Families who had always had money to give to charity now felt the humiliation of lining up at soup kitchens for a free meal.

Men "on the bum" rode boxcars around the country in search of work. One teenage boy, riding on the roof of a boxcar rolling towards Vancouver, spotted his brother Billy on the roof of another train coming east. Billy had just come from Vancouver, but he jumped across to join his brother anyway. In the Depression years, the destination hardly mattered, since there was little work anywhere. Chasing rumours of jobs here and there, the "hoboes" fought with railway police, slept in "hobo jungles" near the railyards, and begged meals at back doors and farm gates. When they found a home that gave a meal and a little kindness, they left a mark on the fencepost to let other drifters know.

In Newfoundland fishing ports, people could at least catch some food, but Newfoundland needed to sell fish too, and few countries could afford to buy. Newfoundland, not yet part of Canada, had been a self-governing dominion, but in 1934 its government went bankrupt. The British government had to take over and manage it from London, making it a colony once again. The three Maritime provinces suffered almost as much. Once Atlantic Canada had been the richest, brightest, most go-ahead part of the country, but since Confederation it had been slipping behind. Maritimers streamed to the United States in search of work. Many were hungry and out of work in Quebec and Ontario, too. Factories closed their doors, and families were forced to live on the charity of their communities. But the Depression was not as hard on central Canada as it was on the West.

The 1930s were terrible times to be a prairie farmer. Parts of the Prairies that usually got all the rain they needed became a "dust bowl." Month after month, hot, dry winds beat against the homesteads. The topsoil turned to dust and black blizzards carried it away. Even where the crops survived, prices were so low that wheat was hardly worth harvesting. The "Golden West" of Wilfrid Laurier's day

Children from remote areas of northern Ontario in the "school train," a passenger car-turned-classroom. This photo was taken in Chapleau.

A dust storm approaches Pearce, Alberta. In the Dirty Thirties, drought did as much damage to the farms of the Prairie Provinces as the low crop prices of the Great Depression.

seemed to be drifting away like dust on the wind.

Calgary lawyer Richard Bedford Bennett became Prime Minister of Canada in 1930, soon after the Depression struck. In 1932 he established work camps run by the army, where 20 000 single men worked for twenty cents a day on backbreaking construction projects. The men hated the camps, and thousands went on strike. They and many other people who were suffering in the hard times set out by train for Ottawa to protest. Bennett did not want thousands of angry men confronting him on the steps of Parliament, and he told the police to stop the "On to Ottawa" marchers in Regina. On July 1, 1935, the police and the marchers clashed in the Regina market square, and two men were killed in the fighting.

The Dionne quintuplets from Callander, Ontario, became the world's sweethearts during the Great Depression.

What was to be done about the bad times? Every political leader had a different prescription. In 1932, J.S. Woodsworth, who had been arrested after Winnipeg's Bloody Saturday in 1919, founded the Co-operative Commonwealth Federation. The CCF wanted the government to take over the economy in the name of the people, to help people in need, and to provide work for the unemployed. In Alberta, Premier William ("Bible Bill") Aberhart preached Social Credit: let the government print money and give it to the people to spend. In Ottawa, Prime Minister Bennett promised his "New Deal" would save the day by reorganizing the economy and providing unemployment insurance. Hungry prairie families were not impressed. They hitched their scrawny horses to the cars they had bought in better times and used them as wagons. (They called these vehicles "Bennett Buggies" to let the prime minister know whom they blamed for their troubles.) In the fall of 1935, Canadians voted Bennett out of office.

He was replaced by a Liberal government headed by William Lyon Mackenzie King, who had been prime minister during most of the 1920s. (King was the grandson of William Lyon Mackenzie, a leader of the Rebellion of 1837.)

In earlier years, Canada had been less than hospitable to immigrants whose skin colour, dress, or language marked them as "different." That tendency grew stronger

The unemployed workers who formed the "On-to-Ottawa" movement to confront the politicians had no money for transportation. They simply climbed aboard boxcars. There was no trouble at Medicine Hat; but in Regina, police were gathering to prevent them from going farther.

Home from school, a boy drops his books in front of the family radio. In the 1930s, radios were larger than televisions are today.

Trick cyclists entertain at Toronto's Canadian National Exhibition in the 1930s.

in Depression days, when people were struggling to survive and competing for scarce jobs. Since 1885, Chinese immigrants had been forced to pay a humiliating fee called a "head tax" to enter Canada. In 1934, the government made a change: it decided that no Chinese at all could enter Canada. And walls were going up against other minorities. At a time when the Nazis in Germany were persecuting Jews, Canada was turning away Jewish immigrants.

In the midst of Depression hardships, Canadian Native people – even war veterans who had risked their lives for the country – were told to "live off the land" and were denied government help. At the same time, Native children were still being taken from their families and put in boarding schools where they lost touch with their traditions and were forbidden to speak their own languages. Leaders like Andrew Paull, a Squamish from British Columbia, and F.O. Loft, a war veteran from the Six Nations Reserve in southern Ontario, began organizing their people to demand respect for themselves and the rights guaranteed to them in the treaties they had signed.

Escaping from the Bad Times

In those hard times, people did not want to think about their troubles. They escaped into "dime" novels, dance parties, movies – mostly American-made movies – and radio. Gathered around their radios, families listened to many American programs, but the most popular programs came from the Canadian Broadcasting Corporation, which was created in 1936. Any family with enough money for a radio could listen to Canadian news, dance to Don Messer's country dance band, or follow football and hockey, play by play. East and West had been competing in football for the Grey Cup since 1921, but the East (which set the rules) won every year until 1935, when the Winnipeg Blue Bombers won the championship for the West.

"Hockey Night in Canada" was becoming a Saturday night tradition. Fans across the country jumped up in excitement when broadcaster Foster Hewitt screamed his catch-phrase, "He shoots! He scores!" One night in 1937, Canada's greatest hockey star of the decade, Howie Morenz, broke his leg during a game in Montreal. The injury became infected and, in those days before antibiotics, Morenz died of blood poisoning. The Montreal Canadiens held his funeral at centre-ice at the Montreal Forum, while hockey fans everywhere mourned.

War Again

In the spring of 1939, King George VI and Queen Elizabeth came to visit Canada. It was the first time a reigning monarch had toured Canada, and it was a bright moment in a dark time. In Ottawa, the king and queen dedicated the national memorial to the dead of the First World War. They travelled across the country by train, stopping in

Doctor Bethune

In 1936, a small band of Canadians called the Mackenzie-Papineau Battalion went off to fight a dictatorship in the civil war that was then raging in Spain. Dr. Norman Bethune, from Gravenhurst, Ontario, also went to Spain to help in the war. Bethune invented a blood-transfusion system that, for the first time, could deliver blood to wounded men right on the battlefield. Although the Mac-Paps were on the losing side in the Spanish Civil War, Bethune's blood transfusions saved many lives.

Bethune went off to another war, this time in China, where he worked for the rebel Communist army of Mao Zedong. He not only assisted the sick and wounded, he also taught and invented new medical procedures. But in the fall of 1939, operating without surgical gloves because medical supplies were scarce, he got blood poisoning and died.

Mao Zedong wrote an essay, "In Memory of Norman Bethune," in which he told his followers that they should all have Bethune's devotion to other people. When Mao's Communist party took power in China, he made sure that the Canadian doctor was known all over the country as a great hero. Canada has been known in China from that day as the home of Dr. Norman Bethune.

Norman Bethune
in Canada / au Canada
诺尔曼·白求恩在加拿大
CANADA
39

In 1940, Warren Bernard, age five, says goodbye to his father, Private Jack Bernard, as the British Columbia Regiment marches through New Westminster, B.C., on its way to the war.

In 1940, when Britain's cities were being bombed, thousands of British children were evacuated to Canada to spend the war years in safety with Canadian families. After the war was over, some returned here to live.

all the cities along the way. In smaller towns, the train slowed while the royal couple waved to people from the rear platform.

Only a few months later, Canada went to war again. Dictatorial regimes which glorified war and conquest ruled Germany, Italy, and Japan, and in the late 1930s they began attacking their weaker neighbours. On September 1, 1939, Adolf Hitler's German army invaded Poland, and Britain declared war on Germany. This time Canada decided for itself whether to go to war. Most Canadians agreed that the dictators had to be stopped, but there was not much cheering. Remembering the terrible times of 1914–1918, Canada went grimly into the war on September 10, 1939. This time, no one thought it would all be over in a few weeks.

After crushing Poland, Germany occupied Denmark, Norway, Luxembourg, The Netherlands, and Belgium. In June 1940 France also surrendered, leaving Britain without European allies. Canada was Britain's chief ally against the dictators for more than a year. But in 1941 Germany invaded the Soviet Union, which then joined the fight against Hitler. The Soviet Union's Joseph Stalin was a ruthless dictator, but because he was fighting the Nazis "Uncle Joe" became a hero in Canadian eyes. At the end of 1941, when Japanese bombers attacked the American naval base at Pearl Harbor in Hawaii, the United States joined the Allies and the war became a global struggle.

"My King and Queen"

by Alixe Hambleton, who remembers the visit.

I was nine years old when King George and Queen Elizabeth came to Regina. It was May 25, 1939, a lovely, warm spring day. Children from all the neighbouring towns and villages, like my town of Lumsden, were taken to the exhibition grounds to see them. Dressed in our best, complete with medals hung on red, white, and blue ribbons, we lined up around the racetrack. We all had flags to wave.

At last the king and queen arrived. They were driven slowly around the track in an open car. The king wore a suit. The queen wore a blue coat over a dress, and a hat with plumes. We cheered and waved our flags. They smiled and waved at us.

Afterwards, I had lunch with my parents in a restaurant. "They didn't look anything like a king and queen." I sighed. "They looked ordinary."

After lunch, Mother and I went shopping. Dad had business to do, so we met at another restaurant for dinner. Two restaurants and ice cream for dessert after dinner all in one day – a rare treat in 1939!

"We have one more stop to make," my father said. "Wait and see," was the only answer I got when I asked about it. We went to the railway station and my father said something to one of the railway officials. The man smiled at me and led us outside to the train yard and over the tracks to where the royal train was standing.

We didn't have to wait long. Suddenly all the lights in the station yard went on. Then the king and queen appeared on the observation platform of the last car of their train, not a dozen metres from where we stood. The king was in full dress suit with all his medals on his chest. And the queen had on a beautiful long white brocade gown with the blue sash of the Order of the Garter across it. On her head she had a diamond tiara. They really looked like a king and queen. Not at all ordinary. They waved, then the train was off down the track.

My father had spent the afternoon finding out when the royal train was leaving and whether the royal couple would be on the observation platform after their formal reception at the Saskatchewan Hotel. I've never forgotten my father's gift of my king and queen.

During the Second World War, Canadians went all over the world to fight by land, sea, and air. In 1941, Canadian soldiers sailed away to defend the British colony of Hong Kong. After the Japanese army overran the colony, more than 500 Canadians died horribly, in battle or in the prison camps. Most Canadian soldiers, however, went to Britain. The army trained there, waiting for a chance to liberate Europe. Farley Mowat, a young soldier in the Canadian Army's First Division, wrote: "The troops fought imaginary battles in the English fields and lanes until they grew numb with fatigue." The soldiers complained about the cold and the damp and the food, and many swore that after the war they would never eat Brussels sprouts again.

On August 19, 1942, 5000 Canadian soldiers crossed the English Channel to attack a little town on the French coast called Dieppe. The Allied generals had hoped to seize the town for a day, but when the Canadians landed

The battle of Dieppe is shown in vivid detail in Charles Comfort's painting Dieppe Raid.

on the stony beaches under the cliffs of Dieppe, the Germans were waiting in fortified bunkers that bristled with guns. It was a disaster for the Allies, and a tragedy for Canada. Barely 2000 Canadian soldiers got safely back to England that night.

In July 1943, the First Canadian Division – with General Guy Simonds in command – invaded Sicily alongside British and American soldiers. In September 1943 Italy surrendered, but the many German troops in Italy fought on. Soon the Canadians were grateful for what they had learned while training in those "imaginary battles" in England. They marched and fought from the scorching heat of Sicily to the mud and rain and snow of northern Italy. The Moro River, Regalbuto, Rimini, and Ortona became Canadian battlefields as memorable as Vimy and Passchendaele in the First World War.

During the grim battle for the Italian town of Ortona, where more than 2000 Canadians were killed or wounded, Captain Paul Triquet and his company fought for seven hours to capture the farm of Casa Berardi at the town's gateway. Only Triquet and 14 of his 81 men were still alive when they captured it – and then the Germans counter-attacked. "*Ils ne passeront pas!* [They shall not pass!]" became Triquet's rallying cry, as he and his men held out for nine more hours – losing 5 more men – before Canadian reinforcements arrived. Triquet was awarded the Victoria Cross.

This Second World War recruiting poster hoped to convince prospective soldiers that joining the war effort was the noble thing to do.

At Sea and in the Air

All through the war, Canadian warships rolled and pitched through the North Atlantic, guarding the convoys of ships that were Britain's lifeline of supplies and troops. The first convoy sailed out of Halifax in September 1939, escorted by two Canadian destroyers. That convoy crossed the Atlantic safely, but soon German submarines called U-boats (from the German *Unterseeboote*) were sinking hundreds of Allied ships. Some nights the naval escorts chased

Paul Goranson, Dorsal Gunner. *Thousands of Canadians flew as gunners, navigators, pilots, bombardiers, and radio operators on night missions over German territory. This gunner is aboard a two-engined Wellington bomber.*

desperately after submarines they could not see, as tankers and freighters exploded and burned around them. In one terrible three-day running battle off Greenland in 1943, HMCS *St. Croix* was struck by a torpedo and sank. Her captain and most of the crew went down with her. Another ship plucked a few survivors from the water, but it too was torpedoed, and only three sailors survived – including one who had come from the *St. Croix.*

Sometimes the navy had to fight within sight of home, when German U-boats sailed into the Gulf and up the St. Lawrence River to torpedo ships and to land spies. One U-boat even sank the passenger ferry *Caribou* on its route between Nova Scotia and Newfoundland, killing 137 passengers and crew.

Many Canadian sailors served in small ships called corvettes, and fought the rough seas of the North Atlantic as hard as they fought the German submarines. "Corvettes roll in a heavy dew," sailors said. Wet, cold, frightened, and crowded, they sailed from Halifax, Sydney, or "Newfiejohn" (St. John's) to get the convoys through to Britain. Canada had started the war with a very small navy, but by the end of the war it had the fourth-largest navy in the world.

Secret Agents

Sergeant-Major Lucien Dumais of Montreal landed on the beach at Dieppe with the Fusiliers Mont-Royal on August 19, 1942. More than a hundred of the Fusiliers died there that day, and Dumais was captured. But on the way to a prisoner-of-war camp in Germany, Dumais jumped from the train and escaped. Although France was occupied by German troops, French civilians helped him make his way to the coast, and he got safely back to England.

Dumais's war was far from over, for he volunteered to go back to France as a secret agent. In November 1943, a small plane dropped him and another Canadian, Raymond Labrosse, in northern France. Soon they had created an escape network for Allied flyers who were shot down in France.

Dumais, Labrosse, and their French comrades made false papers for the flyers. Some they led into Spain. Many of them they guided to the coast, then radioed for small boats that slipped across the Channel from England to pick up the escapees. If they were caught they would be shot. In all, 307 flyers escaped along the network, and Dumais and Labrosse never lost a man.

In 1940, Canadians were among the handful of fighter pilots in sleek Hurricanes and Spitfires who defended Britain against waves of German air attacks. More flyers later served in four-engined bombers that targeted German cities and factories. Thirty bombing missions were a "tour of duty," but long before their tours were done, many young Canadians were blown out of the sky. Some managed to parachute behind enemy lines, and French, Dutch, or Belgian families hid them and helped them to safety. One of the 10000 who died was Andrew Mynarski of Winnipeg. He was about to parachute to safety when he saw one of his fellow crewmen trapped in their burning plane. Mynarski fought unsuccessfully to free him, and he jumped only when his own clothes were aflame. Mynarski died of his burns, but the trapped gunner rode the bomber to the ground and lived.

Another Canadian contribution to the air war took place on this side of the Atlantic. Because the country had the wide-open spaces that novice flyers needed – and because it was far away from hostile action – Canada became, in the words of the American president, Franklin Roosevelt, "the aerodrome of democracy." At places like Debert, Summerside, and Chatham in the Maritimes, St-Hubert and Hagersville in central Canada, and Gimli, Weyburn, High River, and Patricia Bay in the West, Canadians and other British Commonwealth airmen learned to be pilots, navigators, gunners, and bombardiers. The training was fast. Those who passed got their wings and went overseas to war.

Prime Minister William Lyon Mackenzie King – and Pat.

On the Home Front

Canada's wartime prime minister was William Lyon Mackenzie King, a fussy bachelor. Although no one knew it at the time, King used a crystal ball to ask his dead mother for advice. Fortunately, he ignored her "ideas" when he disagreed with them.

In the first years of the war, all of Canada's soldiers

were volunteers. King did not want the country – and his Liberal Party – to be divided over conscription as it had been in the First World War. "Parliament will decide," he liked to say when he wanted to avoid making some decision. If Canadians were drafted, he declared, they would serve at home, not in the fighting overseas. "Zombies," the fighting soldiers called these conscripts contemptuously. Later King added, "Not necessarily conscription, but conscription if necessary." Finally, in 1944, the army was desperate for fighting men, and Parliament changed the rules. Sixteen thousand "Zombies" were sent to fight in Europe. But although there was bitterness on both sides of the conscription debate, King's delaying tactics may have kept the country from suffering a conscription crisis even more divisive than the one during the previous war.

Many German and Italian prisoners of war were shipped to camps in Canada. Only one German prisoner, Lieutenant Franz von Werra, ever escaped from Canada. He jumped from a train near Prescott, Ontario, and crossed the border, then fled through the United States to Mexico. "The one that got away" got all the way back to Germany, only to be killed in action later in the war.

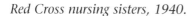

Red Cross nursing sisters, 1940.

Hanorie Umiarjuaq

She was a tough little ship with a tough skipper. The *St. Roch* was a floating RCMP station that patrolled the far northern islands of Arctic Canada. Her skipper was Sergeant Henry Larsen, a Norwegian Canadian who must have had the blood of Norse adventurers in his veins. The Inuit called him "Hanorie Umiarjuaq," meaning "Henry with the big ship." Skipper Larsen and the *St. Roch* cruised the northern waters for twenty-two years, from 1928 to 1950.

In 1940, during the Second World War, Skipper Larsen got the exciting orders he wanted. He was to leave Vancouver and sail for Halifax, through the Northwest Passage. The Norwegian explorer Roald Amundsen had sailed the passage from east to west, but no one had ever gone west to east.

Two years later, after three summers of sailing and two dark winters locked in Arctic ice, the *St. Roch* lay trapped in the ice floes of Bellot Strait. The strait is thirty kilometres long and barely one kilometre wide, with sheer cliffs towering on either side. Larsen was beginning to fear they would have to pass another long winter in the ice.

Then the tide began to drive the ice floes and the *St. Roch* forward. Faster and faster they raced along. The pressure of ice on the hull was immense, and the ship groaned and twisted, but the timbers held and soon the *St. Roch* shot out into clear water. In six weeks she was in Halifax.

In 1944 Larsen and the *St. Roch* set out again, and went east to west through the Northwest Passage in just eighty-six days, the first ship to do the voyage both ways. In 1950 the *St. Roch* sailed south and became the first ship to go right around North America. Today the stalwart little *St. Roch* is on display at the Maritime Museum in Vancouver.

Women as well as men went into uniform. They persuaded the air force and the army to form women's corps, and finally the navy did too. Forty-five thousand women joined the forces during the war. "My parents were rather upset – they felt the army was no place for a girl!" recalled one woman who enlisted in 1942 at the age of twenty. Generals and admirals often felt the same. The services never paid women what men received, and they tried to keep them in "women's jobs" as typists or cooks.

A postman delivering ration books to the Brocketts of London, Ontario, in 1942. During the war many foods, clothing, gasoline, and tires were rationed.

Paraskeva Clark was one of dozens of Canadian artists who painted Canada at war. Maintenance Jobs in the Hangar *shows women working on the Harvard trainers that would be used to train pilots for service overseas, and in Canada, too.*

Yet one father who had been wounded at Vimy Ridge in 1917 said it was the "proudest moment of his life" when his daughter enlisted in the forces. Women did become pilots, codebreakers, and mechanics, and 7000 women served in Europe. Seventy-one were killed by German bombing.

Many more women – 800 000 of them – remained civilians and went into offices and factories during the war. Some of them studied to become mechanics, welders, and electricians, but most working women learned a trade on the job, where they got less pay and less chance of promotion than men did. Nevertheless, so many women went to work in factories during the war that, for the first time, industries started daycare centres to look after their children. For the first time, women drove city buses and taxis, and took over many other jobs that had always been called men's work.

The Canadian economy was going full tilt, producing food, weapons, and equipment for the war. There was a great effort not to waste anything, and every hand was needed. Even children pitched in, collecting paper and

scrap metal. Old fur coats were made into warm vests for Canadian sailors, and anyone buying toothpaste had to turn in the old tube for recycling. Even old bones were collected, to make glue and explosives.

After Japan entered the war and bombed Pearl Harbor, British Columbians were terrified of a Japanese invasion. They vented their fear and rage on the 22000 Japanese Canadians, accusing them of being spies and enemy agents. Most Japanese Canadians lived along British Columbia's Pacific coast. In 1942, these families were rounded up and sent to camps far inland – even though many of these people were Canadian citizens, and many had never even been to Japan. Then the government seized and sold off their houses, cars, fishing boats, and all their property. British Columbia's Japanese-Canadian community was destroyed. Hardly anyone protested. "There's a war on," people said, to excuse this ruthless action. The Japanese Canadians did not receive reparations and an apology from the Canadian government for the injury done to them until 1989.

At Slocan, B.C., Japanese Canadians forcibly removed from the British Columbia coast in 1942 struggle off an open truck with the few belongings left to them.

June 6, 1944

D day, 7:00 a.m., at Juno Beach, Normandy. As a torpedo boat roars past, a landing craft crowded with soldiers of the Royal Winnipeg Rifles rumbles toward the coast of France. The machine guns of the enemy await them.

All night, bombers had pounded the enemy fortifications on the shore. As dawn broke, ships like HMCS *Algonquin* of the Canadian navy began to fire shells at hundreds of targets. But only the infantry could finish the job. Thousands of soldiers had to leave their transport ships and head ashore in smaller landing craft.

The landing craft carrying the soldiers rolled and lurched in two-metre waves. The enemy began firing furiously when the Royal Winnipegs were still 700 metres from Juno Beach. Some landing craft blew up and sank, some were trapped by hidden obstacles beneath the surf. But at 7:49 a.m. the Royal Winnipegs hit the beach and raced through the enemy gunfire. The soldiers entered the French town of Courseulles, then pushed on inland.

The soldiers of the Royal Winnipeg Rifles, along with the rest of the Canadian, British, and American regiments, paid a terrible price that morning of June 6, 1944 – but the Allies had begun the liberation of Europe.

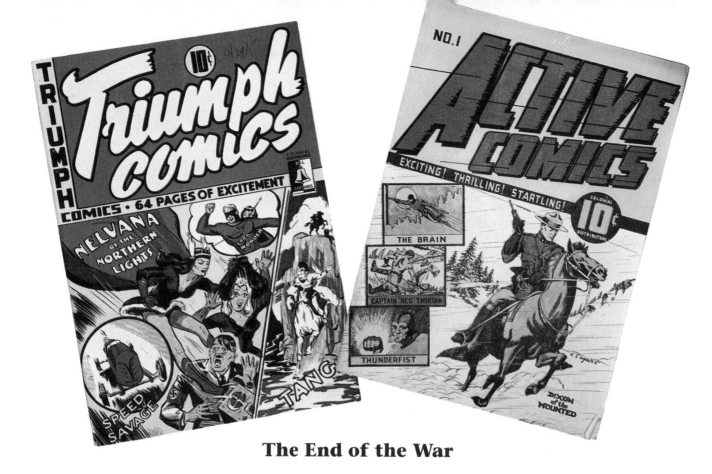

The End of the War

In wartime comics, Canadian superheroes like Dixon of the Mounted and Nelvana of the Northern Lights battled Nazis and saboteurs in every issue of Active *and* Triumph *comics.*

At dawn on June 6, 1944 – D day – the Allied forces launched a massive invasion of German-occupied France. As part of an immense operation that used 7000 ships and 11 000 aircraft, the Canadians fought their way ashore on "Juno Beach," one of the five D-day landing beaches in Normandy, France. The Western Allies advanced slowly towards Germany, while the army of the Soviet Union pushed in on the Germans from the east. Early in 1945, the Canadians liberated most of The Netherlands from German occupation. They reached Amsterdam at the end of the "hunger winter," during which thousands of people had died of illness, cold, and starvation. With the Canadians came food and medical supplies. The country welcomed them with wild celebrations.

Caught between the Western Allies on one side and the Russians on the other, Germany was finally defeated. Adolf Hitler killed himself and Germany surrendered in May 1945. But the war with Japan was still going on. Twenty thousand Canadian soldiers were ordered to the Pacific, and sixty ships of the Canadian navy headed there as well. Then the United States dropped a secret weapon the Allies had been working on all through the war: the atomic bomb. The first bomb fell on the Japanese city of Hiroshima on August 6, 1945. In an instant, the city vanished beneath a rolling, boiling mushroom cloud. For the first time, a nuclear weapon had destroyed a city and its people in a single deadly flash of radiation and fire. Three days later, a second bomb destroyed the seaport of Nagasaki. Japan surrendered at once, and the Second World War was over.

In the spring of 1945, as they fought their way across Europe, driving the Germans out, Canadian soldiers confronted horrors worse than those they had shared on the battlefield. When they liberated the concentration camps, they found them crowded with heaped bodies and starving survivors – and grisly relics of victims gassed and cremated. Hitler's Nazis had planned to create a "master race," and they had set out to murder all the Jews of Europe, and many other groups as well. At least six million people had died in the concentration camps, and Canadians began to realize that some of those people had been turned back from Canadian shores in the years before the war. Now, at last, thousands of death-camp survivors were admitted to Canada as refugees. So were other Europeans, whose homes and families had been shattered by the fighting.

As the war ended, the Soviet Union and its Western allies quickly became rivals. British war leader Winston Churchill said that an "Iron Curtain" had fallen across Europe, dividing the wartime allies into Communists in the East and non-Communists in the West. The "Cold War" was about to begin. But Canadians were rejoicing over the end of the Second World War. And after three stormy decades, they were also about to enter a time of prosperity and hope at home.

Thousands of Canadian soldiers who went overseas married British and Dutch women. In 1946 nearly 50 000 women and 22 000 children, like these aboard ship, followed the soldiers to new lives in Canada.

Chapter 10
The Flying Years

D OWN BY THE FRASER RIVER IN RICHMOND, B.C., KIDS DROPPED THEIR bikes and crowded along the fence at the end of the Sea Island Airport runway. It was June 1, 1948, and the North Star was coming in.

The North Star was Trans-Canada Airlines' brand-new passenger plane, and it was making its first Montreal-to-Vancouver flight. TCA had made the very first passenger flight across Canada just nine years earlier. That trip had taken more than a day, and passengers had had to wear oxygen masks while the Lockheed Electra struggled over the Rockies. Now the North Star's four powerful engines cut the flight to thirteen hours, and the airplane carried forty passengers high above the clouds in a pressurized cabin. It was the biggest, fastest, most luxurious passenger aircraft Canadians had seen – and it had been built in Canada.

In the years after the Second World War, Canada was flying high. Air travel made it possible to leap across continents and oceans. At Chalk River, Ontario, scientists were making electricity, using a nuclear reactor. In Saskatoon, Professor Harold Johns developed the cobalt radiation "bomb" that targeted cancerous tumours. The fearsome scientific discoveries that had won the war seemed to promise a better future in peacetime.

When the war ended in 1945, more than a million men and women came out of the armed forces. Half of the men, and about 7000 women, had been overseas, and almost 50000 of them had married "war brides" (or "grooms", in a few cases) while they were there. In May 1946, four trains of ten cars each left Montreal, filled with brides going to new families and husbands whom many barely knew.

Many war brides found it hard to adjust to their new homes and to Canadians, who seemed so different. A few took "the thousand-dollar cure" – a trip back home that convinced them Canada offered more than war-ravaged Europe.

When Farley Mowat came home from the war, he was happy to turn in his infantry badges for a set of textbooks

Previous pages:
Ottawa's Parliament Hill
has been the site of many
demonstration marches and
protest gatherings, as Canadians
exercise their right to dissent.

and a jam-packed classroom at the University of Toronto. Canada was helping "vets" (war veterans) pay for homes or for schooling. Mowat was one of thousands who were eager to get an education and become doctors, lawyers, and business people – or even, like Mowat, writers. Despite their years of war, many of them were barely out of their teens.

Canadians came out of the Second World War proud of what they had done as a nation. They also remembered the hard times after the previous war, and the agonizing Depression of the thirties, when each region of the country had seemed to suffer on its own. Now more prosperous times had come.

The DC-4 North Star, built by Canadair at Montreal, was the workhorse of the trans-Canadian air routes in the late 1940s and early 1950s.

Proud Growing Regions

In British Columbia, returning veterans found plenty of work cutting timber, refining minerals into precious resources, or catching and canning salmon. By the early 1950s, B.C. had a brash new premier, W.A.C. Bennett, who loved to brag about the way his province was growing. His rivals called him "Wacky," but, wacky or not, Bennett governed the province for twenty years. British Columbians built roads through the mountains, launched ferries to ply the coastal waters, and dammed their wild rivers for electric power. Bennett loved to flash his beaming smile and talk of "Beautiful British Columbia." He told British Columbians that their province was a paradise, and that they were envied by people who had to live anywhere else.

Farley Mowat Meets a Wolf

After the Second World War, Farley Mowat became a naturalist and a writer. The Canadian government sent him to the barrenlands of northern Manitoba to study wolves. Wolves, he was told, were fierce, pitiless killers, and unless they were destroyed they would slaughter the caribou herds. So, even when he heard what seemed to be a young cub crying for its lost mother, Mowat approached cautiously:

As I neared the crest of the ridge I got down on my stomach (practicing the fieldcraft I had learned in the Boy Scouts) and cautiously inched my way the last few feet.

My head came slowly over the crest – and there was my quarry. He was lying down, evidently resting after his mournful singsong, and his nose was about six feet from mine. We stared at one another in silence. I do not know what went on in his massive skull, but my head was full of the most disturbing thoughts. I was peering straight into the amber gaze of a fully grown arctic wolf, who probably weighed more than I did, and who was certainly a lot better versed in close-combat techniques than I would ever be.

For some seconds neither of us moved but continued to stare hypnotically into one another's eyes. The wolf was the first to break the spell. With a spring which would have done justice to a Russian dancer, he leaped about a yard straight into the air and came down running. The textbooks say a wolf can run twenty-five miles an hour, but this one did not appear to be running, so much as flying low. Within seconds he had vanished from my sight.

My own reaction was not so dramatic, although I may very well have set some sort of a record for a cross-country traverse myself. My return over the river was accomplished with such verve that I paddled the canoe almost her full length up on the beach on the other side. Then, remembering my responsibilities to my scientific supplies, I entered the cabin, barred the door, and regardless of the discomfort caused by the stench of the debris on the floor made myself as comfortable as I could on top of the table for the balance of the short-lived night.

It had been a strenuous interlude, but I could congratulate myself that I had, at last, established contact – no matter how briefly – with the study species.

In his fine and funny book *Never Cry Wolf*, Mowat tells how he gradually learned to appreciate the wolf. It was hunters, not wolves, who were killing off the caribou – and the wolf as well.

Throughout his life, Farley Mowat has celebrated the land and the animals of Canada, and those people who live in harmony with them. Long before the "environment" became a popular cause, his books exposed the cruel and destructive ways our society treats nature.

After the war, the Prairie Provinces were finally able to shake off the twenty terrible years of the Dustbowl and the Depression. In Alberta, an oil well "blowout" at Leduc announced the start of a new era. Oil prospectors had drilled 133 dry holes around Leduc before they struck oil in February 1947. They renamed that hole Leduc Number One, and soon 1200 more productive wells "came in" to join it. Alberta discovered that the oil business had the rowdy excitement of the old cowboy days – and there was

William Kurelek, Manitoba Party. *Kurelek painted a magical series of pictures re-creating the simple joys of a prairie boy's childhood.*

Nineteen-year-old champion Barbara Ann Scott, from Ottawa, was the country's most popular celebrity after she won the Olympic gold medal in figure skating in 1948.

Tommy Douglas, one of the first socialists to win political power in Canada, was premier of Saskatchewan and then national leader of the New Democratic Party.

more money in it. Oilmen from Texas came up to Calgary to drill for oil and gas and to build pipelines to transport them. Alberta became the home of a try-anything, free-wheeling style of doing things, in business and in government.

The farmers of Saskatchewan, after all the hard years of struggling together against duststorms and low prices, preferred co-operation to competing for wealth in Alberta's risk-taking style. Saskatchewan had pioneered in creating co-operative businesses, owned by the farmers who used them, to ship grain and bring in supplies. In 1944 it elected Canada's first socialist government, led by a wise-cracking, passionate Baptist minister named Tommy Douglas. Douglas's government introduced new social services, including Canada's first medicare plan, run by the government and available to all. Later, Douglas was elected national leader of the New Democratic Party, which became Canada's third-largest political party.

In Ontario and Quebec, factory gates opened wide to the returning veterans. In the small town of Oakville, Ontario, the Ford Motor Company opened a huge automobile plant, and for a while Oakville was the richest town in Canada. In Hamilton, Ontario, steel mills rolled out the steel for Alberta's oil pipelines. Quebec also had new factories. General Motors built an auto plant in Ste-Thérèse, and gleaming North Star aircraft rolled out of a plant in Montreal. For nearly a century Ontario had had many factories making goods for the whole country, but such industries were newer in Quebec, and they brought many changes.

In the 1940s and 1950s, Premier Maurice Duplessis ruled Quebec. Duplessis assured French-speaking Quebeckers that the Catholic Church and the family farm would preserve their French-Canadian way of life in the midst of English-speaking North America. His iron hand came down hard on anyone who wanted to change things. His ideal Quebec was a place where people lived on farms, obeyed their priests, and raised big families. But not all Quebeckers were like that. Many were leaving the farms to work in

big cities or mining towns. Instead of living the way their
ancestors had always done, Quebeckers were starting to live
much the way people did all over North America. Duplessis
made Quebec look changeless during those years, but
changes were brewing underneath.

The biggest change in Atlantic Canada came in Newfoundland and Labrador. Newfoundland's government had
collapsed, bankrupt, in 1935, and the colony was again
being run by Britain. During the war, the island had been
vital to Allied air and naval forces. But what would Newfoundland do now the war was over? "Join Canada!" urged
Joseph Smallwood, an unsuccessful pig-farmer who had
become a popular radio host. "Joey" burned with the
conviction that Newfoundlanders had to join the modern
world. The way to do it, he declared, was to become
Canada's tenth province. Newfoundlanders were not so
certain – old cries about the "Canadian wolf" were raised
again. Some wanted Newfoundland to remain proudly
alone, while others wanted to join the United States. After
fierce debates that kept nearly everyone on the island glued
to the radio, Newfoundlanders agreed to have a referendum,
or general vote, on whether they would join Canada.

Smallwood and the Confederation forces barely
won the referendum, and Newfoundland and Labrador
became Canada's tenth province in 1949. Smallwood, a
new "Father of Confederation," became Premier of Newfoundland. He would hold the office for more than twenty
years. As part of his plan to bring Newfoundland into the
modern world, he urged his people to burn their fishing
boats and to work in mills and factories instead. Like many
people in the 1950s, he believed that prosperity was just
around the corner.

At midnight on March 31, 1949, Louis St. Laurent
welcomed Newfoundland into Confederation. St. Laurent,
who was nicknamed "Uncle Louis" (though he was rather
cold and stiff in public), had become prime minister when
Mackenzie King retired in 1948, and he led Canada into
the prosperous 1950s. Now that the country could afford
it, Ottawa moved ahead with unemployment insurance,

*After a narrow win in a stormy
campaign to settle Newfoundland's future, Joseph Smallwood
signed the document making
Newfoundland the tenth province
of Canada in 1949.*

old-age pensions, and "baby bonus" payments. If hard times like the 1930s ever came again, there would be a "safety net" of government programs to protect people against suffering.

Canada in the Wide World

Canadian diplomat Lester Pearson won the Nobel Peace Prize for his work in creating the first United Nations peacekeeping force. Pearson went on to be Prime Minister of Canada.

In the 1950s, Canada liked to call itself a "middle power": not the biggest, but not the smallest, either. It had played an important part in the war, and it expected to continue in the same way in peacetime. Canada helped Europe recover from the damage done by the war, and shared in the founding of a new world organization, the United Nations, to help the world's nations work together more effectively. In 1950, Canada helped to create the Colombo Plan, in which the wealthier countries of the British Commonwealth promised to help the poorer ones to develop their economies. This was the start of Canada's foreign aid program.

In 1956, when war erupted over control of the Suez Canal in Egypt, Canadian diplomat Lester Pearson led the way in creating the first United Nations peacekeeping force, and another Canadian, General E.L.M. Burns, led the peacekeepers who stood between the warring sides. Pearson won the Nobel Peace Prize for his work on the Suez crisis, and in 1958 he succeeded Louis St. Laurent as leader of the Liberal Party.

Canadian soldiers would serve on many more United Nations peace missions, but peacekeeping could not make the world a safe place. Soon after the war, Canada became part of a deep, fierce rivalry that divided East from West. The Soviet Union, or U.S.S.R., born in the Russian Revolution of 1917, had become a great power during its battle against Nazi Germany. When the war ended, its armies imposed Communist dictatorships on the nations of Eastern Europe. Germany itself was split into two parts, with the eastern part under Soviet control. The U.S.S.R. promised these states prosperity, and it preached Communist revolution to the rest of the world.

In 1945, Igor Gouzenko, a clerk at the Soviet Union's embassy in Ottawa, fled from the embassy with his wife and children. He carried proof that Soviet spies were at work in Canada and the United States, prying into military secrets and trying to learn details about the atom bomb. At first, no one in Ottawa would believe him, and the Soviets nearly recaptured him. But when the public in Canada and around the world heard his story, fear of Communist spies and secret agents began to grow. By 1949, when Mao Zedong led a peasant army to victory over the corrupt government of China and made China a Communist state, many in the West (Canada, Western Europe, the United States, and their allies) feared that Communism might take over the world the way Hitler and the Nazis had tried to do. Just four years after defeating the Nazi conquest, the Western world began arming itself against Communism.

No one knew what Igor Gouzenko looked like. After he exposed Soviet spying in 1945 and 1946, he wore a disguise to protect himself from revenge. In 1954 he wrote a novel about the Soviet Union.

In 1949, Canada and eleven other Western nations founded NATO, the North Atlantic Treaty Organization, for their mutual self-defence, and Canadian troops went back to Europe once again. All along the borders dividing Eastern Europe from the West, the armies of the Soviet Union and the NATO allies faced each other. Year after year, as politicians blustered and manoeuvred, the world watched to see if fighting would erupt. This tense, dangerous stand-off was called "the Cold War."

In 1950, war between Communists and anti-Communists broke out in the Asian nation of Korea. Canada sent ships and soldiers as part of the U.N. forces. In April 1951, a handful of soldiers from a regiment called the Princess Patricia's Canadian Light Infantry became the first Canadian ground troops to fight in Korea. Chinese troops were driving the United Nations forces southward when the Princess Pat's dug in on Hill 677 to defend the southern capital, Seoul. The South Korean soldiers had been beaten farther north, and as they came streaming back in retreat, the Canadians confronted a Chinese army.

The Princess Pat's spent the night of April 24–25 outnumbered and surrounded, but they held Hill 677 in

Under a camouflage net, a Canadian soldier gets some sleep on the engine of his tank beside the Imjin River in Korea. Canadian soldiers have earned an unmatched record for their services to United Nations peace-keeping forces all over the world.

terrifying hand-to-hand fights against waves of attackers. In the morning the enemy advance slowed and stopped. Reinforcements from Canada's allies came up, and the lines around Seoul held. But it had been a near thing. In the end, the Korean War wound down into a kind of truce in 1953. The Canadians came home, except for the five hundred who died there.

Canadian forces also went into the Arctic. During the Cold War, Canadians and Americans feared that Soviet bombers might suddenly swoop over the North Pole to attack their countries. To defend North America, they built the twenty-two radar stations of the DEW (Distant Early Warning) Line, more than 8000 kilometres long. There were terrible new weapons in the world. Both the United States and the U.S.S.R. had atomic bombs like those that had obliterated Hiroshima in 1945, and soon scientists made even more powerful hydrogen bombs. Long-range bombers could drop them anywhere, and if either side started a war, the other would immediately retaliate. Aircraft, missiles, and submarines stood on alert night and day, waiting for the dreadful orders that could level whole cities. People everywhere began to realize that nuclear war could destroy the world. That fear – the "balance of terror" – kept both sides from launching a nuclear attack, all through the Cold War.

Home in the Suburbs

Boom! In the 1950s, the population exploded. At least, it seemed that way. Hard times and war had kept Canadians from having big families in the 1930s and 1940s. But in the "baby boom" years, streets, schools, and playgrounds were crowded with more kids than anyone could remember. The millions of children born between the Second World War and 1960 became adults between the late 1960s and the 1980s, and they made a bulge in the population.

Four million Canadian babies were born in the 1950s, and many families needed new homes. Few homes had

been built in the 1930s, when no one had money to build or buy them, and during the war materials and workmen had been scarce. In the 1950s, Canada went on a building spree, producing more than a million new houses in ten years. In a few years, the shape of Canadian cities changed completely.

Don Mills, eight hundred hectares of farmland a few miles up the Don River from Toronto, was built as a new kind of community, the model Canadian "suburb." In Don Mills, the working bustle of the city seemed far away. Everyone lived in bungalows with big "picture windows" that looked out over wide lawns to curving streets where children played street hockey. Soon suburbs were sprouting around every city in the country – Fraserview and Surrey near Vancouver, Wildwood near Winnipeg, Cowie Hill and Sackville outside Halifax.

One of Canada's first pop stars, Paul Anka was sixteen when he first had a big hit, with "Diana," a song about his babysitter in Ottawa.

For people who had to live downtown or couldn't afford a house, there was another new kind of home, the "high-rise." Tall apartment towers sprouted like forests in downtown Vancouver and Toronto, housing far more people than the old low-rise buildings – but also making city crowding and traffic jams worse. Old neighbourhoods close to downtown were bulldozed for "public housing" apartment buildings. New and modern seemed better than old and traditional in the 1950s, and many useful, well-built buildings – a record in brick and stone of the country's history – were demolished just because they needed repairs or were out of fashion.

In every playground, the hula hoop was the hottest trend of the late 1950s. It was not an easy task to keep four hula hoops spinning at once, but this girl seems to be a real champion.

Instead of shopping downtown on Main Street, suburban Canadians headed for another invention of the 1950s: the shopping centre. Park Royal, in West Vancouver, claimed to be Canada's first shopping centre, but soon every suburb had one. At first a shopping centre meant a row of stores facing a parking lot, but soon the centres turned indoors and became malls.

As the cities spread out into suburbs, more people needed cars. Canadians bought three million cars in the fifties. A big, bright new Ford or a Chevrolet with swooping fins and plenty of chrome was often the first car a family

Cars of the American "Big Three" automakers, many of which were made at Windsor, Oakville, or Oshawa, Ontario, ruled the roads in the 1950s. Fins, chrome, and gadgets were the fashion.

had ever owned. Gasoline was cheap, and the whole country seemed to be on wheels. Canadians drove to work, to the shopping centre, the drive-in movie, the hamburger stand, and to the cottage or camp. For the first time, many Canadians – not just wealthy ones – took vacations away from home.

The country's first superhighway, the Queen Elizabeth Way from Toronto to the U.S border, had opened just before the war. In the fifties and sixties, the exit ramps, interchanges, and overpasses of superhighways blossomed around every big city. The federal government and the provinces got together to build the Trans-Canada Highway from St. John's to Victoria. Trains still hauled freight and grain across the country, but the day of the railway was passing, and soon passenger trains would be running half empty. If Canadians couldn't travel by air, they wanted to go by highway.

Canadians became "consumers." They had money to spend on cars and appliances and all kinds of gadgets and hobbies. Most of them had grown up with electric light and power, but now they could afford to fill their new homes with freezers, convenience foods, washer-dryers, and "hi-fi" record players. Most of the new fads and luxuries came from the United States, the biggest, richest, most powerful country in the world. In the fifties, things labelled "Made in Japan" were still laughed at as junk.

The hottest new appliance was the television set. Canadians who lived near the border hooked their small sets up to wobbly antennas and tried to pick up a black-and-white picture from an American station just across the border. CBC Television went on the air in 1952, and gradually every city saw its own stations begin broadcasting. It was great being able to see the Toronto Maple Leafs and Montreal Canadiens play, instead of trying to follow hockey action on the radio. If your family was the first on the block to have a set, you invited the neighbours in to watch.

The 1950s also invented rock and roll – and teenagers. Too often, before then, children had had few chances to be children. Many had worked hard to help support their families, and many never finished school. By the 1950s and 1960s, however, teenagers lived a life much different from what their grandparents had known. Instead of following in their parents' footsteps and learning grownup tasks and responsibilities, postwar teenagers were busy with their own interests and activities. They had their own slang and their own fashions. They were still going to school, and they might go to college later. If they worked, it was to add to their allowance, and they spent their money as they liked. They could buy a new record by Paul Anka, a kid from Ottawa who became a pop star in the United States, or save up for one of the new little transistor radios so that they could carry their music everywhere. Boys dreamed of buying an old car and turning it into a "souped-up" hot rod. Girls wore their cardigans buttoned up the back, soaked their crinolines in sugar-water to make them stiff, and swooned over American movie stars like Marlon Brando and James Dean.

During the 1950s, Canadians began to take more

Sixteen-year-old Marilyn Bell fought oil slicks and lamprey eels, as well as fatigue, to become, on September 9, 1954, the first person to swim across Lake Ontario. It took her twenty-one hours, and radio and newspapers followed every stroke she took.

interest in being Canadian, as the links with Britain weakened. Canada now ran its own international affairs, and the country was becoming more of a player in the world – partly because of its peacekeeping and other United Nations activities. In 1952, Vincent Massey became the first Canadian-born governor general (at least since Pierre Rigaud de Vaudreuil, the last governor general of New France).

New Canadians

In the 1950s, new Canadians mostly still came down the gangplanks of transatlantic passenger ships in Halifax or Montreal. Many groups had enriched Canada with their hard work on farms and in towns across the nation, but three-quarters of all Canadians had British or French roots, and most immigrants still came from Europe.

By the middle of the twentieth century, Canada's population had reached fourteen million. Some were the children, grandchildren, and great-grandchildren of immigrants who had poured into Canada in the years before the First World War. Jewish communities were now strong in Montreal, Winnipeg, and some other cities. Finnish culture thrived in northern Ontario. Ukrainian was widely spoken on the Prairies, and Vancouver had one of the largest Chinese communities outside China. But except for Chinese and South Asians on the west coast, American Blacks in Ontario and Nova Scotia, and a few other groups, Canada had not accepted many immigrants from non-white or non-European backgrounds.

After the Second World War, Canada reopened its doors to immigrants. Nearly three million arrived in just twenty years. Instead of just coming by ship, they came by plane, to airports all across Canada. And the proportion of British and northern European immigrants became lower. Southern Europeans were the first groups to grow more numerous; Italian communities expanded rapidly in the cities during the 1950s, and Greek and Portuguese communities soon appeared. Non-European immigrants also began to arrive. They came from the islands of the Caribbean, from India and Pakistan, from Korea and Hong Kong, and from many other countries. People of hundreds of languages and backgrounds now enriched Canada with their traditions.

The newcomers brought their customs and beliefs with them. Sikh and Buddhist temples stood beside Jewish synagogues or Catholic or Baptist churches, and whole sections of cities sprouted street signs in Chinese, Portuguese, or Italian. Suddenly, there were shops selling food, clothing, music, books, and artworks that were new, startling, and fascinating to many Canadians. The 1950s and 1960s opened Canada to the tastes and styles of the world. It was becoming a multicultural nation.

Many of the immigrants came to Canada for the same reason as the early colonists: they hoped that hard work in a new land would provide a better life for their children. But in the troubled postwar world, Canada also became a haven for refugees from oppression and war. Often the refugees arrived poor and penniless, but many were skilled and ambitious people who quickly made their mark in their new country. In 1956, when the tanks of the Soviet Union crushed an uprising in Hungary, 30000 Hungarian exiles came to Canada. In 1968, when Soviet tanks rolled into Czechoslovakia, more refugees fled to Canada. During the 1960s, when the United States was fighting a war in Vietnam, 32000 young Americans immigrated here, rather than be drafted and forced to take part in the conflict. Some of the refugees dreamed of returning to their homelands one day, but most hoped to make new lives in Canada.

In 1957, Canadians voted out Louis St. Laurent and the Liberal Party, which had ruled Canada since 1935, and elected a prime minister who passionately believed that people of every background could share "One Canada." John Diefenbaker's parents had come to Saskatchewan as homesteaders in 1904. "When we got rich," he liked to say, "we moved to a sod hut." He never forgot his humble roots. He spoke out for "ordinary" Canadians, and he

A colourful parade marks the celebration of Chinese New Year in Vancouver.

Crises in other parts of the world have often brought new communities to Canada. These Hungarians fled after the failure of their rebellion against Soviet rule in 1956.

John Diefenbaker campaigning in 1957. Canadians across the country rallied to the fiery speeches of the man from Prince Albert, Saskatchewan. They gave his Conservative Party the biggest win in Canadian history.

wanted all Canadians to share the opportunities the country offered. In 1958, "Dief the Chief" won the biggest election victory in Canadian history. His Conservative Party took 208 of the 265 seats in the House of Commons.

Diefenbaker had a "vision of the North." Instead of huddling along the border, watching American television, he said, Canadians should go north, to lay down roads, open mines and mills, and create new towns. Workers started uranium mines in Uranium City, Saskatchewan, and Elliot Lake, Ontario. They built a new city around the iron ore mines of Schefferville, Quebec, which shipped eight million tonnes a year down the railway to the new port of Sept-Iles. In Kitimat, British Columbia, a brand-new city grew up around a new aluminum smelter. The North seemed like a treasure trove of riches waiting to be discovered. Still, most Canadians stayed in the south.

Diefenbaker's vision of the North never made much room for the Native nations there, though his government did allow Native people to vote in Canadian elections for the first time. In the 1950s, the number of Native people in Canada began to increase, after centuries of slow decline. Soon Native leaders would be finding new ways to defend their people and to reclaim their lands and rights.

"Il faut que ça change!"

Quebec's powerful premier, Maurice Duplessis, died suddenly in the late summer of 1959. Duplessis had been Quebec's uncrowned king, and few could imagine life without *le Chef*, the boss. He had always told his people that they must cling to their traditional ways or their unique culture would be swamped by English-speaking North America. But after his death, Quebec began to stir.

In the 1960s, Quebec decided to take on the world, not shelter from it. But its people were as determined as ever not to be swallowed up by the English-speaking population around them. French Quebeckers declared that they were ready and able to run their own affairs. They were not

going to be pushed around by the government in Ottawa, or by the wealthy English-speaking minority which had run most of the big businesses in Quebec. *"Maîtres chez nous,"* cried the new Quebec premier, Jean Lesage – "Masters in our own house."

Quebeckers saw that they would need skilled, educated people, and they began opening new schools and universities around the province. A huge power dam, Manic-5, which provided power for the growing cities and industries, became a symbol of the energy surging through Quebec. *"Il faut que ça change!"* was a popular saying in the new Quebec. "Things have to change!"

René Lévesque, a fiery broadcaster with a cigarette always at the corner of his mouth, was Premier Lesage's most controversial, colourful minister. Lévesque demanded that the federal government give more power to Quebec. He spoke passionately of Quebec's rights and the wrongs done to French Canadians, and he became a hero to a new generation of people who chose to be called "Québécois," not "French Canadians."

"What does Quebec want?" asked English Canadians. Before long, Lévesque proposed an answer – sovereignty! He believed the future for Quebec was as an independent country, running its own affairs without interference from the rest of Canada.

English Canada was alarmed by this talk of "separatism." The government in Ottawa promised to renew Confederation, to make French Canadians feel they were truly equal to English Canadians throughout the country. It began to promote "bilingualism and biculturalism" as the future for all of Canada. That annoyed many English Canadians, who complained that French was being "shoved down their throats." However, these measures were not enough to satisfy René Lévesque. He walked out of Premier Lesage's government and founded a new political movement which became the Parti Québécois. The Parti Québécois promised to take Quebec out of Confederation. It wanted Quebec to gain all the powers of an independent country, and then

Rarely seen without a cigarette, René Lévesque fought for Quebec's independence with a passion that made him one of the most loved – and most feared – politicians in Canada.

Mannumi Shagu's Woman and Children, *an Inuit sculpture from Cape Dorset, Baffin Island.*

negotiate a new kind of relationship with Canada.

There was another organization, the Front de Libération du Québec, which wanted more than an independent country. This secret group wanted a complete change in Quebec – a revolution – and it was ready to use violence to get it. In 1963, FLQ bombs began exploding in mailboxes and office buildings around Montreal. People across Canada wondered whether the turmoil in Quebec would produce a new version of Confederation, an independent Quebec, or bloodshed in the streets.

In the 1960s, not only Quebec but the whole country seemed eager for change. In Canada and many other parts of the world, the older "baby boomers" had reached their teenage years. Because those were prosperous times, they had more spending money than previous generations of youth. Their favourite musicians became international celebrities, like the Beatles from England, who swept to the top of Canadian music charts late in 1963. Their fashions, like miniskirts, blue jeans, and long hair, even began to spread to adults who wanted to appear youthful or "with

When "hippie" and "straight" lifestyles clashed in communities like Toronto's Yorkville and Vancouver's Gastown, conflict with the police often followed.

it" (as they said in the 1960s). Late in the decade, some of the young people became "hippies," rejecting the technology and ambition of the time and preaching international peace and love. They grew their hair long and wore beads and earrings from Eastern countries like India and Afghanistan. Some dropped out of school. Some gave up meat and alcohol, and turned to herbal tea and marijuana. Some rejected the idea of marriage, and lived in groups in rundown urban neighbourhoods like Yorkville in Toronto and Gastown in Vancouver. Others went "back to the land," where they tried living in communes and raising organic foods.

Many sixties youth had high ideals. In 1961, university students founded Canadian Universities Service Overseas, or CUSO, which sent young Canadians abroad to help poor people in underdeveloped countries. Later, many university campuses became stormy places as students marched in protests, trying to change how the universities and all of society worked. They also wanted to change the way Canada and the United States got along. They argued that Canada was too closely tied to the United States. Canada was becoming an American colony, cried the new Canadian nationalists. They wanted a country independent of foreign control, making its own plans.

It wasn't only young people who were unhappy with old ways. Canadian women were changing their lives, too. More and more women were taking paid jobs and working outside the home. By 1967, there were as many women in the work force as there had been during the Second World War. However, newspapers still ran separate ads for "Help wanted, male" and "Help wanted, female," and most of the powerful, well-paid positions still seemed to be reserved for men. Ellen Fairclough, a chartered accountant, became the first woman Cabinet minister in 1957. Lawyer and writer Judy LaMarsh was a prominent politician in the sixties. However, they were exceptions. Women still faced discrimination when they aspired to "men's" jobs – and met with opposition when they talked about changing the way men ran the world.

Montreal college students march in protest along Rue Ste-Catherine in October 1968. Students everywhere marched, for various causes, in the 1960s.

In the late fifties, when nine-year-old Abigail Hoffman wanted to play on a minor-league hockey team, she had to pretend to be a boy named "Ab" Hoffman. By the 1960s Abby Hoffman was a star athlete competing for Canada in the Olympics, but girls still could not play organized hockey. Things were starting to change, however – in sports, at work, everywhere. By 1967, the women's movement had pushed the government into studying the status of women in Canada. There would be great changes in the next few decades.

Canada's Birthday Party

The year 1967 was Canada's one-hundredth birthday, and the nation threw itself an exuberant birthday party. Canadians surprised themselves with a sense of pride and a sense of fun.

Across the land, towns and communities started work on imaginative centennial projects. One Manitoba town put in a sewer system and made a July-first bonfire of its outhouses. An Alberta town produced a flying-saucer landing pad. Charlottetown, the "Cradle of Confederation," had led the way with its Confederation Centre, and hundreds of other towns opened centennial community centres, centennial libraries, or centennial arenas. The new maple leaf flag blossomed everywhere. It had been chosen as the national flag just two years earlier, after fierce debates about its design and colour, and now young Canadians travelling in Europe or India, or hitchhiking down the Trans-Canada Highway, carried the red and white emblem sewn on their backpacks.

The world's fair in Montreal, Expo 67, became the highlight of Centennial Year. A few months before the fair opened, the islands in the St. Lawrence where it would be held were a muddy, chaotic construction site, and many nervous Canadians predicted disaster. Instead, Expo blossomed into perhaps the most exciting world's fair ever. Its pavilions displayed the best of all nations, and its theme

How Canada Got Its Flag

After Confederation in 1867, Canada remained part of the British empire, and the flag it flew was either Britain's Union Jack or the Red Ensign with the Canadian coat of arms. As the country slowly shed its colonial past, Canadians started to consider what a truly Canadian flag should look like.

In 1964, Parliament began to debate the design of a national flag, and hundreds of designs were presented. The Union Jack, the fleur-de-lis, and the beaver all had their supporters. Gradually the maple leaf won out. But would it be one maple leaf or three? For months, legislators wrangled, editorials thundered, letter-writers argued, and protesters shouted over the look of the flag.

At first Parliament proposed three red maple leaves on a white background with blue bars on each side. But red soon replaced the blue, and a citizens' group named "The Committee for a Single Maple Leaf" fought for a simple, clear image at the centre of the flag. At last the government closed off the debate. On February 15, 1965, Canada's new flag was officially unfurled – the bold, distinctive red maple leaf (see following page) that is now recognized around the world.

YUKON

Great Bear Lake

• Whitehorse

NORTHWEST TERRITORIES

Yellowknife

Great Slave Lake

MANITOBA

BRITISH
COLUMBIA

ALBERTA

• Edmonton

Victoria

SASKATCHEWAN

Regina

Lake Winnipeg

Winnipeg

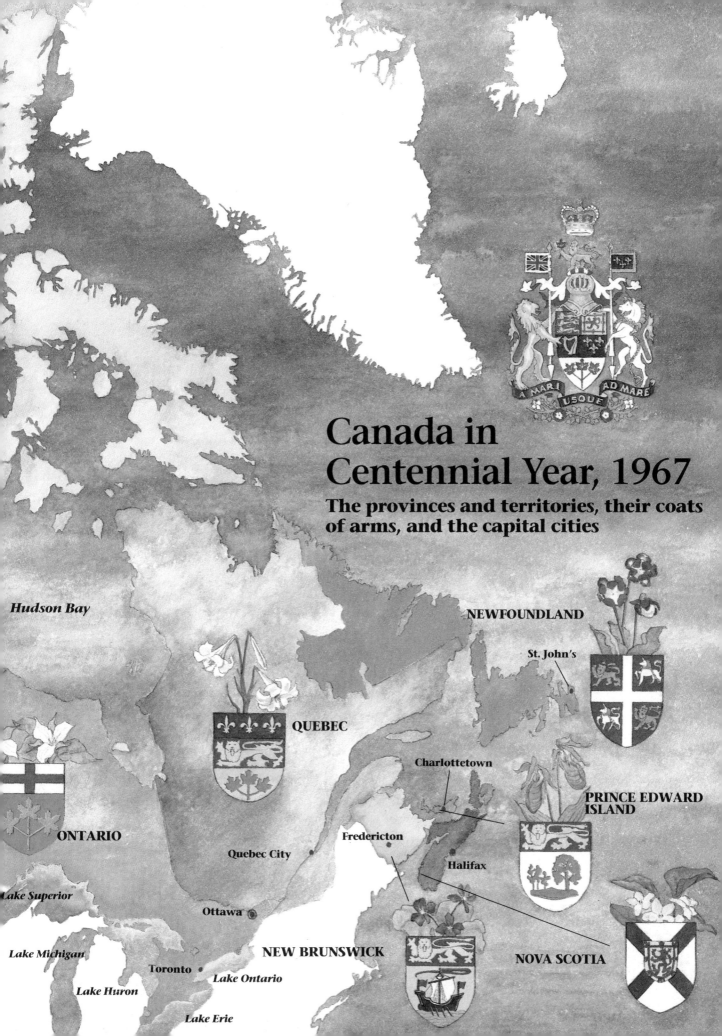

Canada in Centennial Year, 1967

The provinces and territories, their coats of arms, and the capital cities

Hudson Bay

NEWFOUNDLAND

St. John's

QUEBEC

Charlottetown

PRINCE EDWARD
ISLAND

ONTARIO

Fredericton

Halifax

Quebec City

Lake Superior

Ottawa

Lake Michigan

NEW BRUNSWICK

NOVA SCOTIA

Toronto

Lake Ontario

Lake Huron

Lake Erie

"Terre des Hommes/Man and His World," expressed a new mood that was bubbling up in Canada. Canada welcomed the world to Expo 67, and fifty million visitors came – two visitors for every Canadian.

By 1967, the North Star that had been so exciting in 1948 had long since gone to the scrap heap. Canada had joined the jet age in 1960, when Trans-Canada Airlines' DC-8 cut the Toronto-Vancouver flying time to five hours. Under its new name, Air Canada, the national airline would soon be making the same trip with jumbo jets carrying 350 passengers. Astronauts were travelling into space, and just two years after the centennial, men would walk on the moon. No one knew just where Canada was going – but suddenly the ride looked exciting.

Coming Together – Flying Apart

Expo 67 in Montreal was successful – and a lot of fun. Centennial year was like that.

Now that Canadians could fly across the country in the time it took to eat a meal and watch a movie, it seemed that Canada should be more united than ever before. Instead, it seemed to be flying apart. Everything was being questioned. New groups challenged the status quo. The pride people felt in their own regions collided with the struggle to build a unified nation. More and more Canadians were asking hard questions about the way the country was put together.

Canada had a new prime minister. John Diefenbaker's Conservative Party had been replaced by Lester Pearson's Liberals in 1963, and when Pearson retired in 1968, Pierre Elliott Trudeau took over. With him came "Trudeaumania." Trudeau was younger than most Canadian prime ministers had been. Perfectly bilingual, he was clever in both French and English. On the campaign trail, he could debate with students, draw admiring crowds at the shopping centre, and show off on the diving board back at his hotel. He had the same excitement as Expo 67, and he won the federal election of 1968. For a while, Canada's new prime minister was as popular as a rock star.

Underneath the glamour, Pierre Trudeau could be tough. His obsession was Confederation and Quebec's place in it. He rejected the idea of independence for Quebec. Instead, he wanted a Canada in which French Canadians were full and equal partners, and he was willing to fight for that. In October 1970, when the FLQ kidnapped a politician, Pierre Laporte, and a British diplomat, many young Québécois cheered. Some of the province's leaders talked of making a deal with the terrorists. Trudeau sent in the army instead.

The ordinary freedoms that Canadians take for granted were suspended. In Montreal, police arrested hundreds of "suspects" in the middle of the night. Soldiers patrolled the streets, and helicopters roared overhead. The "October Crisis" shook all of Canada. Here and there, civil-libertarians spoke out against the government's assault on civil rights, but as the crisis raged, Quebec and its people looked revolution in the face and turned away. The terrorists murdered Pierre Laporte, but there was no more support for violence and terror in Quebec. After the kidnappers were allowed to escape to Cuba in exchange for freeing their British hostage, the FLQ simply vanished. Quebec would decide its future democratically.

Prime Minister Trudeau set about making the French language equal to English in the government of Canada. He brought French-speaking Canadians to Ottawa, and he made English-Canadian civil servants learn French. French signs joined English ones in federal buildings and projects across the country. Many English Canadians responded positively, by sending their children to French-immersion schools so they could take their place in a bilingual Canada. Many others complained that "the French" were taking over the government and the country.

During the 1970s, Pierre Trudeau's government borrowed and spent money lavishly. Canadians wanted new and better programs for the elderly, the handicapped, minorities, women, children, and the poor. Companies demanded government support for risky or expensive projects. "Crown corporations" (companies owned by

Pierre Elliott Trudeau was a man with a style of his own, here with a rose in his lapel and "Trudeau-mania" surrounding him.

the government) invested in oil exploration, railways, and many other industries. All this was costly, but the government believed that using the taxes paid by citizens to achieve the country's ambitions was a good thing.

Battle of the Titans

While Pierre Trudeau was determined to build a united, bilingual Canada, René Lévesque held to his own vision of an independent Quebec – with a passion equal to Trudeau's. When Lévesque's Parti Québécois swept to power in Quebec in 1976, Trudeau and Lévesque confronted each other in a battle for the future of Quebec and Confederation.

The Parti Québécois had promised to consult the people of Quebec before breaking up Canada. On May 15, 1980, the people of the province voted in a referendum that asked them to say *"Oui"* or *"Non"* to a plan that would make Quebec "sovereign" (that is, independent) yet still associated with the rest of Canada in some way that would be decided later. Lévesque led the forces for the *"Oui"* and "sovereignty-association," and Trudeau led the forces for

The Greatest Goal

Canadians always knew Canadian hockey players were the best in the world. In 1972 the Soviet Union challenged Canada to prove it, in an eight-game series pitting their best players against the best Canadian professionals of the National Hockey League.

Most Canadians thought the only question was how many goals their team would win by. But by the time Team Canada headed for the Soviet Union, after four games at home, the country was in shock. The Soviet

team had lost only one game! The score was two to one, with one tie.

Canada lost the first game in Moscow, too, but then Paul Henderson of the Toronto Maple Leafs scored the winning goal in games six and seven. He became a national hero with his final goal, the most famous goal in hockey history, which won game eight – and the series – with just thirty-four seconds left to play.

On the lawns of Parliament on April 17, 1982, Prime Minister Pierre Trudeau watches as Queen Elizabeth signs the agreement that brought Canada's constitution, the British North America Act, to Canada.

the *"Non"* and for renewed Confederation. Canada held its breath as Quebec voted. The result was 60-40 for the *"Non."* Separatism had been rejected.

Trudeau had promised that, if Quebec voted for Canada, the nation's constitution, the British North America Act, would be changed. The BNA Act still sat in Britain, and ever since it had been written in 1867 there had been no way for Canadians to amend it except by acting through the British Parliament. In 1981, Trudeau led the effort to set rules by which Canada would change the BNA Act itself, and despite René Lévesque's protests, he succeeded. In April 1982, the constitution finally came to Canada. In a rain-soaked ceremony on Parliament Hill, Canadians took over the power to change their own constitution, and added a Charter of Rights and Freedoms to protect individual liberties. In Quebec the Parti Québécois held on to power for a few more years, but it seemed that separatism was dead.

Energy and Ecology

While Trudeau and Lévesque fought their battle, Canada and the world had been changing fast.

In 1973, during a crisis in the Middle East, the Arab countries – which produced most of the world's oil – stopped selling oil to Japan, Europe, and North America. Since gasoline is made from oil, there were soon long lineups at service stations. Governments brought in new laws to conserve oil, and fuel prices shot upwards. Oil soon began to flow from the Middle East again, but something

No ordinary mall – you can ride a balloon, a roller-coaster, or a submarine at the West Edmonton Mall.

had changed. Oil, the lifeblood of the modern world, suddenly seemed scarce and very precious.

Alberta, which had most of Canada's oil and natural gas, enjoyed a "boom." In Calgary, new bank towers and oil company buildings displayed Alberta's wealth. From all over western Canada, shoppers flocked to the West Edmonton Mall, the largest shopping centre in the world – which soon had its own indoor roller coaster, a pool with submarines and sharks, an ice rink, and a hotel. Alberta also took pride in its new medical research industries, its theatres, and its museums, including the Tyrrell Museum of Paleontology near Drumheller.

As money and people flowed to western Canada, Albertans declared that westerners would no longer simply provide cheap resources for central Canada. Western Canada wanted a bigger share in Confederation. Some nervous easterners murmured about "western separatism," but western leaders declared that "the West wants in." Alberta led the way in demanding new powers for the provinces, and changes in Ottawa to make all the provinces full partners in Canada.

In 1979, Edmonton's hockey team, the Oilers, joined the National Hockey League. Until 1967 Montreal and Toronto had had the only Canadian teams in the league, but by the end of the 1970s there were teams from Quebec City to Vancouver. Edmonton's team, led by an eighteen-year-old sensation named Wayne Gretzky, was soon the best of all. No one had ever scored or set up goals the way "the Great Gretzky" did.

The world was still desperate for oil, and oil companies soon turned their explorations to the stormy Grand Banks of Newfoundland. The search paid off when floating oil platforms struck oil on the Hibernia field, 200 kilometres out from St. John's. After half a century of hard times, Maritimers hoped their region would begin to prosper from the oil that would flow from Hibernia. They were eager to support themselves and, like Alberta, Atlantic Canada "wanted in." Newfoundland led the fight for local control of oil and fisheries.

When Number 99, "the Great One," played for the Edmonton Oilers, it was the hottest team in hockey. Gretzky turned professional at age seventeen, the youngest major-league athlete in North America.

There was oil beneath the seas and islands of the Arctic, too. The Americans had never officially recognized Canada's claim to the northern waters, and in 1969 they challenged both Canada and the forbidding Arctic when they sent a huge oil tanker, the *Manhattan*, through the Northwest Passage without asking Canadian permission. In the end, however, the *Manhattan* needed help from the Canadian icebreaker *John A. Macdonald* to avoid being trapped in the ice.

One way Canada could get oil from the Arctic Sea was by carrying it, in what would be the world's longest pipeline, across the Yukon and south through the Mackenzie Valley. In 1974 Judge Thomas Berger was appointed to investigate the pipeline plan. Judge Berger talked to the people most affected, the Dene people of the Mackenzie Valley. They

Nuclear Energy

When the Second World War ended with the dropping of two atomic bombs, Canadian scientists began to study how to use atomic power peacefully to generate electricity. The result was the CANDU (Canadian Deuterium Uranium) reactor. CANDU reactors use Canada's abundant supplies of natural uranium, protected by immersion in deuterium, or "heavy water."

Today CANDU reactors in Ontario, Quebec, and New Brunswick provide about 12 per cent of Canada's electricity. But they also create concern. Many people fear that a nuclear accident, like the one that happened at Chernobyl in the Soviet Union in 1986, could endanger many lives and pollute the atmosphere for centuries. And since used nuclear fuel remains radio-active for thousands of years, safe places to store it have to be found.

Each CANDU reactor is a brilliant example of Canadian science and engineering, and CANDU scientists are confident that no Chernobyl-type accident is possible. But the risks of nuclear power show us the dangers of technology. As we worry more about pollution, and as our supplies of oil run out, the problem of creating cheap, safe electrical power will continue to face Canadians.

told him that they still hunted and trapped in their valley homeland, and that a pipeline might destroy their fragile valley. "Deep in the glass and concrete of your world, you are stealing my soul, my spirit," said Dene chief Frank T'Seleie. Judge Berger recommended that the Mackenzie pipeline be postponed, and the government agreed. Despite southern Canada's thirst for oil, the concerns of Native people were beginning to be heard.

As the hunt for resources went on, Canadians began to think more about "ecology." In the fall of 1971, a rundown, crazily painted old ship named *Phyllis Cormack* sailed out of Vancouver for the remote Alaskan island of Amchitka. The United States intended to test a nuclear bomb on Amchitka. The small band of British Columbian protesters aboard the ship wanted to stop them and warn the world about the dangers of nuclear radiation.

The voyage of the *Phyllis Cormack* did not stop the bomb from being exploded, but it gave the world a new word and a new organization: Greenpeace. In hundreds of colourful ways, Greenpeace told the world's people about the damage being done to our planet and the need to protect it. To save the whales from being hunted to extinction, Greenpeace's ships confronted the whaling fleets on the high seas. To preserve the forests, its members blocked logging roads in British Columbia's rainforest. Canadians were beginning to see that progress brought comfort and leisure, but also polluted the air and water. Four billion people crowded the planet in the early 1970s, and there would be six billion by the year 2000. Canada's population was small, but each Canadian used up far more of the world's resources than a person in one of the poorer, developing countries.

Greenpeace began in British Columbia but it defended the environment in protest actions around the world. British Columbia was like that; after a hundred years as

Whenever they send their fragile Zodiacs to confront whaling ships or naval ships with nuclear weapons, Greenpeace's campaigners always get lots of attention.

Whooping Cranes

Each spring, the whooping cranes fly north from the Gulf of Mexico to their nesting grounds in the bulrush marshes of northern Alberta. Whooping cranes are pure white, except for small red and black markings on their heads and their two-metre wings, and they are the tallest birds in North America. Their migration makes a spectacular sight for any nature lover.

But fifty years ago only fifteen whooping cranes, the last wild whooping cranes in the world, made that flight. Another irreplaceable species stood at the edge of extinction as the cranes' distinctive whoop fell silent.

Since then, Canadian and American wildlife experts have fought to save the whooping cranes from hunters, droughts, and the draining of the marshlands they need. Slowly the whooping cranes have recovered.

Today they number more than 150, and wildlife experts are beginning to believe the species will survive. If so, they will be one of the first species ever rescued by careful conservation efforts. For the whooping crane and many other endangered species, the fight goes on.

Canadian writing for children blossomed in the 1970s and 1980s through the work of authors such as Dennis Lee and Margaret Laurence.

part of Canada, the province still looked out to the Pacific Ocean and the rest of the world. In the 1970s and 1980s, Vancouver grew and prospered as Canada's gateway to the rapidly growing nations of the Pacific. British Columbians were also fiercely proud of the beauty of their rugged province, and ready to fight to safeguard it from pollution.

A Canadian thinker, Marshall McLuhan of the University of Toronto, had become famous for declaring that the world was becoming a "global village," big and small at the same time, where everyone was linked together with everyone else. One place where the idea seemed easy to understand was the Sun Yat-sen Garden, the only classical Chinese garden outside China, which lay nestled amid the urban hustle of downtown Vancouver. The city's Asian-Canadian communities, once downtrodden minorities, had become a precious link between Canada and the Far East. Japan and Asia were surging forward in the world economy, and British Columbia schools put Asian culture and languages on the course of study.

In the 1970s, the combination of global pressures and regional claims made life hard for Canada's prime ministers. "I can lose. I just never do," said Pierre Trudeau boldly when someone asked him about elections. But he almost lost the election of 1972, and Joe Clark and the Conservative Party did beat him in 1979. Clark was a young unknown, and reporters nicknamed him "Joe Who?" He promised to make Canada "a community of communities," where every region would take charge of its own affairs, but his government lasted only nine months before Trudeau was back as prime minister.

Finally – in the middle of a snowstorm on February 29, 1984, the extra day of leap year – Pierre Trudeau decided he would retire. Except for John Diefenbaker's six years and Joe Clark's brief victory, the Liberal Party had held power in Ottawa since the 1930s. But in September 1984 the Progressive Conservatives were voted in and their new leader, Brian Mulroney, became Canada's nineteenth prime minister.

Lean and Mean

On October 5, 1984, the American space shuttle *Challenger* rocketed skyward on a pillar of smoke and flame. In minutes the shuttle was in orbit, with Marc Garneau of Quebec City one of the seven astronauts aboard. Garneau, the first Canadian to see the earth from space, saw the vast country stretched out beneath him, and he crossed over Canada hundreds of times during the eight-day voyage. More than ever, Canada's future seemed linked with that of the shrinking planet.

A month before Marc Garneau's flight, Brian Mulroney became prime minister of Canada. Mulroney came from a working-class Irish-Canadian family in Baie-Comeau, Quebec, on the north shore of the St. Lawrence. He had been bilingual all his life, and in both languages he loved to talk. By the time he became prime minister, he used the telephone so much his cronies across the country joked that he had "black-wire disease."

Brian Mulroney promised to open Canada up to the world outside its borders. At the end of the Second World War, Canada and the United States had been two rich countries in a poor, war-battered world. By the 1980s, however, Japan and Europe were racing to catch and surpass North America, and Canada's prosperity was no longer guaranteed in the fast-changing world. Prime Minister Mulroney said that Canada had to be lean and mean to survive. That might mean cutting back on the expensive social services that many Canadians held dear. Although some Canadians argued that trans-Canada passenger trains were a symbol uniting the country, the Conservative government said the trains didn't pay their way, and many stopped running. The government sold off Air Canada, the national airline, and Petro-Canada, the national oil company. It also postponed a number of costly projects, such as government-funded daycare centres.

Something else that vanished was the dollar bill. A one-dollar coin went into circulation in 1987, and the last dollar bills were printed two years later. Because the coin

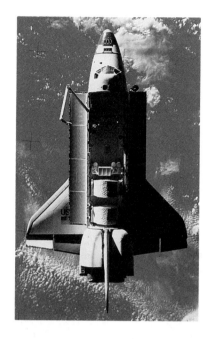

A satellite, just released by the "Canadarm," took this photo of the space shuttle in orbit. Astronaut Marc Garneau was the first Canadian to fly aboard the space shuttle.

carried the image of a loon, Canadians quickly named it the "loonie," and when a two-dollar coin came along in 1996, it promptly became the "toonie."

In the late 1980s, Prime Minister Mulroney's government negotiated a Free Trade Agreement with the United States. Canadian companies and jobs that had been protected from competition might vanish, but the Conservatives were confident that, in the long run, the agreement would be good for the country. They said that Canada must compete in the world marketplace, and that free trade with the United States was the place to start.

In the federal election of 1988, the political parties debated the Canada–U.S. Free Trade Agreement. Liberal

Terry Fox

Lift, hop. Lift, hop. Lift, hop. Rocking back and forth between his one good leg and his artificial one, the young man ran on. He tried to ignore the pain as he slowly wore away the distance between St. John's, Newfoundland, and his destination at the Pacific Ocean.

Terry Fox of Coquitlam,

B.C., was nineteen when he lost his right leg to cancer in 1977. While he was re-covering, he dreamed of doing something that would inspire other cancer sufferers, and raise money to fight the disease. In April 1980, he set out on his "Marathon of Hope" – a run all the way across Canada.

All that summer, the slim, curly-haired runner struggled on, running forty kilometres a day. Canada began to pay attention. Television cameras reported on Terry's progress and, before long, crowds were gathering to see him in each town he passed through. Moved by his courage, people began to donate to cancer research.

By September, when the Marathon of Hope reached the north shore of Lake Superior, Terry Fox had covered over 5300 kilo-metres. He was halfway home, and he had raised nearly $2 million. But there he had to stop. Cancer had returned, this time in his lungs. He could not run any more, and in less than a year Terry Fox was dead.

When they heard how his run had been halted, Canadians donated more than $25 million for cancer research. And marathons named for him still raise funds all over Canada. Canada has had many fine athletes, but few touched the hearts of as many Canadians as Terry Fox.

leader John Turner and NDP leader Ed Broadbent swore the agreement would mean that Canada would be swallowed by the United States. They each promised to "tear up the deal." Mulroney and the Conservatives swore that the future of the nation depended on it. It was the most fiercely fought election in years. Support swung back and forth – first to Mulroney, then to Turner, then back to the Prime Minister. When the votes came in on November 21, Brian Mulroney's Conservatives had been re-elected. Free trade between Canada and the United States began on January 1, 1989.

Living in the 1980s and 1990s

In the 1980s, compact, sophisticated electronic gadgets – from digital watches to microwave ovens – swept away the electric devices that had seemed so amazing in the 1950s. There had been computers in the 1950s, but they had cost millions of dollars, filled whole rooms, and needed teams of experts in white coats to keep them going. By the 1980s, the microscopically-small silicon chip had made lap-sized computers more powerful than the old room-filling machines. Soon computers came into classrooms, offices, and homes, and "user-friendly" programs made them easy to operate. Then in the 1990s came the Internet, which linked home, school, or business computers to world-wide networks. Suddenly, kids could connect to their friends by e-mail and do school projects by surfing sites on the World Wide Web. What's more, they quickly discovered that computers could also be used for games, contests, and even shopping.

By the 1990s, there were 30 million Canadians, more than twice as many as at the end of the Second World War. Immigrants and refugees were still coming to Canada to find better or more peaceful lives. In 1978, hundreds of thousands of refugees fled Vietnam after the war there, often risking their lives in small crowded boats. Canadians rallied to help. They called the refugees "the boat people," and church groups, neighbours, and friends sponsored

Everybody dances when the Caribana parade rolls through Toronto to celebrate Caribbean-Canadian culture.

Prime Minister Jean Chrétien chats with Govenor-General Adrienne Clarkson just before she reads her first the Throne Speech in the Senate Chamber on Parliament Hill, October 12, 1999.

A new leader for the 1990s, Nellie Cournoyea became government leader in the Northwest Territories in 1991.

thousands of them and helped them settle in communities across Canada.

As people of different colours and customs mingled on buses, in stores, in schools, and in the workplace, both old and new Canadians tried to break down the walls of prejudice and fear. Multicultural radio and television stations began broadcasting across the country, and people began to hear new languages and new accents. More and more, minorities and immigrants were celebrating the special qualities and customs they brought from their homelands even as they became full members of Canadian society. Minority communities took noticeable pride in members who achieved success in every walk of life. When Adrienne Clarkson, once a child immigrant from China, became Canada's governor general in 1999, she symbolized for many people the success of Canada's diverse population.

The roles of men and women were changing rapidly in the 1980s and 1990s. In 1981, when Canada's constitution was being brought home from Britain, women's organizations made sure that the Charter of Rights included "Article 28," which guaranteed equality between women and men. They had fought hard for Article 28. Then, at the last minute, the politicians announced a change, one which allowed any government to ignore Article 28 whenever it chose. Women's groups organized a blizzard of telegrams, phone calls, protests, and demands, and forced the governments to back down. Article 28 was protected.

By the end of the century, it was no longer rare for women to be doctors, engineers, politicians, or bus drivers, or for men to be nurses or stay-at-home fathers who cooked and shared in child-rearing. Women demanded action against the violence suffered by women and children. They worked to improve health and child care. They fought for equal pay with men and for access to jobs that had been closed to them. Every step seemed difficult, yet gradually the lives of men and women had changed. Late in the 1980s, a young hockey player named Justine Blaney won the right to play along with the boys, and by 1991 Manon Rhéaume, a goaltender from Trois-Rivières, Quebec, had played in the National Hockey League. At the 1998 Olympics in Nagano, Japan, Canadian women played in the first-ever gold medal game in women's hockey – but a heartbreaking loss left them holding the silver.

The Global Village

At the end of the 1980s, the shape of global politics changed dramatically. The Cold War was suddenly over. Since 1945, the West (the mostly democratic countries led by Western Europe and North America) and the East (the Communist states led by the Soviet Union and China) had opposed each other with unrelenting hostility and suspicion. The two political systems had dominated the world, and their hostility had threatened it with instant nuclear destruction if war were to break out.

Then, one by one, the Communist governments in Eastern Europe began to collapse. Not only had those governments restricted the freedom of their citizens, they had been unable to ensure even such basic needs as food and housing. Their citizens wanted change. In Poland, an electrician named Lech Walesa led a pro-democracy organization of workers called "Solidarity" against the Communist government. Democracy triumphed first in Poland and then in the other countries of eastern Europe. When Mikhail Gorbachev came to power in the Soviet Union in 1984, he too promised changes, and soon the changes had gone farther and faster than any leader could control.

Canadian women have just won the 1999 Women's World Hockey Championship in Helsinki, Finland, and Geraldine Heaney (right) races to congratulate goalie Sami Jo Small.

Astronaut Roberta Bondar, a doctor and a pilot, trained for eight years for her flight into space in 1992.

In 1989, the Berlin Wall, the symbol of how Europe had been divided, came down. Germany, which had been split into West Germany and East Germany since 1945, became one country again. The mighty Soviet Union came apart to form Russia, Ukraine, and other smaller independent states. The Communist government in China held on to power, but gradually it had to relax some of its fierce control over the lives of its people. In Europe governments began to plan how to unite under one general government. The threat of global nuclear war was fading. It was a hopeful, joyful moment. World peace and prosperity suddenly seemed possible.

World peace was not to be. Conflicts arose in Europe, Africa, and the Middle East, and Canadian forces were kept on alert. Canadian peacekeepers served in the African nations of Somalia and Rwanda, and on the Pacific island of East Timor. When Iraq invaded the small middle-eastern country of Kuwait in 1990, Canada joined the United Nations forces which drove the Iraqi army out. When Yugoslavia split apart and its people fought each other, Canadian troops were there, struggling to keep peace in the separated states of Bosnia-Herzegovina and Croatia. Then, in 1999, when the conflict spread into neighbouring Kosovo, Canadian pilots flew combat missions alongside their western allies.

By the 1990s, electronic communication and supersonic jets were linking every spot in the world, and business dealings went on around the globe and around the clock. The foods we ate, the clothes we wore, the toys we played with, might be produced by hand a few miles away or might come from Paris, Bangkok, or Beijing. The music of Africa and India and the music of the West blended in exciting new sounds, sometimes downloaded instantly onto home computers everywhere. Television used satellites to beam digital images of a soccer match, a pop concert, or a war all over the world. Japanese tourists were as common in Prince Edward Island as Canadian ones were in Greece or Jamaica.

Canada was becoming part of a new world culture driven by global business and instant communication. The country took pride in Canadians who became international celebrities. Quebec's singing sensation Céline Dion, Vancouver rocker Bryan Adams, writer Alice Munro, opera singer Ben Heppner, and cellist Ofra Harnoy delighted fans all over the world. In 1986, physicist John Polanyi won the Nobel Prize for Chemistry, and in the 1990s Nobel Prizes went to two other Canadian scientists, Michael Smith and Bertram Brockhouse. Polanyi's prize-winning subject was "infrared chemiluminescence," but he was also a passionate advocate of disarmament, peace, and science.

The year Polanyi won his Nobel Prize, wheelchair-bound athlete Rick Hansen completed a 40 000-kilometre, round-the-world journey. The "man in motion" wheeled along the Great Wall of China, crossed the length of Canada, and raised millions of dollars for research and therapy. By the time he completed his marathon at Expo 86, the World's Fair in his home town of Vancouver, he had worn out 11 pairs of gloves and 117 wheelchair tires. "Dreams do still come true," he said.

As the world grew smaller, Canadians, like everyone else, became more aware of human suffering and inequality. The terrifying new disease called Acquired Immune Deficiency Syndrome (AIDS) spread rapidly around the world, and so did news of famines and natural disasters. Many people in Africa and Latin America were growing poorer and more desperate, and even rich countries no longer seemed able to stem the rising poverty within their borders. Even prosperous Canada began to doubt whether it could afford its high standard of living. During the 1990s, nearly every government was deeply in debt. Preston Manning, the founder and leader of the new Reform Party, became a hero to those who believed governments should provide fewer services, leaving citizens free to do more for themselves. While most other government leaders took a softer approach, nearly all began to cut back services. Homeless people began to be seen in the streets and at food banks. Canadians began to worry that their medical care, their pensions, and their public libraries might not survive.

An even greater concern had begun to worry people all over the planet: the fate of the planet itself. From the time

His spine broken in an accident, B.C. athlete Rick Hansen began his "Man in Motion" tour, circling the world in a wheelchair to raise funds for spinal-cord research. Here fans gather in Quebec City as he rolls through.

When oil tankers go on the rocks, everyone who cares comes out to save the seabirds and water mammals. These rescuers are working on the west coast of Vancouver Island.

the first European colonists had arrived in North America, they had prospered by selling the resources of the land and sea. Now, however, fishermen on the once-bountiful Grand Banks of Newfoundland noticed that their catches were becoming smaller. By 1992, catches were so small that it became clear that a 500-year old industry was going to die. Almost all cod fishing on the Banks was banned to protect the fish from becoming extinct.

At the same time, acid rain was killing the blue lakes and the maple forests of Ontario. Prairie farmers found that the rich topsoil on their fields was losing its nutrients, and they counted the cost of the fertilizer they needed to grow crops. British Columbians saw empty "clear-cut" patches spreading across their mountains, as loggers cut down the towering old trees of the coastal rainforest. Native communities were devastated when the game vanished from their hunting territories and rivers because of poison from industrial chemicals. Garbage dumps grew alarmingly as Canadian consumers threw out more and more "disposable" products. Scientists and environmental activists alike became more and more alarmed at the hot summers and mild winters. Had human beings actually changed the earth's climate?

In the 1950s and 1960s, it had seemed that Canadians could have everything they wanted. Now they began to realize that they could not. Trying to have it all was destroying the planet. Environmentalists urged people everywhere to learn that the world's problems were all linked. By the 1990s, a popular slogan in Canada was "reduce, reuse, and recycle."

Floods rampaged through the streets of Chicoutimi, Quebec, in July 1996, and more than 10,000 of the city's 60,000 people had to flee from their homes.

Cities and towns wrote rules to get people to cut down pollution and reduce waste. Manufacturers struggled to provide the riches Canadians expected while at the same time obeying the new environmental laws.

First Nations and Distinct Societies

In September 1987, Pope John Paul II, the leader of the Roman Catholic church, came to Fort Simpson in the Northwest Territories to visit the leaders, elders, and people of the Dene nation. He said Mass wearing Native robes of deerskin, and prayers were chanted in the Dene language. John Paul declared that Native Canadians had governed themselves and practised their own faiths long before the Europeans brought theirs to Canada. He praised their determination to protect their culture. He prayed that Canada might become "a model for the world in upholding the dignity of aboriginal people."

During the 1980s, the Native people of Canada, still the poorest minority in the country, were fighting harder than ever to regain control of their lives. Young political leaders like Georges Erasmus, a Dene from the Northwest Territories, and Ovide Mercredi, a Cree from Manitoba, came forward, and traditional elders regained their positions of influence. Native men and women were winning fame as artists, architects, playwrights, and musicians. Others stayed home (or returned) to serve their people on the reserves as

Canadian rowing champion Silken Laumann fought bravely back from an accident that threatened to destroy her chance for an Olympic medal in 1992. The whole world cheered as sheer determination powered her to a bronze medal.

Eyeball to eyeball, a Canadian soldier and a masked Mohawk warrior stare each other down on the front lines of the nerve-racking confrontation at Oka, Quebec, in the summer of 1990.

lawyers, teachers, social workers, healers, or storytellers. Native entrepreneurs ran airlines, built fishing fleets, opened craft co-ops, and started other businesses.

As the strength and confidence of the Native nations grew, they challenged the Canadian government to honour its promises. The Cree of northern Quebec rallied international support to stop the damming of more of their rivers for electrical power. The Haida of British Columbia, the Lubicon of Alberta, the Anishinaube of Ontario, the Innu of Labrador, and many others defended their traditional lands from loggers, miners, and other intruders. They wanted the world to take care of the earth as their traditions had taught them to do. They wanted to practise their own beliefs and teach their children in their own way. They wanted their treaties respected.

In the summer of 1990, to protect land the Native people claimed at Oka and Kahnewaké (just outside Montreal), Mohawk "Warriors" set up roadblocks and armed themselves with machine-guns, ready to kill or die for their cause. The Quebec police and later the Canadian army confronted the heavily-armed Warriors, and Canadians feared a violent and tragic outcome. At last, the Warriors surrendered, but Natives everywhere declared there would be more Okas unless Canada respected Native land and Native rights.

During the 1990s, judges in Canadian courts began to uphold Native claims to land and self-government. In British Columbia, where many Native nations had never signed treaties or surrendered their land or powers, the Gitk'san and Wet'su'wetan peoples won an important court victory recognizing their rights. Soon after, the neighbouring Nisga'a people agreed to sign their first treaty with Canada and British Columbia.

In the North, Inuit leaders began to plan the creation of a new territory where the Inuit people would be a majority of the population. Nunavut, with its capital at Iqaluit on Baffin Island, became Canada's third territory in April 1999. Paul Okalik, an Inuk lawyer, became Nunavut's first government leader. Meanwhile, the remaining part of the Northwest Territories considered changing its name to Denendeh, the land of the Dene.

The Canadian government only slowly gave Native Canadians the powers they wanted, but in the 1980s Prime Minister Mulroney and his government had decided it was time to give more power to the provinces. In the referendum battle of 1980, Pierre Trudeau had promised Quebec a new kind of Confederation. In 1987, Brian Mulroney set out to make the changes that Quebec, and then the other provinces, had demanded. The "Meech Lake Accord" (named for the place outside Ottawa where it was signed) would give powers once held by Ottawa to each province, and it declared that Quebec would have the powers of "a distinct society."

"It's a done deal," the prime minister said proudly when he presented the Accord to the Canadian people – but it wasn't. Each province had to approve the Meech Lake Accord within three years. During that time, opposition exploded across the country. In three provinces, the voters elected new premiers who wanted changes made to the Accord. Debate raged over what the words "distinct society" meant. Three years passed, and as the deadline approached, the prime minister held another meeting. Again he thought he had a deal to save the Meech Lake Accord. But the Accord had ignored the Native people, and they were

Prime Minister Brian Mulroney had to fight hard to win the 1988 election. The big issue was his Canada–U.S. free trade agreement.

French President Jacques Chirac (left), a collector of Inuit art, was among the first foreign visitors to the new territory of Nunavut. Jean Chrétien and resident Rita Mike welcomed him to Pangnirtunq.

determined that it must not be passed without including them. Manitoba was one of the provinces that had not yet approved the Accord, and at the last moment Elijah Harper, a Cree member of the provincial legislature, said no. On June 23, 1990, the Meech Lake Accord was dead.

Meech Lake had promised Quebec all the powers of a distinct society, but at the last minute those powers had been snatched away. Many Quebeckers decided it was time to take charge of their own future – without the rest of Canada. Their premier, Robert Bourassa, gave Canada two years to offer Quebec what it wanted. For two stormy years, Canadians in Parliament and across the country debated constitutional deals. The political leaders met in Charlottetown and called their new plan the "Charlottetown Accord," and they hoped it would save the country. Canada held a nationwide referendum on the Accord in the fall of 1992. After a passionate debate in kitchens and coffee shops across the country, however, Canadians decided the Accord was either too much or too little. They voted it down.

A few months later, Brian Mulroney retired. The Progressive Conservatives chose Kim Campbell from Vancouver to be their new leader, making her Canada's first woman prime minister. But not for long. In the election

of 1993, Jean Chrétien, a Quebecker from the town of
Shawinigan, led the Liberal Party back to power. The
powerful Conservative Party was reduced to two seats in the
House of Commons. The Reform Party, however, had grown
strong in the west, while Lucien Bouchard, who spoke
passionately for Quebec's separation from Canada, won
many Quebec seats for his new "Bloc Québécois." Bouchard
had once been Brian Mulroney's federalist partner. Now he
fought to divide the country.

Separatism, thought to be dying since 1980, was
stronger than ever. On October 30, 1995, there was a
referendum in Quebec. For the first time in fifteen years
Quebeckers were asked the question: Quebec or Canada? At
the start of the campaign, federalists were confident. Then
Quebeckers rallied to the dynamic campaign style of Lucien
Bouchard. The separatist cause seemd to be taking the lead.
Just days before the vote, tens of thousands of Canadians
from every province drove, flew, or rode the trains to
Montreal to show that they cared about keeping Quebec in
Confederation. Did they help? Did they make things worse?
The referendum was almost a tie. Separation for Quebec had
been rejected, but only by the merest fraction of the votes.

Lucien Bouchard left Ottawa to become the premier of
Quebec in 1996. In the years that followed, Ottawa and
Quebec City continued the debate over Quebec's future.
When the Supreme Court of Canada was asked to rule on
the issue, neither side liked the decision. The court told
Ottawa that it would have to negotiate separation if
Quebeckers wanted it, and it told Quebec it should ask the
voters a clear question in any future referendum. More
debate about Quebec's place in Canada seemed certain.

Prime Minister Jean Chrétien led his Liberal Party to
re-election in 1997, and he looked forward to being prime
minister when the new millennium began. Chrétien was an
experienced politician, even though he liked to call himself
"just a little guy from Shawinigan." He loved to boast that
the United Nations had declared Canada the best country in
the world in which to live. He urged Canadians to show
more pride in their country.

*Late in 1994, Bloc Quebecois
leader Lucien Bouchard lost one leg
to a terrible illness. After a
remarkable – and brave – recovery,
he returned to his crusade for
Quebec sovereignty, and he became
Quebec's premier in 1996.*

In 1998, the government of Canada brought in more money than it spent. For the first time in thirty years, that is, Canada had a budget surplus rather than a defecit. Putting an end to rising debt raised hopes that cutbacks in public services might stop. At the same time, however, many political leaders were saying that in a fast-changing world, Canada had to make even greater changes to the way governments worked. The Free Trade Agreement between Canada and the United States, and the North American Free Trade Agreement that included Mexico, had helped bring down trade barriers around the world. But perhaps Canada had to go farther, as many other countries were doing, and accept that governments must control less and leave businesses and private citizens to run the affairs of communities. Ontario Premier Mike Harris and Alberta Premier Ralph Klein had sharply cut the size of their governments. Preston Manning's

Days before the Quebec referendum of 1995, hundreds of thousands of passionate federalists carried the maple leaf through the streets of Montreal.

Reform Party, which held similar views, had become the
Official Opposition in Ottawa in 1997. The twentieth century,
which had been shaped by nations and national rivalries,
ended with debate about whether nations or businesses would
manage the affairs of the world.

Into a New Millennium

Was everything going to break down the moment 1999
became 2000?   In the last years of the twentieth century,
that alarming possibility created "Y2K" panic ("Y" means
"Year", and "2K" means "2000"). If computers proved
unable to read the new date, the systems that ran bank
machines, delivered heat, light, and electricity, and made
jet aircrafts fly would collapse. For several years,
programmers had worked frantically on the problem, and
when the date changed, the computer systems continued
to run smoothly. Although the new millennium had
caused fear as well as excitement, New Year's Eve found
most Canadians cheering in the new century and the
new millennium with music and fireworks, or enjoying
televised coverage of the colourful celebrations around
the world.

*Fireworks burst over the Peace
Tower on Parliament Hill to bring
in the new millennium and the
year 2000 in Ottawa.*

*In 1995 thirteen-year-old Craig
Kielburger of Thornhill, Ontario,
won world-wide admiration for his
campaign against the oppression of
children in Asia.*

At the start of the 1900s, Prime Minister Wilfrid Laurier
had predicted that the twentieth century would belong to
Canada. At the end of the century, Canada had grown into
one of the safest, most prosperous, most democratic, and
most respected countries in the world. Life was good for a
very large number of citizens. Yet French and English
Canadians still distrusted each other, and many others felt
excluded from the running of the country. Each region had
its own claims and complaints. Minority language groups
wanted recognition. Business leaders warned that the
country was falling behind in the fierce competition of
global trade. Was there a unique and distinctive Canadian
style? Sometimes it was hard to believe there had been a
national dream, a faith that Canada was something special
in the world.

In 1867, D'Arcy McGee had looked forward to "a new
nationality" emerging from Confederation, and John A.
Macdonald had imagined "one people." But at the dawn of
the twenty-first century, Canada was more than ever a
country of many peoples, many communities. The
Canadian experiment had been to build a nation out of
many nations and to find a way for them to live in
harmony with each other and with this northern land. It
had never been easy. It was still hard.

Northern Voyagers

IN JULY 1986, JEFF MACINNIS, A 23-YEAR-OLD STUDENT from Toronto, and Mike Beedell, an Arctic photographer from Ottawa, sailed out of the Mackenzie River delta to challenge the Northwest Passage.

There is no easy way through the Northwest Passage, but for MacInnis and Beedell the voyage would be exceptionally daring. They were setting out with sails and paddles alone, aboard a bright yellow catamaran less than six metres long. *Perception* had no motor, no cabin, and no shelter, just twin hulls of yellow fibreglass and a single mast. The pair looked as if they should be sailing for fun on a pond by a cottage, not steering out into treacherous Arctic waters.

Since 1906, when Roald Amundsen's *Gjoa* first completed the passage, many other adventurers have challenged the Northwest Passage. The idea of the passage has never ceased casting its spell. In the 1970s songwriter Stan Rogers put it into words in these lines from his song "Northwest Passage":

> . . . for just one time, I would take the Northwest
>   Passage
> To find the hand of Franklin reaching for the
>   Beaufort Sea
> Tracing one warm line through a land so wide
>   and savage
> And make a Northwest Passage to the sea

Mike Beedell and Jeff MacInnis haul the Perception *across ice on King William Island.*

Until his death at age thirty-three in an aircraft disaster, folksinger and writer Stan Rogers touched audiences with his music of farmers, sailors, and fishing towns.

Westward from the Davis Strait, 'tis there 'twas said to lie
The sea-route to the Orient for which so many died
Seeking gold and glory, leaving weathered broken bones
And a long-forgotten lonely cairn of stones.

Even in the Far North, MacInnis and Beedell saw how human beings had overcome nature. Aircraft roared low over their heads, and powerful radios kept them in touch with the world. The two voyagers passed artificial islands built around oil wells, and they visited radar stations ready to give a few minutes' warning of any nuclear attack. Franklin and Frobisher never knew such wonders – or the threat of such horrors.

In their Northwest Passage adventure, MacInnis and Beedell did not try to overpower the North. When the Arctic wind blew against them, they stopped. When it died, they paddled by hand. Sometimes they dragged their boat, metre by painful metre, across jagged and rolling floes of ice. Just as often, the ice drove them back or sent them dashing for refuge ashore. Yet, when wind and ice allowed,

they sailed on to complete their voyage. Over three exciting summers, *Perception* carried them 3500 kilometres, from Inuvik at the Mackenzie River delta to Atlantic tidewater at Pond Inlet on Baffin Island.

The scenic Mackenzie River delta, where the North's greatest river flows into the Arctic Sea.

MacInnis and Beedell were close not only to nature but to history, to thousands of years of Arctic adventurers, all the way. Only *Perception*'s thin hulls and the men's insulated, watertight suits kept them from the killing cold. Razor-edged ice ripped their suits and froze their fingers. Seals and beluga whales bobbed up around them, and sometimes they were stalked by polar bears. They saw history in the remains of Inuit campsites and at the graves of men who had sailed with Sir John Franklin in 1845.

"Nature must be ridden, not driven" became the motto of *Perception*'s voyage. When all Canadians can learn that lesson, the new century will bring adventures beyond our imaginings. Perhaps our children's children will see a Canadian land as fresh and beautiful and full of dreams as the land the first people knew a hundred centuries ago. There are northern passages, yet uncrossed, awaiting them.

Chronology

About 75 million years ago Dinosaurs live in steamy forests and warm seas that cover much of what we now call Canada.

About 20 000 years ago The first human inhabitants of North America probably cross from Siberia by land bridge as the last Ice Age draws to a close.

About 1000 years ago Native people of southern Ontario begin to plant and harvest corn. The Thule people – ancestors of the Inuit – migrate east across Arctic Canada.

About 1000 years ago Leif Ericsson's first voyage to Vinland. A Norse colony is established in Vinland, but lasts only a couple of years.

About 600 years ago Five Iroquois nations form the powerful Confederacy of the Longhouse.

1497, 1498 John Cabot (Giovanni Caboto) of Genoa makes two voyages for England to the fishing grounds off Newfoundland.

1534 Jacques Cartier explores the coasts of Newfoundland, Prince Edward Island, and New Brunswick. He lands on the Gaspé Peninsula and claims the land for France.

1535 Cartier journeys up the St. Lawrence to the Native settlements of Stadacona and Hochelaga. He gives Canada its name (from the Indian word *kanata*, meaning "village").

1576 Martin Frobisher journeys as far as Frobisher Bay, Baffin Island, on the first of three voyages in search of the Northwest Passage.

1583 Sir Humphrey Gilbert visits Newfoundland and claims it for England.

1604 Pierre Du Gua de Monts and Samuel de Champlain establish a colony in Nova Scotia. Marc Lescarbot starts the first library and first French school for Native people, and in 1606 produces the first play staged in Canada. After Lescarbot returns to France, he writes the first history of Canada.

1608 Samuel de Champlain founds a permanent French colony at Quebec.

1610–1611 Explorer Henry Hudson is set adrift by his mutinous crew in Hudson Bay.

1615 The first Roman Catholic missionaries try to convert the Native people to Christianity.

1616 Champlain completes eight years of exploration, travelling as far west as Georgian Bay. The French and Hurons form an alliance.

1617 Louis and Marie Hébert and their children become the first French settlers to farm land in New France.

1630s The first French schools are founded in Quebec by religious orders.

1642 Ville-Marie (Montreal) is founded by Paul de Maisonneuve.

1645 The Hôtel-Dieu Hospital in Ville-Marie, founded by Jeanne Mance, is completed.

1649 War between the Huron and Iroquois confederacies leads to the destruction of the Huron nation. The Iroquois begin raids on New France.

1663 King Louis XIV decides to rebuild New France. He sends a governor and troops to protect the colony, an intendant (Jean Talon) to administer it, and settlers to increase its population.

1670 The English king grants a charter to the Hudson's Bay Company, giving it exclusive trading rights to vast territory drained by rivers that flow into Hudson Bay.

1682 René-Robert Cavelier de La Salle reaches the mouth of the Mississippi, and claims for France all the land through which the river and its tributaries flow.

Early 1700s Horses come to the northern plains, and the region's Native peoples become nations on horseback.

1713 A peace treaty forces France to turn over Newfoundland and Acadia to Britain. The French begin construction of Louisbourg, strongest fortress in North America, on Cape Breton Island.

1726 The first English school in Newfoundland is established, known as "the school for poor people."

1743 Louis-Joseph, son of Pierre de La Vérendrye, explores westward in search of the "Western Sea," crossing the plains almost to the Rocky Mountains.

1749 The British found Halifax as a naval and military post; about 3000 people settle there in one year.

March 25, 1752 First issue of the *Halifax Gazette*, Canada's first newspaper.

1755 The expulsion of the Acadians by the British begins: 6000–10 000 Acadians driven from their homes.

1756–1763 The Seven Years' War between Great Britain and France, fought partly in their North American colonies: *July 8, 1758* French troops, under the command of Louis-Joseph de Montcalm, win victory over the British at Carillon (Ticonderoga). *July 26, 1758* The British capture Louisbourg from the French. *September 13, 1759* At the Battle of the Plains of Abraham, Quebec falls to the British. Both commanders, Wolfe and Montcalm, are killed. *September 8, 1760* New France surrenders to the British. *1763* New France becomes a British colony called Quebec.

1763 Alliance of Native nations under Pontiac, chief of the Ottawa, makes war on the British, seizing many forts and trading posts.

1769 Prince Edward Island, formerly part of Nova Scotia, becomes separate British colony.

1770–1772 Samuel Hearne, guided by Chipewyan leader Matonabbee, explores the Coppermine and Slave rivers and Great Slave Lake and is the first white man to reach the Arctic Ocean overland.

1773 Scottish settlers reach Pictou, Nova Scotia, aboard the *Hector*.

1774 Quebec Act is passed by British Parliament, recognizing the French Canadians' right to preserve their language, religion, and civil law.

1775–1783 The American Revolution gains independence from Great Britain for the Thirteen Colonies. The people of

Quebec, Nova Scotia, and Prince Edward Island decide against joining the revolution.

December 31, 1775 American invaders under General Montgomery assault Quebec. The city is under siege until spring, when British reinforcements drive the Americans away.

1776 The fur traders of Montreal band together in the North West Company to compete with the traders of the Hudson's Bay Company.

1778 Captain James Cook explores the Pacific Coast from Nootka (Yuquot Cove) to the Bering Strait.

1783 Immigration of 40 000 United Empire Loyalists from the Thirteen Colonies. Most settle in Nova Scotia, Quebec, and New Brunswick (established as a colony separate from Nova Scotia in 1784). Three thousand Black Loyalists settle near Shelburne, Nova Scotia.

1784 After helping the British during the American Revolution, the Iroquois are given two land grants. Thayendanegea (Joseph Brant) settles his followers at the Six Nations Reserve, near Brantford.

1791 Quebec is divided into two colonies, Upper and Lower Canada, each with its own Assembly.

1792, 1793, 1794 Captain George Vancouver makes summer voyages to explore the coasts of mainland British Columbia and Vancouver Island.

1793 By canoe and on foot, Alexander Mackenzie crosses the Rocky Mountains and the Coast Range, reaching the Pacific Ocean on July 22.

1793 York (now Toronto) founded by John Graves Simcoe, lieutenant-governor of Upper Canada.

1803 First paper mill established in Lower Canada, producing paper from cloth rags.

1808 Simon Fraser travels the Fraser River for 1360 km to reach the Pacific Ocean on July 2.

1811 Lord Selkirk plans a settlement of Highland Scots in Red River area, near present site of Winnipeg. First settlers arrive at Hudson Bay in the fall of 1811.

1812–1814 The War of 1812, between the United States and Britain: *August 16, 1812* Detroit surrenders to British general Isaac Brock and Tecumseh, leader of the Native nations allied to Britain. *October 13, 1812* Brock is killed during the Battle of Queenston Heights. *June 22, 1813* Laura Secord overhears

American troops planning an attack, and walks 30 km, crossing enemy lines, to warn Colonel James FitzGibbon. Two days later, the Americans are ambushed and surrender to FitzGibbon. *October 5, 1813* Tecumseh dies during the British defeat at Moraviantown. *December 24, 1814* The Treaty of Ghent officially ends the war.

June 6, 1829 Shawnandithit, the last of the Beothuks, dies at about age twenty-eight in St. John's, Newfoundland.

1830 Escaped slaves Josiah and Charlotte Henson and their children journey north from Maryland to Canada. The Hensons later help found a community of ex-slaves called Dawn, near Dresden, Ontario.

1832 The Rideau Canal, built by Colonel John By, opens; the community of Bytown (later Ottawa) grows out of the camp for the canal workers.

1836 The first railway in Canada opens, running from La Prairie to St. John's, Quebec.

1837 Rebellions in Upper and Lower Canada are put down by government troops. The rebel leaders, Louis-Joseph Papineau of Lower Canada and William Lyon Mackenzie of Upper Canada, are forced to flee.

1838 Lord Durham comes to Canada as governor. He recommends that the governments of the colonies should be chosen by the people's elected representatives.

1840 *Britannia* – the first ship of the Cunard Line, founded by Samuel Cunard of Halifax – arrives in Halifax harbour with transatlantic mail.

1841 The Act of Union unites Upper and Lower Canada (which became Canada West and Canada East) into the Province of Canada, under one government, with Kingston as capital.

1842 Charles Fenerty of Sackville, New Brunswick, discovers a practical way to make paper from wood pulp. Today the pulp and paper industry is Canada's largest manufacturing industry, and Canada exports more pulp and paper than any other country in the world.

1843 James Douglas of the Hudson's Bay Company founds Victoria on Vancouver Island.

1845 Sir John Franklin and his crew disappear in the Arctic while seeking the Northwest Passage.

1846 Geologist and chemist Abraham Gesner of Nova Scotia invents kerosene oil and becomes the founder of the modern petroleum industry.

1851 Canada's first postage stamp is issued, a three-penny stamp with a beaver on it.

1856 Timothy Eaton opens his first general store, in Kirkton, Ontario. Thirteen years later he opens a store at the corner of Queen and Yonge in Toronto.

1857 Queen Victoria chooses Ottawa as the new capital of the United Province of Canada.

1858 Gold is discovered in the sandbars of the Fraser River. Some twenty thousand miners rush to the area, and it comes under British rule as the colony of British Columbia.

1859 The French acrobat Blondin crosses Niagara Falls on a tightrope. On later tightrope walks, he crosses the falls on stilts, blindfolded, and with his feet in a sack.

1864 Confederation conferences in Charlottetown, Prince Edward Island, September 1–9, and in Quebec, October 10–29. Delegates hammer out the conditions for union of British North American colonies.

March 29, 1867 The British North America Act is passed by Britain's Parliament, providing for Canada's Confederation.

July 1, 1867 Confederation: New Brunswick, Nova Scotia, Quebec, and Ontario form the Dominion of Canada, and John A. Macdonald becomes the first prime minister.

1867 Emily Stowe, the first woman doctor in Canada, begins to practise medicine in Toronto.

1869 The Métis of Red River rebel, under Louis Riel, after their region is purchased by Canada from the Hudson's Bay Company.

July 15, 1870 Manitoba joins Confederation. The new province was much smaller than today's Manitoba.

1870 As buffalo become scarce, the last tribal war is fought on the Prairies between the Cree and the Blackfoot over hunting territories.

July 20, 1871 British Columbia joins Confederation.

May 1873 American whisky traders kill fifty-six Assiniboine in the Cypress Hills of the southern Prairies. The North-West Mounted Police (later the RCMP) is formed to keep order in the new Canadian territories.

1873 Prime Minister Sir John A. Macdonald resigns as a result of scandal over the partial financing of the Conservative election campaign by the Canadian Pacific Railway Company.

July 1, 1873 Prince Edward Island joins Confederation.

August 1876 Scottish-born Alexander Graham Bell, who has been working on the invention of the telephone since 1874, makes the world's first long-distance call, from Brantford to Paris, Ontario.

1879 The first organized games of hockey, using a flat puck, are played by McGill University students in Montreal. Before this, hockey-like games have been played on ice with a ball.

1880 Britain transfers the Arctic, which it claims to own, to Canada, completing Canada's modern boundaries – except for Newfoundland and Labrador.

1884 A system of international standard time and official time zones, advocated by Canadian engineer Sir Sandford Fleming, is adopted.

1885 The Métis North-West Rebellion is led by Louis Riel and Gabriel Dumont. After early victories for the rebels, the rebellion is crushed by troops who arrive on the newly built railway.

November 7, 1885 The last spike of the Canadian Pacific Railway main line is driven at Craigellachie, B.C. The next year, Vancouver is founded as the railway's western terminus.

1891 The City of Toronto establishes the first Children's Aid Society in Canada.

1893 Lord Stanley, the governor general, donates the Stanley Cup as a hockey trophy.

1896 Gold is discovered in the Klondike. By the next year, 100 000 people are rushing to the Yukon in the hope of getting rich.

1899–1902 The Boer War in South Africa is fought between Dutch Afrikaners (Boers) and the British. Seven thousand Canadian volunteers fight on the British side.

September 1, 1905 Saskatchewan and Alberta join Confederation. Immigrants rush to settle on the plains, mainly as wheat farmers.

1906 Norwegian Roald Amundsen, in the schooner *Gjoa*, finds his way through the Northwest Passage to the Pacific.

1907 Tom Longboat, an Onondaga from the Six Nations Reserve and a world champion distance runner, wins the Boston Marathon in record time. In 1906 he won a 12-mile (almost 20 km) race against a horse.

1908 *Anne of Green Gables*, by Lucy Maud Montgomery, is published. In the next ninety years the book sells more than a million copies, is made into a television movie, and becomes a popular musical.

1909 The first powered, heavier-than-air flight in Canada is made by J.A.D. McCurdy in the *Silver Dart*. The biplane flew almost a kilometre.

1909 The first Grey Cup game; the University of Toronto football team defeats Toronto Parkdale. A trophy has been donated by the governor general, Earl Grey.

1911 A proposal for free trade between the United States and Canada is rejected in a fiercely contested general election. The Liberal government, under Wilfrid Laurier, is replaced by a Conservative government led by Sir William Borden.

1913 Vilhjalmur Stefansson leads a Canadian expedition to the Arctic, and explores the North by deliberately drifting on ice floes.

1914–1918 The First World War. Britain declares war on Germany on behalf of the British Empire, including Canada. ***April 22–May 25, 1915*** Battle of Ypres (Belgium). The first major battle fought by Canadian troops. They stand their ground against poison-gas attacks. ***April 9–14, 1917*** Battle of Vimy Ridge (France). A Canadian victory, at cost of more than 10 000 killed or wounded. ***October 26–November 7, 1917*** Passchendaele (Belgium). A Canadian victory, at the cost of more than 15 000 casualties. Nine Victoria Crosses are awarded to Canadians. ***1917*** Flying ace

Billy Bishop of Owen Sound, Ontario, wins the Victoria Cross for attacking a German airfield single-handed.

November 26, 1917 The National Hockey League is established in Montreal. The original teams are: Montreal Canadiens, Montreal Wanderers, Ottawa Senators, and Toronto Arenas.

1917 Sir William Borden leads a unionist coalition, which combines support by Conservatives and western Liberals, into a wartime election against the Laurier Liberals. Borden wins.

December 6, 1917 A French munitions ship explodes in Halifax harbour, flattening the city, killing 1600, and injuring 9000.

1918 Women win the right to vote in federal elections.

May 15–June 25, 1919 The Winnipeg General Strike. A strike in the building and metal trades spreads to other unions, and 30 000 workers stop work, crippling the city.

August 1919 Following the death of Laurier, William Lyon Mackenzie King is chosen to be leader of the Liberal Party.

1920 The Group of Seven artists hold their first exhibition, in Toronto.

1921 Agnes Macphail of Owen Sound, Ontario, becomes the first woman elected to the House of Commons, in the first election since women gained the vote.

1923 The Nobel Prize for Medicine is awarded to doctors Frederick Banting and J.J.R. Macleod. Along with Dr. Charles Best and others, Banting discovered insulin as a treatment for diabetes.

1927 The first government old-age pension pays up to $20 per month.

July 1, 1927 To celebrate Canada's Diamond jubilee (sixtieth birthday), the first coast-to-coast radio broadcast is made.

1928 At the first Olympics in which women may compete, a Canadian women's six-member track team wins one bronze, two silver, and two gold medals.

1929 England's Privy Council rules that women are indeed "persons," and therefore can be appointed to the Canadian Senate. The next year, Cairine Wilson becomes Canada's first woman senator.

October 29, 1929 North American stock markets crash and the Great Depression begins.

1930 R.B. Bennett leads the Conservative Party to victory over William Lyon Mackenzie King's Liberals as the country is plunged into the Great Depression.

November 2, 1936 The Canadian Broadcasting Corporation is established.

April 1, 1939 Trans-Canada Airlines (later Air Canada) makes the first scheduled passenger flight from Vancouver to Montreal.

1939–1945 The Second World War. After Germany invades Poland and Britain declares war, Canada declares war as well. ***December 7, 1941*** The Japanese attack the U.S. naval base at Pearl Harbor, in Hawaii, and Canada declares war on Japan. ***December 1941*** The Fall of Hong Kong. More than 500 Canadians die in battle or of starvation and ill-treatment in Japanese prison camps. ***1942*** Twenty-two thousand Japanese Canadians are rounded up by RCMP and placed in work camps until after the war. ***August 19, 1942*** In a disastrous raid on Dieppe, France, 900 out of 5000 Canadians are killed and almost 2000 are taken prisoner. ***May–October 1942*** German submarines in the Gulf of St. Lawrence sink twenty-three Allied ships, with a loss of 258 lives. The gulf is then closed to ocean shipping until 1944. ***July 1943*** Canadian troops invade Sicily and, with other Allied troops, fight their way north through Italy. They reach Rome on June 4, 1944. ***June 6, 1944 (D day)*** Canadian troops, along with British and Americans, land successfully on the coast of France and begin to drive the Germans back.

July 1941 The first national unemployment-insurance program comes into operation.

1945 Family-allowance payments begin. All families receive a monthly sum for each child under sixteen who is in school.

February 1947 Prospectors strike oil in Leduc, Alberta, beginning Alberta's oil boom.

March 31, 1949 Newfoundland and Labrador join Confederation as the tenth province.

1949 William Lyon Mackenzie King, Canada's longest-serving prime minister, retires at the age of 74.

1950–1954 The Korean War. Twenty-seven thousand Canadians serve and more than 1600 are killed or wounded.

1950 Inuit win the right to vote in federal elections.

1952 Vincent Massey becomes the first Canadian-born governor general since Pierre Rigaud de Vaudreuil governed New France.

September 6, 1952 The first Canadian scheduled TV broadcast.

September 9, 1954 Marilyn Bell, age sixteen, is the first person to swim Lake Ontario.

1957 Lester Pearson wins the Nobel Peace Prize for proposing a United Nations peacekeeping force to prevent war over control of the Suez Canal.

1957 John George Diefenbaker leads the Conservative Party to decisive victory over Louis St. Laurent's Liberals in a federal election, winning more seats in the House of Commons than any party has before.

October 23, 1958 The Springhill Mining Disaster. Shifting rock kills seventy-four coal miners. Some of the survivors are trapped for eight days before being rescued.

June 26, 1959 Queen Elizabeth II and U.S. President Dwight Eisenhower officially open the St. Lawrence Seaway, which lets ocean vessels reach the Great Lakes.

1960 Native people living on reserves get the right to vote in federal elections.

1960 Social changes and a new government in Quebec lead to the beginning of Quebec's "Quiet Revolution." Stirrings of interest in independence for Quebec soon follow.

1962 Saskatchewan is the first province to have medical insurance covering doctors' bills. In 1966, Parliament passes legislation to establish a national medicare program. By 1972, all provinces and territories have joined the program.

September 29, 1962 The first Canadian satellite, *Alouette I*, is launched by the American space agency.

1963 The FLQ, a terrorist group dedicated to revolution to establish an independent Quebec, explodes bombs in Montreal.

February 15, 1965 Canada gets a new red-and-white, maple leaf flag.

1967 Canada celebrates a hundred years of Confederation. Across the country, communities sponsor centennial projects. In Ottawa, on July 1, Queen Elizabeth II cuts a giant birthday cake.

April–October 1967 Expo 67, the Montreal world's fair, attracts more than 55 million visitors.

1968 René Lévesque founds the Parti Québécois, with the goal of making Quebec a "sovereign" (independent) state "associated" with Canada.

1968 Pierre Elliott Trudeau succeeds Lester Pearson as prime minister and leader of the Liberal Party. "Trudeaumania" sweeps the country in the subsequent federal election.

1970 Voting age lowered from twenty-one to eighteen.

1970 The October Crisis. After the FLQ kidnaps a Quebec government minister and a British trade commissioner, Prime Minister Trudeau invokes the War Measures Act, which allows Canadians to be arrested and held without being charged.

1971 Gerhard Herzberg of Ottawa wins the Nobel Prize for Chemistry.

1976 René Lévesque and the Parti Québécois are elected in Quebec.

1976 Wayne Gretzky, age seventeen, plays hockey for the Edmonton Oilers; he is the youngest person in North America playing a major-league sport.

April 12, 1980 Terry Fox begins his cross-country run, the "Marathon of Hope." On September 1, he is forced to stop the run when his cancer returns.

May 15, 1980 Quebec voters reject "sovereignty-association" in favour of renewed Confederation.

November 1981 First flight of the Canadian Remote Manipulator System (Canadarm) on the space shuttle. The highly computerized 15m arm can be operated from inside the shuttle to release, rescue, and repair satellites.

November 5, 1981 The federal government and every province except Quebec reach agreement for patriating the Canadian constitution (bringing it to Canada from Great Britain).

April 17, 1982 Canada gets a new Constitution Act, including a Charter of Rights and Freedoms.

May 14, 1984 Jeanne Sauvé is Canada's first woman governor general.

1984 At the Summer Olympics in Los Angeles, Canada wins its greatest-ever number of gold medals: ten, including two for swimmer Alex Baumann.

October 5, 1984 Astronaut Marc Garneau, aboard the U.S. space shuttle *Challenger*, becomes the first Canadian in space.

March 21, 1985 Wheelchair athlete Rick Hansen leaves Vancouver on a round-the-world "Man in Motion" tour to raise money for spinal-cord research and wheelchair sports.

1986 John Polanyi of Toronto is co-winner of the Nobel Prize for Chemistry.

May–October 1986 Expo 86, the Vancouver world's fair, attracts more than 20 million visitors.

April 30, 1987 Ten provincial premiers and Prime Minister Brian Mulroney agree to the Meech Lake Accord, which would make large changes to Canada's Constitution and address Quebec's concerns. Parliament and the legislatures of all provinces have three years to accept the Accord. It dies in June 1991, when both Newfoundland and Manitoba refuse to endorse it.

February 13–28, 1988 The Calgary Winter Olympics. Canada wins two silver medals (Brian Orser and Elizabeth Manley, for figure skating) and three bronze medals.

January 1, 1989 After a federal election fought over the issue of free trade, the free-trade agreement between Canada and the United States comes into effect, gradually ending controls on trade and investment between the two countries.

December 2, 1989 Audrey McLaughlin becomes the first woman leader of a federal party – the New Democratic Party.

April 1990 The federal government settles a land claim with the Inuit that will give them 350 000 square km of territory in the North, to be called Nunavut.

Summer 1990 A land dispute causes a 78-day armed confrontation between Mohawks and the army on a reserve near Oka, Quebec.

January–February 1991 War in the Persian Gulf. Canada sends three warships, twenty-six fighter jets, and 2400 people to the Persian Gulf as part of a United Nations effort to force Iraqi troops to withdraw from Kuwait.

January 22, 1992 Dr. Roberta Bondar becomes the first Canadian woman in space, aboard the U.S. space shuttle *Discovery*.

August 28, 1992 Canadian leaders adopt the Charlottetown Accord to reform Canada's constitution, but in a national referendum in October, Canadians reject it.

October 24, 1992 Toronto's Blue Jays became the first Canadian team to win baseball's World Series.

1993 Canada, with Kurt Browning (gold), Elvis Stojko (silver), and Isabelle Brasseur and Lloyd Eisler (gold), has its best skating World Championship since 1962.

June 25, 1993 Kim Campbell, the new Conservative party leader, becomes Canada's first female prime minister, but in October, Jean Chrétien's Liberals win the general election.

1994 The North American Free Trade Agreement (NAFTA) comes into effect, linking Canada, the United States, and Mexico in a new economic partnership.

September 15, 1994 Separatist Jacques Parizeau becomes the premier of Quebec.

1995 "Turbot war" erupts when Canada arrests a Spanish ship in a bid to prevent European fleets from over-harvesting Newfoundland fish stocks.

1995 Donovan Bailey becomes "the world's fastest man" when he breaks the record for the 100-metre race.

October 30, 1995 Quebec votes in a referendum on sovereignty and the federalists win a razor-thin victory.

January 29, 1996 Lucien Bouchard is sworn in as the new premier of Quebec.

May 19, 1996 Astronaut Marc Garneau makes his second trip into space.

1996 Lucien Bouchard becomes leader of the separatist Parti Québecois and premier of Quebec.

Astronaut Marc Garneau makes his second trip into space.

Donovan Bailey wins the 100-metre gold medal at the Atlanta Olympics.

1997 Jean Chrétien's Liberal Party wins re-election in the federal election.

The "flood of the century" hits Manitoba's Red River valley, but "the big ditch" built many years earlier protects Winnipeg.

1998 An extraordinary ice storm devastates the Montreal region and eastern Ontario, destroying trees and leaving millions in cold and darkness as electrical systems collapse.

1999 Eaton's, a familiar name to Canadian shoppers for more than 100 years, goes out of business.

The new territory of Nunavut is established in Canada's eastern Arctic.

Adrienne Clarkson becomes Governor General of Canada.

2000 Canada enters a new millennium.

Publishers' Acknowledgments

The publishers wish to acknowledge the financial support of the Canadian Studies and Special Projects Directorate of the Department of the Secretary of State of Canada.

Basil Johnston, O. Ont., of the Department of Ethnology of the Royal Ontario Museum read and commented upon an early draft of the manuscript. On numerous occasions, Jack Granatstein generously provided advice.

For kind permission to reprint material used herein, the publishers are grateful to: Farley Mowat, for the excerpt from Never Cry Wolf; and Ariel Rogers for the excerpt from the Stan Rogers song "Northwest Passage."

The excerpt from David Thompson's Narrative is taken from John Warkentin, ed., The Western Interior of Canada: A Record of Geographical Discovery, 1612–1917, Carleton Library No. 15 (Toronto and Montreal: McClelland and Stewart Limited, 1964, 1969), pp. 102-03. The passage from Roughing It in the Bush, by Susanna Moodie, is from the New Canadian Library edition, No. 31 (Toronto: McClelland and Stewart Limited, 1962, 1970), p. 194.

Authors' and Illustrator's Acknowledgments

Malcolm Lester and Louise Dennys first suggested this book to us, and we began it with the support of the editorial team they assembled at Lester & Orpen Dennys, particularly Carol Martin and Sandra LaFortune. We completed it with the help of Kathy Lowinger at Lester Publishing and Phyllis Bruce and her staff at Key Porter Books, who handled a thousand last-minute details and guided the manuscript through to publication.

The authors wish to thank the Ontario Arts Council for a grant that helped them to complete the work. We also thank the staffs of the public libraries of Trenton and Kitchener, Ontario, and of the Metropolitan Toronto Central Reference Library, as well as many writers, readers, and friends who listened well.

The illustrator would like to thank the staff of the Kitchener Public Library, especially those in the Grace Schmidt Room. Staff at many other institutions were enormously helpful: at the Canadian Museum of Civilization, Dr. Bryan C. Gordon, Dr. David Keenlyside, and their fellow curators; at Parks Canada, Richard Lindo and René Chartrand; at Fort Edmonton Park, Jane Repp; at the National Aviation Museum, Rénald Fortier. I received assistance from the archives of the CPR; Fort Ticonderoga, N.Y.; Ste-Marie Among the Hurons; Historic Naval and Military Establishments at Penetanguishene; the Citadel, Halifax; the Royal Ontario Museum (Sigmund Samuel Collection); and from most of the provincial archives.

I would also like to express my appreciation to Commander Tony German, RCN (Ret.), and to the late J. Merle Smith, my father-in-law, who inspired me with his love for historical illustrations.

Picture Credits

All the illustrations in the book are by Alan Daniel, with the exception of those credited below. The following abbreviations have been used:

AGO: Art Gallery of Ontario, Toronto
AO: Archives of Ontario, Toronto
BCARS: British Columbia Archives & Records Service
BCARS/V: British Columbia Archives and Records Service/Visual Records Unit
CL: The Confederation Life Gallery of Canadian History
CMC: Canadian Museum of Civilization
CP: Canapress Photo Service
CPR: Canadian Pacific Railway Corporate Archives
CTA: City of Toronto Archives/James Collection
CW: Canada Wide
CWM: Canadian War Museum
FL: First Light Associated Photographers
GA: Glenbow Archives, Calgary
ISTC: Industry, Science and Technology Canada
MM: McCord Museum of Canadian History, McGill University, Montreal
MTL: Metropolitan Toronto Reference Library, Toronto
MTL/JRR: ——/John Ross Robertson Collection
NAC: National Archives of Canada
NASA: National Aeronautics and Space Administration
NGC: National Gallery of Canada, Ottawa
NMC: National Museums of Canada
NPA/MM: Notman Photographic Archives/McCord Museum of Canadian History
PAA: Provincial Archives of Alberta
ROM: Royal Ontario Museum, Toronto
ROM/C: ——/Canadiana Department
ROM/E: ——/Ethnology Department

Front
Page 1: AO/6520 S13458; 5: NGC/© Ozias Leduc 1992/VIS*ART.

Chapter One
Page 10: Mike Beedell; 11: Royal Tyrrell Museum/Alberta Culture and Multiculturalism; 12: Royal British Columbia Museum, Victoria, B.C., #11733; 18: Saul Williams/ROM/974.177; 20: CMC/S89-1828.

Chapter Two
Page 25, left: R. Ferguson, Canadian Parks Service; 30: NAC/C-8336; 31: NGC/#6663; 38: NAC/C-17338; 39: Bodleian Library; 42: Henrietta Martha Hamilton/NAC/C-87698.

Chapter Three
Page 46: NAC/C-9711; 48: CL; 50: MTL; 51: The Jesuit Archives; 52: Frank Craig/NAC/C-10622; 53: CWM;

54: CL; 55: Edmond-J. Massicotte/NAC/C-14360; 56: National Film Board of Canada/NMC; 57: Bank of Canada Currency Museum; 58: Paul von Baich/FL; 59: L.R. Batchelor/NAC/C-11925; 60, top: National Film Board of Canada, NMC; bottom: C.W. Jefferys/NAC/C-10687; 63: A.H. Hider/NAC/C-6896; 64-65: a detail from Henri Julien, *La Chasse-galerie*, collection of the Musée du Québec, #34.254, photography by Patrick Altman; 66: Parks Canada; 70: Claude Picard/Courtesy Environment Canada—Parks Service, Atlantic Region; 74: Laurie & Whittle/NAC/C-1078; 75: Desfontaines/NAC/C-3759.

Chapter Four
Page 79: John Lambert/NAC/C-113742; 80, above: CL; 82: William Booth/NAC/C-40162; 83: Dorothy Siemens; 84: MTL/JRR/T30840; 85: AO/135; 86: NAC/C-11222; 87: *Picturesque Canada*, Vol. II, 1882; 91: CWM; 92: NGC/#7157; 93: Malak Photographs Ltd.; 96: James Duncan/ROM/C/951.158.14; 97: AO/S-18444; 99: William Berczy, Sr./NGC/#5777; 102: C.W. Jefferys/NAC/C-73725; 103: AGO/Gift of Mrs. J.H. Mitchell in memory of her mother Margaret Lewis Gooderham, 1951; 104: NAC/C-5434; 105: Scholastic Canada; 106: New Brunswick Museum; 107: National Film Board/NMC; 109: Dorothy Siemens; 110-11: George Heriot/ROM/C/951.158.14.

Chapter Five
Page 115: A.J. Miller/NAC/C-403; 117: Dorothy Siemens; 118: William Armstrong/NAC/C-19041; 121: GA; 123: Henry James Warre/NAC/C-1629; 124: William Hind/NAC/C-13965; 125: C.W. Jefferys/NAC/C-16750; 126: Manitoba Archives, John Kerr Collection; 127: NPA/MM/78494-BI; 128: NGC/#6920/Transferred from the Parliament of Canada, 1955; 129: Royal Geographic Society, London/T129; 132: MM/M605; 133, top: GA/985.221.168; bottom: GA/M1083; 134: Samuel G. Cresswell/MTL; 135: Owen Beattie/University of Alberta/CP.

Chapter Six
Page 141: Fraser Clark; 142: ROM/E/912.1.93; 143: George Mercer Dawson/NAC/PA-37756; 144: Fraser Clark; 145: Royal British Columbia Museum/#1908; 146: BCARS/V/PDP2252; 147, bottom: BCARS/V/HP6462; 151: BCARS/V/PDP2258; 152: BCARS/V/HP127; 154: BCARS/HP2654; 155: MTL/JRR/MTL2313; 156: BCARS/HP759; 157: BCARS/HP7106; 158: BCARS/HP92108; 159: BCARS/HP17933.

Chapter Seven
Page 163: C. Williams/NAC/C-5086; 164: Cincinnati Art Museum, Subscription Fund Purchase, #1927.26;

165: Hunter & Co., Toronto/NAC/C-9553; 166, top: MTL/T13731; bottom: NAC/PA-11566; 167: MTL/JRR; 168-69: ISTC; 171: G.H. Andrews, Niagara Falls with Terrapin Tower/ROM/C/962.111.3; 172: CL; 173: William Notman & Son, Montreal/NAC/C-6166; 174: NAC/C-22002; 175: Thomas Kitchin/FL; 177: NAC/C-15369; 178: Manitoba Museum of Man & Nature/#3661; 179: GA/NA1406-71; 180: NAC/PA-66544; 181: Thomas Kitchin/FL; 182: GA/NA1104-1; 184: PAA/#A12006; 186: J.W. Bengough/NAC/C-8449; 187: BCARS/HP72553; 190-91: Alan Daniel/Courtesy of The Reader's Digest Association (Canada) Ltd.; 191: CPR/#1960; 192, top: Sergt. Grundy/NAC/C-2424; bottom: Robert William Rutherford/NAC/C-2769; 193, top: GA/NA-428-1; bottom: CPR.

Chapter Eight
Page 196: NAC/C-932; 197: NAC/PA-68351; 198, top: Dartmouth Heritage Museum; bottom: Special Collections Division, University of Washington Libraries, photo by Cantwell, #46; 199: CL; 200: NAC/C-23354; 201: NAC/C-9671; 202: GA; 203: AGO/Gift from the Fund of the T. Eaton Co. Ltd. for Canadian Works of Art, 1948; 204: GA/NA-978-4; 205: NAC/C-6605; 206: Thomas Kitchin/FL; 207, top: Provincial Archives of Manitoba/N10911; bottom: MM; 208: The Eaton Collection/AO/F22G-1-0-23; 209, top: Jessop/NAC/PA-30212; bottom: Muriel Wood; 210, top: NAC/C-9480; bottom: NPA/MM/1027, View; 211: NAC/PA-41785; 212: Archives, The Hospital for Sick Children; 213: John Boyd/NAC/PA-60732; 215: CTA/#1797; 217: AO/S-1243; 218: National Aviation Museum, Ottawa; 219: NAC/PA-110154.

Chapter Nine
Page 222: GA/NA2676-6; 223, top: CWM/CN8567; bottom: NAC/PA-568; 224: Dept. of National Defence/NAC/PA-1020; 225: Robert Semeniuk/FL; 226, top: NAC/PA-1654; bottom: Kitchener Public Library; 227, top: MTL/JRR/Ephemera Collection; bottom: CTA/#640; 228, top: NAC/PA-1892; bottom: Janet Lunn; 229: NAC/C-95266; 230, right: CTA/#2451; 231, top: MTL/T31725; bottom: Manitoba Provincial Archives/Foote Collection; 232, top: Canada's Sports Hall of Fame/NAC/PA-50440; bottom: General Motors of Canada Ltd.; 234: AGO/Gift of the Canadian Club of Toronto, 1926; 236: City of Edmonton Archives; 237: H. Wright Corp./NAC/PA-142372; 238: GA/NA-1831-1; 239, top: AO/S801; bottom: PAA/A5145; 240, top: Canadian Government Motion Picture Bureau/NAC/C-80917; bottom: CTA/#2040; 241: Canada Post; 242, top: Claude Detloff/NAC/C-38723; bottom: Montreal Gazette/NAC/PA-129617; 243, top and bottom: MTL/JRR/Ephemera Collection; 244: CWM/CN12276; 245: AGO/Study Collection/T-1340; 246: CWM/CN11356; 247: NAC/C-52832; 248: York University Archives, Toronto Telegram Photographic Collection; 249: NAC/PA-117812; 250, top:

NAC/C-261110; bottom: CWM/CN14085; 251: Tak Toyota/NAC/C-46350; 253, right: NAC/PA-136280; 254, left and right: NAC/Comics; 255: W.J. Hynes/Dept. of National Defence/NAC/PA-147114.

Chapter Ten
Page 259: National Aviation Museum; 260: Farley Mowat; 261: NGC/(c) Estate of William Kurelek, permission granted by the Isaacs/Innuit Gallery of Toronto; 262, top: Canada's Sports Hall of Fame; bottom: CP; 263: National Film Board of Canada/NAC/PA-128080; 264: Duncan Cameron/NAC/C-94168; 265: Montreal Star/NAC/PA-129625; 266: NAC/PA-143954; 267, top: CP; bottom: CP; 268: Ford Motor Company of Canada Ltd.; 269: CP; 270: Stratford Festival Archives; 271, top: Robert Semeniuk/FL; bottom: CP; 272: CW; 273, top: CP; bottom: Indian and Northern Affairs Canada; 274: Leo Harrison/CW; 275: Daggett/Montreal Star/NAC/PA-139982; 277, top left: T.G.A. Henstridge/NAC/Heraldry (3); bottom left: J. Evariste-Alain/NAC/Heraldry (2); top right: NAC/Heraldry (15); middle right: Osy-Mandias/NAC/Heraldry (7); bottom right: Germain Tremblay/NAC/Heraldry (12); 280: NAC/C-30085; 281: Peter Bregg/CP; 282: F. Lenon/The Toronto Star; 283: Doug Ball/CP; 284: ISTC; 285: Buston/CP; 286: Glen Ross/New Brunswick Power; 287, top right: K. Dykstra/FL; bottom left: Karl Sommerer; 288, top: reprinted by permission of Macmillan Canada; bottom: from The Olden Days Coat by Margaret Laurence, used by permission of the Canadian Publishers, McClelland & Stewart, Toronto; 289: NASA; 290: CP; 291: Jim Russell/FL; 292: top: Tom Hanson/CP; bottom left: 293: Vellis Crooks/CP; 294: NASA; 295: Jacques Nadeau/CP; 296: Peter McLeod/FL; 297: top: Jacques Boissinot/CP; bottom right: Hans Deryk/CP; 298: Shaney Komulainen/CP; 299: William C. Stratas; 300: Paul Chiasson/CP; 301: Tom Hanson/CP; 302: Ryan Remiorz/CP; 303: Wayne Cuddington/CP;   304: Tom Hanson/CP.

Northern Voyagers
Page 305, top: Mike Beedell; bottom: CP; 306-07: Paul von Baich/FL.

Page 328: AGO/Gift of the Klamer family, 1978/Reproduced with the permission of the West Baffin Eskimo Co-operative Ltd., Cape Dorset, N.W.T.

Index

Page numbers in italics refer to illustrations, paintings, or photographs.

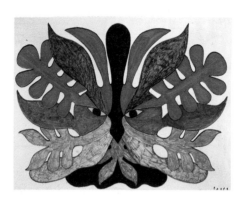

General editor: Barbara Hehner
Illustrations and maps: Alan Daniel and Lea Daniel
Design: Scott Richardson
Picture editor: Renée Dykeman
Colour separations: Colour Technologies
Text set in Stone Serif by MacTrix DTP
Text printed on Luna Matte
Printed and bound by D.W. Friesen & Sons

Above:
Kenojuak Ashevak, Owl.
An Inuit from the Baffin Island
community of Cape Dorset,
Kenojuak Ashevak began making
her vibrant prints in the 1950s. She
became one of Canada's most
popular artists. Cape Dorset art was
soon world-famous.